- ¤ -

LAP STEEL GUITAR

≈

BY ANDY VOLK

Cover, Graphic Design & Layout
Andy Volk
Volk Media Design
Production: Ron Middlebrook

Text Copyright © 2003 Andy Volk

ISBN 1-57424-134-6
SAN 683-8022

Published by **CENTERSTREAM Publications, LLC**, P.O. Box 17878 Anaheim, CA 92807

This book is in no way intended to infringe on the intellectual property rights of any party. All products, brands, and names represented are trademarks or registered trademarks of their respective companies: information in this book was derived from the author's independent research and was not authorized, furnished or approved by other parties.

All rights for publication and distribution are reserved. No part of this book may be reproduced in any form or by any electronic or mechanical means including information storage and retrieval systems without permission in writing from the publisher, except by reviewers who may quote brief passeges in review.

- ¤ TABLE OF CONTENTS ¤ -

- ¤ TABLE OF CONTENTS ¤ -

Dedication

This book is dedicated to my wife, Lynn, and children, Gregory and James,
and to my late friend, Ralph Kolsiana, who taught me that age
differences are irrelevant between like-minded musicians.

Acknowledgements

A project of this scope would be impossible without the advice, assistance, and friendship of a large group of people. I'd like to thank Martin Abend, Rick Aiello, Bill Asher, Tim Ausburn, Brad Bechtel, John Bechtel, Carroll Benoit, Kelli Bert, Jody Carver, Cindy Cashdollar, Paul & Adrian Chandler, Bruce Clarke, Dancing Cat Records, Ricky Davis, Keith DeLong, Mike Dotson, T. Sage Harmos, Mike Idhe, Michael Johnstone, Jack Jones, Myrna Kame, George Lake, Ken Latchum, Dwight Mark, John Marsden, Matson Navigation Company, Ron Middlebrook, Jack Montgomery, Jesse Morris, Northern Blues Music, George Pieburn, Ron Preston, Howard Reinlieb, Lorene Ruymar, Dewitt Scott Sr., Tim Sheerhorn, David Siegler, Sierra Instrument Company, Chas Smith, Loni Specter, Dave Stewart, Bob Stone, Fritz Svacina, Roy Thomson, Bud and Greg Tutmarc, Dirk Vogel, and Bob Pulevai Waters. (My apologies to anyone who may have been inadvertently left off this list).

Special thanks and acknowledgement is due to Stan Werbin at Elderly Instruments in Lansing, Michigan, who generously shared many vintage instruments from his personal collection; and to Dave Matchette who photographed them.

Many thanks for their encouragement and keen proofreading skills to Sarah Ahlgren, Bob Stone, and Lynn Volk.

Thank you as well to all the artists who so generously shared their time and their love for the steel guitar with me:

Debashish Bhattacharya, Gary Brandin, Roy Brown, Bob Brozman, Darick Campbell, Cindy Cashdollar, Bruce Clarke, John Ely, Ed Gerhard, Elder Aubrey Ghent, Pete Grant, Marian Hall, Don Helms, Steve Howe, Lee Jeffreiss, Greg Leisz, David Lindley, Harry Manx, Clarence Junior Martin, Tom Morrell, Herb Remington, Billy Robinson, Freddie Roulette, Greg Sardinha, and Jeremy Wakefield.

Finally, a tip of the tone bar to the *Steel Guitar Forum* (www.steelguitarforum.com), a web bulletin board run with aplomb by Bobby Lee Quasar. The *Forum* is *the* place to be on the net to discuss and learn about steel guitar in all its many permutations. For more than six years, the *Forum* has been a deep well of information and lively discourse about the steel guitar and its players.

- ¤ INTRODUCTION ¤ -

What is it about the sound of the steel guitar that so gets under your skin? Is it the sublime sound of sliding into a single note? The quavering sigh of a chord that seems to sustain for the duration of a human breath? Or is it that *moan*; so voice-like that, in comparison, a standard guitar can seem as cold and staccato as the clacking computer keyboard on which I write these words?

For me, growing up in Philadelphia, the sounds of early rock & roll and smooth, melodic soul music were everywhere, but steel guitar sounds were few and far between. The only exceptions being Pub-Tiki and Kona-Kai - long-gone restaurants where the languid sounds of the islands formed a caressing sonic landscape to the pseudo-Polynesian carvings and ersatz Micronesian cuisine.

After that early immersion in the music of the South Pacific of the imagination, it was the opening strains of *Greensleeves* from Mike Auldridge's 1974 album, *Mike Auldridge, Dobro* that next caught my ear. I was hooked. Over the next thirty years, I read everything I could get my hands on about lap-style guitar - from the Hawaiian Steel Guitar Association newsletters, to back issues of *Guitar Player*, to a dusty old copy of the *Alvino Rey Method for Singing Electric Guitar* – long forgotten on the shelves of the Boston Public Library.

Thus began a joyous journey of discovery that has taken me through a fascinating and ever eccentric backwater of the guitar stream with many twists, turns and convoluted byways. I discovered that lap-style guitar had been enchanting musicians and listeners for more than one hundred years in practically every genre of music. I've had the honor to speak with some of the greatest players ever to touch a steel guitar. I've whiled away hour upon hour lost in the beauty and power of the sound of a bar on strings - a sound that reflects every nuance of a player's touch, tone and expression.

This journey has culminated with the writing of this book. I hope it may serve as a road map for your own journeys with this fabulous instrument.

Andy Volk
Needham, Massachusetts

The world of steel guitar is one of contradictions and eccentricities. This book is about the *non-pedal acoustic and electric steel guitar* in all it's many incarnations. There is a certain amount of disagreement regarding the preferred terms for non-pedal instruments. *Lap Steel Guitar* is used in this book as a general category to mean *any* non-pedal acoustic or electric steel guitar that is played flat, perpendicular to the player and parallel to the floor, on either the player's lap or on a stand or set of telescoping legs. This includes all guitars commonly referred to as *lap steels, Hawaiian steel guitars, non-pedal steel guitars*, and *table steels*.

An important branch of the non-pedal steel guitar family is *not* represented in this book: resophonic guitars. These fascinating and beautiful instruments have their own family tree with a rich history and pantheon of excellent players who deserve documentation. Resonator guitars are truly a world unto themselves and you will find several fine books listed in the bibliography section for those who wish to more fully explore these instruments.

Lap-style guitar can be heard today in American roots styles, blues, bluegrass, Cajun, Indian classical music, country, rockabilly, Hawaiian, jazz, rock, western swing, sacred music and composed instrumental music, as well as in film scores and commercials. While there has also been a revival of interest in the older styles of playing, many modern bands have discovered how steel guitar can add to their music. All signs point to a healthy future for lap-style playing as upcoming generations will explore new aspects of this beautiful, haunting and most-expressive of musical instruments.

Because of the limitations of space, available information and/or photos, many fine and historically significant steel players could not be included here. Nevertheless, the past and present day musicians profiled within represent a significant sample of the most important contributors to the instrument.

Steel Guitar Tunings

Please note that all steel guitar tunings in this book are listed from highest string (1) to lowest string (6, 8 or 10), with the tuning name to the left of the note names, as in this example for C6th tuning:

Strings	1	2	3	4	5	6
C6th	E	C	A	G	E	C

- ¤ -

- ¤ A BRIEF HISTORY OF LAP-STYLE GUITAR ¤ -

While walking beside a railroad track in Hawaii one day in 1885, so the story goes, eleven-year old Joseph Kekuku could scarcely imagine the revolution he was about to spark in guitar technique and instrument design when he picked up a metal bolt and slid it along his guitar strings. Kekuku became the first to popularize the then radical new technique of sliding a metal bar along the strings to change the pitch of individual notes and chords while resting the guitar flat on the lap. The San Francisco Panama Pacific International Exposition, which lasted for most of 1915, introduced this Hawaiian style of playing to the mainland U.S., where it became wildly popular until well into the 40's.

Hawaiian steel guitar, or lap-style slide guitar, shares a parallel history in the African American tradition with the Diddly Bow, a one-string instrument made by stretching the wire used to fasten a broom or hay bale across a wall or door. The player would then slide a knife or bottle along the string to change the pitch of a single note while plucking with the other hand.

By the early decades of the 20th Century, slide guitar playing had divided into two streams: bottleneck-style, played on standard Spanish guitars using a glass or metal tube on the player's finger, and lap-style, played on instruments specifically designed for that purpose. While bottleneck-style became associated mostly with blues music, lap-style playing made inroads into other musical genres, including commercial Hawaiian music, vaudeville, country, Cajun, big band and western swing.

While the first lap-style Hawaiian guitarists simply raised the strings on their standards guitars for lap-style playing, over time, musicians replaced their modified standard guitars with new instruments intended for lap-style technique.

Short-scale, solid-neck and hollow-neck wooden acoustic steel guitars gave way to much louder, metal-bodied instruments that used internal aluminum resonators. As audiences and concert venues increased in size, the need for ever-increasing volume led most professional steel players to abandon their resonator guitars for the electric steel guitars that became widely available in the early 1930s. These early, 6-string, single neck electric instruments evolved to double, triple and even quadruple-neck guitars culminating, in the early 1950s, with the modern pedal steel guitar. Today's pedal steel guitars have ten to fourteen strings per neck, three to eight pedals, and knee levers for individually raising or lowering the pitch of strings.

The pedal steel is a fantastic instrument with its own remarkable history in many genres of music. The focus of this book, however, remains the lap steel guitar, a musical instrument that continues to challenge today's luthiers and players to reach new heights of personal expression.

- ¤ -

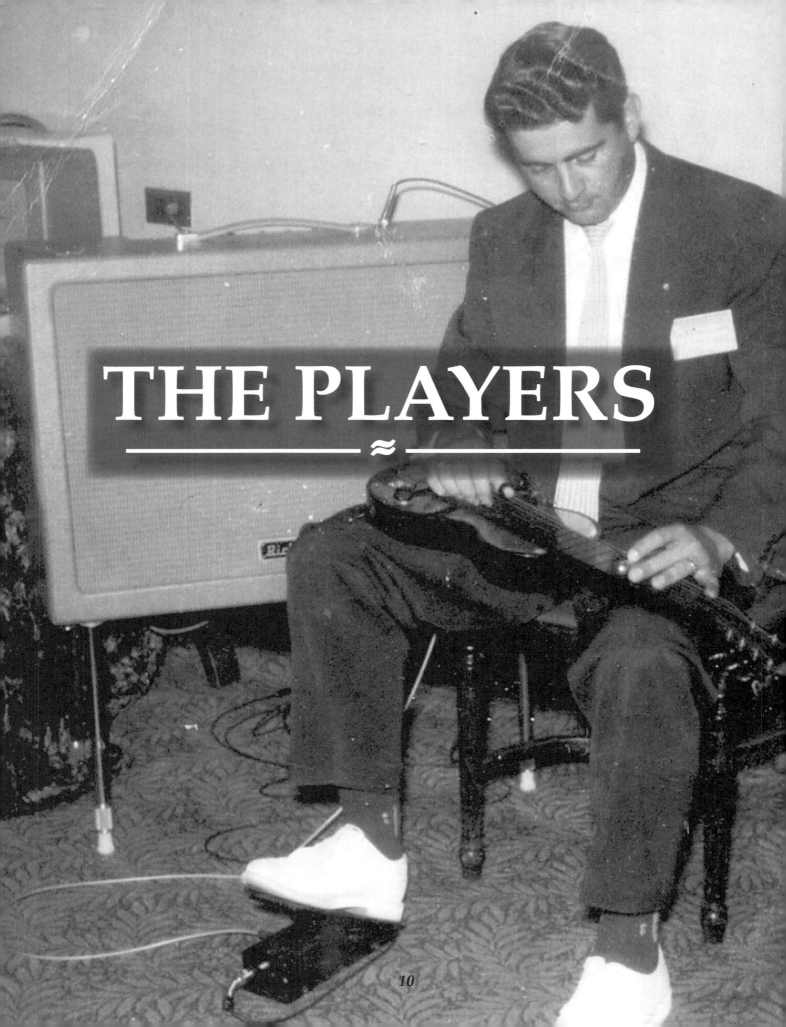

THE PLAYERS

- ¤ HAWAIIAN MUSIC ¤ -

The guitar was first brought to the Hawaiian Islands in the 1830's by Spanish and Mexican cowboys hired by King Kamehameha III to work the cattle ranches. The Hawaiians adopted the instrument into their music, an evolving mix of traditional chants, church songs of the missionaries, and later, even military marches and ragtime.

Hawaiian guitarists detuned - or *slacked* - the strings of their standard guitars to suit the keys of their vocals, thus creating one of the world's great fingerstyle guitar traditions. Slack key playing is a largely improvisational style played in a variety of open chord tunings, many of which became closely guarded secrets even within families. The paradigm shifted that day in 1885 when Joseph Kekuku discovered the joys of sliding.

While there are theories about an Indian origin for the style, for all intents and purposes, lap-style guitar was born and developed in Hawaii by Kekuku and others. Though Kekuku left the islands for the mainland United States in 1904, it was the 1915 Panama Pacific International Exposition, held in San Francisco, that created a thirty-year-long fad for Hawaiian culture.

Some of the more prominent early acoustic Hawaiian-style players include Keoki Awai, Sol K. Bright, Tau Moe, Sam Ku West, David Kane, Bob Paoli (of the duo Jim and Bob), Pale K. Lua, Mike Hanapi, Ben Hokea, David Kahanamoku Kaili, M.K. Moke, and Frank Ferera, a Portugeuse-Hawaiian who was the most frequently recorded of any lap-style player between about 1915 and 1930.

Tin Pan Alley obliged the demand for Hawaiiana by supplying a seemingly limitless number of Hapa Haole (half white) tunes. In Hawaii, Charles King composed many melodies in the Hawaiian language that became standards. Hollywood eventually joined the music publishers in helping to perpetuate a fantasy of an idealized island lifestyle in many of its films. Professional and amateur musicians throughout America formed Hawaiian combos and the sale of lessons and instruments flourished, thanks to door-to-door sales and mail order.

Hawaiian-style met American jazz in the recordings of "King" Bennie Nawahi and the great Sol Hoopii, whose technique and showmanship was echoed by vaudeville artists such as Roy Smeck, "the Wizard of the Strings".

The introduction of electrical amplification in the mid 1930's had a profound effect on commercial Hawaiian music which had, by this time, largely merged with Hapa Haole music. Rickenbacher's aluminum frypan electric steel guitar was an instant success with musicians and heralded one of the most fertile periods in the history of steel guitar design. Great Hawaiian-style steel guitarists of the past noted for their electric steel guitar playing include Dick McIntire, Andy Iona, Sam Koki, Ralph Kolsiana, Jules Ah See, Pua Almeida, Hal Aloma, Danny Stewart, Gabby Pahinui, Eddie Bush, David "Feet" Rogers, David Keli'i, and Billy Hew Len.

Modern Hawaiian players recognized for their skills on the instrument include Alan Akaka, Jerry Byrd, Greg Sardinha, Owana Salazar, Casey Olsen, Duke Ching, John Ely, Bob Brozman, Bobby Ingano, and Herbert Hanawahine.

Sol Hoopii

[Hoopii is pronounced: Ho-Oh-Pee-Ee]

Solomon Hoopii Kaai was the first steel guitarist to combine Hawaiian music with American jazz; a potent combination that had a profound influence on the first generation of Dobro and lap steel guitarists in both Hawaiian music and western swing.

Born in Honolulu in 1902, Sol was one of 21 children. As a teenager, he stowed away on a Matson liner to San Francisco along with two compatriots. After they were discovered, so the story goes, their fellow passengers paid their fares upon hearing them play. Adept at ukulele and standard guitar, as well as steel guitar, Sol formed a highly successful trio with Lani McIntire and Glenwood Leslie. The trio was in great demand in clubs, theatres, and movie soundstages where Sol made many film appearances throughout the early 1930s. Sol's recording career extended from 1925 until the early 1950's and included traditional Hawaiian standards, contemporary Hawaiian songs and hot jazz. His style was inspired by the jazz players of his era, especially clarinet and horn players, such as jazz legend, Bix Beiderbecke. His many recordings, while sounding very much of their era, nevertheless radiate a certain timelessness in no small part due to the audacity of Sol's steel technique and the creativity he brought to the instrument.

After a successful career in commercial music, Sol left secular music behind in 1938 to become a disciple of evangelist Aimee Semple McPherson, and his last recordings were almost all religious songs.

Sol's earliest recordings were in low-bass or high-bass A major tuning. He also played in a number of variations on E major tuning and innovated the C# minor tuning, which afforded him the close-voiced swing sound that so caught the ear of other players.

Sol Hoopii's Tunings						
Strings	1	2	3	4	5	6
A (low-bass)	E	C#	A	E	A	E
A (high-bass)	E	C#	A	E	C#	A
E major	E	B	G#	E	B	E
C# minor	E	C#	G#	E	D	B

Beyond his innovations in steel technique and tunings, Sol was a trendsetter in his use of the metal-bodied National Tricone and later in his career, the Rickenbacher Bakelite and Dickerson electric steels.

Even today, more than half a century after Sol last recorded, his tone and technique remain virtually unrivaled on acoustic steel. His stamp on American popular music remains indelible even though many musicians remain unaware of the Hawaiian wellspring of the tunings and licks they're playing.

- ¤ -

Ralph Kolsiana

Because he recorded only a handful of 78 RPM records and never played live radio dates, Ralph Kolsiana is unjustly forgotten as a pioneer electric lap steel player. Born in Hawaii of Dutch, Brazilian and Peruvian heritage, Kolsiana was raised in Philadelphia, PA and died in Los Angeles in 2002 at age 90. His swinging approach to the instrument was equally influenced by traditional Hawaiian music and hot jazz. He remained a lifelong jazz fan who appreciated Charlie Parker and Dizzy Gillespie as well as Laurindo Almeida and Barney Kessel. Somewhat of a Renaissance man, he was a photographer, sculptor, fabric designer, and Black Belt in Kung Fu in addition to his musical pursuits.

As a child, he studied in Philadelphia with Jimmy Kahanalopua, who had a style similar to Sol Hoopii's. Ralph's career included recording for the RCA Bluebird label, playing on motion picture soundtracks, gigging at hundreds of clubs all over America and rubbing shoulders with the greats and not-so-greats, such as Al Capone, who hired Ralph's band to serenade him and his gang from behind blue velvet curtains while they cavorted with their lady friends.

The following interview took place in 1992 and appeared originally under the author's byline in *Steel Guitar World Magazine*.

- ¤ Ralph Kolsiana ¤ -

How and when did you first learn to play steel guitar?

I started back around 1930 or '32. My father had a friend Jimmy Kahanalopua, who ran the Royal Conservatory of music in Philadelphia. I studied with him.

Who were your earliest steel guitar influences?

My earliest influence was, of course, Sol Hoopii. After hearing Sol, every Hawaiian band wanted to use a steel guitar. Not many people know that Hoot Gibson, the famous cowboy movie star, brought Sol out here to Los Angeles to play with his western group. That's how the western guys got into using the steel guitar. I don't think anybody's ever covered that story. This was way, way, back as I recall, in the early 20's. There weren't very many players during those days and nobody had a native Hawaiian steel player except Hoot Gibson.

What other players did you listen to besides Sol Hoopii?

Pale K. Lua was one, though not as much as Sol. There was another Hawaiian player in Philadelphia who wasn't with the Royal Conservatory whose name was Paul Kula. Later, I was influenced by Dick McIntire, Danny Stewart and Andy Iona. There was also a real good steel player from up in Connecticut somewhere, David Burrows. It was *David Burrows and his Five Hot Shots*. Today, my favorite player is David Keli'i.

What was your first instrument?

At first, I was using a steel guitar that I converted from a Spanish guitar. I cemented a post in the center under the sound hole and attached the top from our old hand-cranked brass doorbell. Later we got an electric bell and I screwed that onto the post and found I got quite a resonance out of that. I went out with a group on the Steel Pier in Atlantic City. I joined that group in about 1934. At the time, they were just coming out with the Dobros and the Nationals, wooden instruments with metal resonators.

When I first went out to Steel Pier, I still had that old wooden guitar with the raised nut and that bell inside of it! Back then, the instrument companies supplied all the instruments - to give them public exposure, of course. We had Dobros for a while, then they came out with the Rickenbacher electrics and they were superior to anything we had before. We even had electric mandolins in the band as well as steel and Spanish guitar. After I had my first pancake [*Rickenbacher Frypan electric steel*], I got hold of black Bakelite steel with chrome plates and I liked that a lot. I alternated between that and the frypan. I still have that first electric frypan, it's serial number 004.

What guitar are you playing and what tunings are you using today?

I play a 1950 double-8 Fender. E9th tuning has been my favorite for a number of years. I used E9th before I even knew what E9th was because, being an ear player and not a music reader, I discovered this tuning for myself way back around 1940. I had been using the old E7th tuning as well as the A7th and the A-major tuning. When I found the E9th [*technically, E13th*] I kinda stuck with it and it's the one I still use most today on my inside neck. On the outside neck, I've experimented with a lot of other tunings like D9th and B11th, but since I played at the Hula Hut in Santa Monica in the 50's, I've been using C13th on the outside neck.

- ¤ Ralph Kolsiana ¤ -

Ralph Kolsiana's Tunings								
Strings	1	2	3	4	5	6	7	8
E13th	E	C#	G#	F#	D	B	G#	E
C13th	E	C	A	G	E	C	Bb	C

Do you have any tips for beginning steel players?

I would recommend E9th tuning because of its versatility - being able to find harmonies and chords without jumping around too far.

You played a very wide variety of music, not just Hawaiian, right?

In those days you had to play the popular tunes of the day, standards like *Honeysuckle Rose, Sweet Sue, Sweet Georgia Brown,* and on occasion we did Chinese tunes, Japanese tunes, Samoan, Tahitian, even some Maori music from New Zealand - they're all Polynesian, of course - and some tunes from Fiji, which are Mikeronesian.

That's an incredible range of music.

We even learned some Hebrew songs when we played the Young Men's Hebrew Association in Brooklyn! Later on, I joined Ida's Hawaiians up in Reading, PA, which had many German people who loved Hawaiian music. We learned all kinds of German songs and polkas.

How did the Waikiki Swingsters come to record for RCA?

In 1935, Mr. Oberheim, the agent for RCA, caught our act on Steel Pier and brought us to RCA's studios in Camden, NJ.

[*The Waikiki Swingsters originally included Ralph's brother Johnny Kolsiana playing Django Reinhardt-inspired lead guitar on a Gibson archtop acoustic, along with a rhythm guitarist and upright bassist. Their music was a mix of hot swing tunes and Hawaiian standards.*]

You would record direct to acetate, wouldn't you? If you made a mistake you'd have to stop?

Oh yeah, we didn't have any rehearsal time. We were on such a tight schedule. So we picked all the songs we were used to playing regularly so we wouldn't have to stop. We didn't make any mistakes evidently - except my brother - a little hesitation he did on one take. Oberheim didn't think it was very serious so he let it go.

Your brother Johnny's guitar playing came very close to Django's style. People today are still trying to play those licks but it was pretty unusual to hear back in the 30's.

Yeah, Johnny came very close. He was fortunate during the war to wind up in Paris with the Air Force. He had taken his guitar with him and went and sat in with Django. That was the thrill of his life. They were really surprised. He really knocked 'em out; the whole club went wild. How many people get to satisfy the thrill of a lifetime - get to meet their idol and play with them?

Very few. What a great experience!

Later in the war, he was shot down over Mindanao but he made it back.

Waikiki Swingsters, 1936, L to R: Don Ferarer, Larry Shuller, Bill Holt, Ralph Kolsiana

What do you think of modern steel playing and the pedal steel?

I think the pedal steel has great potential but could be played to sound a little more natural. Joaquin Murphy, for example, has a real human touch. Some other pedal steel playing I've heard has a mechanical edge to it that you can't get away from. It's partly the nature of the instrument but there are some players I hear who don't have - the only thing I can call it is soul - in their playing. It's harder to put expression into a pedal steel because of the mechanical make-up of changing chords with pedals. That is my opinion.

How can steel players play more soulfully?

A steel player should try to know the song they're playing so well they're able to put a little more of themselves into it. You can take two or three players, even on lap steel, with the same songs; they'll sound like themselves and not anybody else. Andy Iona didn't play like Eddie Bush and Eddie didn't play like Danny Stewart and Danny Stewart didn't play like Dick McIntire. When you're playing a number that you know, you kind of project yourself into playing what you feel and hear, what it is you're trying to say to the listener. You're trying to tell it in your own way.

- ¤ Ralph Kolsiana ¤ -

What do you think makes Hawaiian music unique?

Jimmy Kahanalopua always told me, "The steel guitar is the voice of Hawaii - an extension of the physical voice." That's what I was told and it's exactly the way I feel about it. An authentic Hawaiian singer will sound like a steel guitar. It's like an extension of a people's singing voice to the world.

- ¤ -

Keoki Awai & group, circa 1915

Dick McIntire

Before Jerry Byrd earned the appellation "Master of Touch and Tone", Dick McIntire *owned* the title. His sensitivity, time, perfect intonation, and sublime note choice were legendary to the generation of Hawaiian steel players of the 1930's & 1940's. Born in Hawaii around 1900, Dick spent his career in Los Angeles where he opened several teaching studios, appeared regularly on radio, and played on hundreds of recordings with artists such as Bing Crosby, Frances Langford, Ray Kinney and Lena Machado. His recordings as a leader with his own group, *The Harmony Hawaiians*, stand as textbook examples of harmony singing accompanied by deep, throbbing acoustic rhythm interlaced with Dick's economical but impossibly perfect intros, fills and solos. Out of print for years, some of McIntire's best work is currently available on CD from Australia's *Cumquat Records.*

Dick pioneered a smooth, legato approach to electric steel guitar that had a profound impact on Jerry Byrd in his formative years as well as on many other Hawaiian-style steel players. McIntire was noted for his use of the E7th, C#m and F#9th tunings.

Dick McIntire's Tunings						
Strings	1	2	3	4	5	6
E7th	E	B	G#	D	B	E
C# minor	E	C#	G#	E	B	E
F#9th	E	C#	G#	E	A#	F#

- ¤ -

Andy Iona

Andrew Aiona Long was one of the most talented and prolific of the second generation of Hawaiian-born steel guitarists who migrated to the east and west coasts of the U.S. to take advantage of the opportunites for work in nightclubs, radio and recording studios. Along with Sol Hoopii, he was a key figure in the melding of traditional Hawaiian music with the popular American idioms of jazz, blues and swing.

Born in Honolulu in 1902, Andy became proficient on both saxophone and clarinet despite a youthful machine shop accident that cost him his right thumb. He also mastered steel guitar which he played with three finger picks and a thumbpick turn backwards to help accentuate multi-string strums. He favored a Rickenbacher Frypan played with a wide, fast vibrato.

Iona did stints as a sax player with the *Royal Hawaiian Band*, *Johnny Noble's Orchestra*, and other bands in both Hawaii and the mainland U.S. In 1928 and '29, Iona recorded four highly regarded sessions on Columbia, backing up Sol Hoopii as part of a saxophone quartet. He formed his group, *The Islanders*, in 1934 and spent much of the next 30 years working as a bandleader, arranger, and steel guitarist for radio, studio recordings and Hollywood film scores, including an 8-year tour with skater Sonja Henie's *Hollywood Ice Revue*. Iona died in 1966.

David "Feet" Rogers

David "Feet" Rogers' style on the Hawaiian steel guitar was unique and transcendently beautiful. He could spin a gossamer thread of melody played entirely in harmonics that seemed to float above the rhythm. His style represents a folksy, back porch kind of playing, much closer to Hawaiian music as it was played by the people at family gatherings and informal luaus and jam sessions than the music found at the nightclubs of Waikiki.

Born in 1935 in Kalihi, Hawaii, Rogers grew up in a home he described as having "plenty music, plenty Hawaiian food, plenty love." His skill at barefoot football earned him the lifetime nickname "Feet".

Feet came from a line of steel players who included his father George, and Uncle Benny Rogers. For many years, the unique tuning they all used was a family secret. According to Feet: "How we tune the steel is kind of like a chant or a family song, you know. It belongs to us and we have to take care of it or else it will change like everything else."

David "Feet" Rogers' Tuning						
Strings	1	2	3	4	5	6
D major	F#	D	A	F#	D	D (low)

In 1960, when he was playing with Eddie Naeole, Feet was approached by slack key master, Gabby Pahinui, Ukulele virtuoso Eddie Kamae, and bassist, Joe Marshall to join their new group called the *Sons of Hawaii*. Their approach to Hawaiian music proved a tremendous hit with audiences and the *Sons of Hawaii's* albums remain among the best selling Hawaiian music of all time. David Rogers died in 1983.

Barney Isaacs

Barney Isaacs steel guitar playing eptomized Hawaiian soul music presented with a unique treble-dominated tone. According to Alan Akaka, former President of the Hawaiian Steel Guitar Association, Isaacs was "... known to play intricate chordal backgrounds behind the singers. He favored the C6th (aka C13th) and E9th tunings. Occasionally, Barney would play the B11th tuning. Over the years he used a Magnatone double-neck short scale and Fender Stringmaster triple-neck long scale. This artist had a jovial personality and was loved by many. One could find him on many recordings amongst artists such as Charles Kaipo Miller, Danny Kaleikini, Sterling Mossman, Marlene Sai, Haunani Kahalewai, Ed Kenney and many, many more."

The son of steel guitarist and composer, Alvin Isaacs, Barney was the first-call steel player for many years for the *Hawaii Calls* radio programs and served as musical director at the Kahala Hilton. He died in 1996.

- ¤ -

Billy Hew Len

One of the all-time greats of Hawaiian steel, Billy Hew Len, like Django Reinhardt, overcame an incredible physical handicap (the loss of his left hand) to become a virtuoso of his instrument. Through intense practice and dedication, Billy became a master of the instrument, thanks to a leather glove with an attached steel bar that replaced his missing hand.

Billy Hew Len's Tunings								
Strings	1	2	3	4	5	6	7	8
A6th	E	C#	A	F#	E	C#	A	F#
F major 7th	E	C	A	F	E	C		
D9th	E	C	A	F#	E	C#		
A13b9th	E	C#	A	F#	E	C#	Bb	G
E6th	E	C#	B	G#	E	D	E	G#

24

- ¤ Billy Hew Len ¤ -

His style is characterized by lush, throbbing chord work alternating with very fast arpeggios and volume swells using the knob on the face of the guitar, all informed by a very Hawaiian sense of swing. Billy Hew Len died in 1987.

The following interview was edited from a long-lost lesson given by Billy in a Honolulu hotel room to an eager student sometime in the late 1960s or early 1970s - its exact provenance is lost. Thanks to Canadian musician, George Lake, for supplying the tape.

What are some of the tunings that you use?

My main tuning is A6th. The reason why I use A6th is because you can play the sweet Hawaiian way or get jazz sounds. Because of the tuning Feet Rogers uses, everything's harder - not as pretty. Feet Rogers learned from his uncle, Benny Rogers. They play the way they do because of the tuning they use. There's another reason I use A6th: I used to play a C6th a long time ago, but I couldn't play in the low register in the key of F. The advantage of this for ad libbing is you're in a lower register in A6th than C6th in the key of F. In C, you don't have the lower register. As you go higher up the neck, it doesn't tend to sustain as well in the higher register.

Changing tunings is a matter of plucking certain strings and knowing the tuning you're using. Where we play, you don't have time to start tuning all over the place, when you're on a job. So, you have to be there right away. You want a fast action by having melody notes close together.

Very few people know about this [A13b9] tuning - it's got fantastic 7th chords; very pretty but it takes time to learn to play. You have to pluck your strings and really listen to the harmony that you hear. You can play diminished chords with this tuning. It's hard to play diminished chords without pedals. You usually have to play two-part harmony. With this tuning, you can get diminished chords in four-part harmony.

F major 7th is a good tuning. The sound that Gabby [*Pahinui*] makes is similar to this.

I heard Alvino Rey play E6th one time. He hit this one chord and I grabbed my guitar and tuned it the same way. I never had an 8-string guitar or a pedal guitar back then. It's a good tuning for background sounds. If you have two guitars, this is the one you use for playing background. You get a real Hawaiian sound. To play this tuning solo, you would have to really concentrate because the harmonies are not close - they're wide apart. On one neck you play the solo and when the guys sings, you play big fat beautiful chords on the other. I love this sound. I used to stay up all night, hours and hours, and hours playing it. My brothers would want to kill me. I have nine brothers! Whew! (Laughs)

How important is register?

Some guys play way up high; a constant high sound. You want a difference in the variety of the sound - not just one high sound. You need high, low and medium.

Your style is among the jazziest of all the Hawaiian players.

For jazz style on A6th, I use all octaves and substitute chords. Wes Montgomery, he's the guy that originated this sound [*on standard guitar*] but I played like him thirty years ago. That's how much my mind was ahead in sound.

- ¤ Billy Hew Len ¤ -

Do you feel you have a personal style?

People talk about style. I don't have a style. I don't know what the hell a style is. I just play Hawaiian -style like I want to play it.

- ¤ -

Jerry Byrd

Born in 1920 in Lima, Ohio, Jerry Byrd is undoubtedly the single most influential electric lap steel player in history. Along with Don Helms, Billy Robinson and Howard White, Jerry Byrd created the foundation for the Nashville steel guitar sound. His instantly identifiable touch and tone feature impossibly perfect intonation and slant bar technique with a trademark vibrato and mastery over harmonics. He has been an innovator with his development of the C6th and C-Diatonic tunings as well as a composer of lap steel standards, such as *Steelin' The Blues* and *Steelin' the Chimes*.

- ¤ Jerry Byrd ¤ -

His career has been almost equally divided between country and Hawaiian music. His work in the country music field can be heard in his legendary recordings with such artists as Hank Williams, Chet Atkins, Jethro Burns, Marty Robbins, Hank Snow, Roy Clarke, Ernest Tubb, Red Foley, Burl Ives and numerous others. His influence on professional steel players is incalculable and his recordings have set an olympian standard for the steel guitar faithful.

A lifelong exponent of Hawaiian music, Byrd grew tired of the pressure of commercial country music and moved to Honolulu in the early 1970s. Since then, he has become revered for his efforts to teach native Hawaiians about steel guitar, to the extent that some credit him with single-handedly saving the steel guitar from extinction in Hawaii. Byrd's style has been so influential, it has arguably, become the most-imitated way to play Hawaiian music.

The following interview (practically a soliloquy) with Jerry Byrd aired in 1973 on Canada's CBC Radio Network. It was conducted in Hawaii and edited by broadcaster, Laurie Mills. Transcribed by the author, it is reprinted with the kind permission of Mr. Mills.

Professionals like Buddy Emmons, Curley Chalker, Julian Tharpe and perhaps Lloyd Green – those players whose names are known around the world - got their start by listening to the king, Jerry Byrd. This man, using a non-pedal steel guitar, has done more to popularize the instrument and spread the gospel of steel guitar than any other dozen steel players. This is Jerry Byrd's story but it is also the steel guitar's story.

The first steel guitar that was played on a country record was by Lani McIntire who later became famous in the Hawaiian music field - he wrote the song *The One Rose*. He had two brothers, Dick and Al. Dick was a great steel guitar player. Al played bass and they all joined the navy and left Hawaii together and ended up in California. Lani played on Jimmy Rogers' first records.

I was a kid born in Ohio and one day a tent show came through my hometown and that was quite a big thing. When a tent show came to your hometown you went! If you had the money that is (which I didn't) but I had a buddy who came from a pretty well-to-do family so he said, "Let's go see the show." I said, "I don't have any money" but he said, "That's okay, I'll pay your way." So we walked all the way across town to the tent show. I walked in and it was a troupe of Hawaiians. This guy playing this beautiful steel guitar - the old National metal resonator guitar - all silver, with that shine! Between the shine and the music it captivated me. So that was the day that changed my life. I knew that I wanted to play that instrument so I went from there. I learned the hard way, the hunt and peck system.

So when I graduated from high school, I joined a country music show – the Renfro Valley Barn Dance - which was a big show at that time and went on from there. The first records I made on a big scale were with Ernest Tubb. I played the same things that I had been playing for years. At that time I was working in a radio station in Detroit, WJR. That job ended and I got a call from Ernest Tubb. The first thing we did was go to Chicago and make records. I played the same type of fills and everything I had been playing for years and all at once I was discovered. Then I worked with Red Foley and I started recording on my own in 1949 with Mercury.

I listened to the Hawaiians because they were really the only ones who were playing the steel guitar at that time. Dick McIntire was my particular favorite although there were so many great ones: Andy Iona, Sam Koki, Sol Hoopii - all of them contributed to steel guitar. A lot of the kids like me that were learning to play, you couldn't play Hawaiian music in the middle of Ohio so you play the next thing to come along which was country music. I know Joaquin Murphy out in California picked up a lot of his stuff from Sol Hoopii. Roy Wiggins got a lot of his stuff from Hawaiians; that was the only place you heard it.

The first real impressive steel guitar player that I heard in country music was in western swing: Leon McAuliffe. When he made a movie with Bob Wills I went and sat through that about four times to hear him play one chorus of *Ida Red*. Really, my style was a Hawaiian style of playing and it lent itself so well to country music - when I say country, I mean the country music of the time - it has changed considerably. I don't mean today's country music, as I sit and listen to it. If I had to sit down and play a chorus I really don't know what I would play that would fit that type of material. When I talk about country music I'm talkin' about the 40's & 50's, before Elvis Presley put everybody out of work. The Red Foley-type of ballads was really the thing that I liked, like *The Blues in My Heart*, that type of song.

In the 40's and 50's when you were playing with various groups, you were mostly playing on records rather than playing dances where one could experiment. Do you think your music would have turned out differently had you been doing more dances?

Oh yes, I'm sure it would have. Like you say, you can experiment. Take Curley Chalker for instance, who's a fantastic steel guitar player; a great technician who has complete command of the instrument. Curley did a lot of work in Las Vegas working half the night or all night. So you're really playing practically constantly. Curley got to do a lot of experimenting and formed his jazz style of playing from that background. We all play our personalities and background. Your background reflects what you do. And I think that's why Curley is so great and so fast - because he had a lot of time to practice. I didn't. You can't experiment on record sessions. In fact, later on in Nashville I started working with a five-piece dance band just to do that - to get to play something different and be able to experiment more. I'm doing that over here too [*Hawaii*].

When you stay in one area and only play in one area like I was in Cincinnati and Detroit you hardly even get out of the state. I wasn't doing road work, just radio and TV. All at once you start getting' letters from all over the world and you start to say gee, why would they pay any attention to me? It's all kinda of grown since then. It kind of came to a head when they had the International Steel Guitar Convention in St. Louis and they wanted me to close it out on a Sunday. I played the last hour and they gave me a standing ovation and a plaque in recognition for what I've contributed to steel guitar and it just overwhelmed me.

I'm glad and I'm grateful that I could contribute what I had to my instrument. If I was able to encourage or inspire or help anybody, I always did. I don't know anybody that I ever refused to help. I've always been for steel guitar. I think when you're dedicated to one thing – whatever it is - and if you spend your lifetime in sincere dedication, it all comes back good. When they gave me the plaque, I told 'em I could name at least eight or ten other guys that deserved the same thing.

Why did you come to Hawaii?

Why did I come to Hawaii? It's a combination of things, but mostly, I wanted to put something back into the instrument and into the music that I had taken out of it for so many years. My first love was Hawaiian music – still is. It does something to me that no other music does and I'm not talking about the tourist-type Hawaiian music but the country-type Hawaiian music, which is their country music. Knowing the people even before I came over here, in their love and sincerity, I seemed to identify with them. Nashville has gotten to be a giant. I've seen it grow from the beginnings and was a part of it, for which I'm grateful, but I couldn't seem to identify with it anymore. I wasn't happy. So I thought, "Why don't I go over where I can play what I want to play?"

- ¤ Jerry Byrd ¤ -

Also, it concerned me that a lot of the kids over here never heard of steel guitar. I want to teach the kids and be sure the steel guitar is always in Hawaiian music, where it belongs and where it identifies Hawaiian music the world over. When I played the Blue Dolphin Room here, I met people from all over the world who come to see me and visit and they're upset that they hear Hawaiian music but don't hear any steel guitars anymore. So we're doing something about that.

I'm teaching some boys now. I've got one that's playing professionally and a few more that soon will be, so I'm enjoying that. I feel like I'm contributing something back and I'm glad that I can do that. I could probably teach 10 hours a day, 6 days a week. I've gotten a lot of calls; even professional musicians over here. Although I appreciate that, that's not where I want to spend my time. I want to get to the kids 'cause that's where it's gonna live. There are plenty of kids that want to learn. I've been beating the drum for the three years or so I've been over here.

You know the Hawaiians have been exploited every which way that you can imagine and they probably thought, "Well, here's another Haole that's come over here and gonna tell us what we need to do." They sit back and listen - don't say anything - just listen. But now they've finally come to the conclusion that I'm sincere in what I want to do so now they're all with me.

I saw my first pedal steel guitar in 1939, believe it or not. Back then you didn't have the mechanical know-how, machine tools and what have you they have now. They had all kinds of things to pull strings, they were very ingenious but they just didn't work. You were forever out of tune if not breaking strings and I couldn't stand that. So I said they're going to have to come a long way with these things before I'll play one.

So the next one I saw in a really good form was in 1949, when I went to California. Ernest Tavares was playin' it. Ernest and Freddie worked with Harry Owens forever and Freddie's with the Fender guitar company now. So Ernest had a pedal steel, which was good. But by that time I had started making recordings that were doing well so being a stylist as I am, like Chet Atkins or other people who are stylists, when you have a style, you have to stay with it. If you move away from it, you lose all of your people – the people that buy your records.

Pedals started to get popular when Bud Issacs brought it to Nashville. By that time I had a big fan club and I asked the members what they thought about me going to pedal guitar. They wrote back, 99 out of 100, "No, if we want that, we'll go buy *their* records."

Pedals raise and lower the strings but I'm not sure they get the same effect that I can by using the bar. I can do it more relaxed, more natural. It's a hard thing to describe. I think I can sit down with a pedal player and have him move one string in harmony like a two-part or three-part harmony and he can do it with pedals and I can do it without pedals and it wouldn't sound the same at all. Because I think I could do mine a little slower than he can pull that pedal down, you know? I'm not sure that it's a lazy man's way of playing - they're sure busy enough with their feet and their picks. I don't think there's a lazy way you can play any musical instrument. (Laughs)

So like everything else in country music, you're an identity; part of everybody's family. They want you for what you do. Like Ernest Tubb, Red Foley, and Hank Williams were all separate entities and they loved each but they didn't want them to change. It came to a place where I had to make a decision whether to join everybody else and go to pedals or to be a stylist and stay with what I was doing. After much deliberation I decided I'd just continue with what I was doing. I still think it was the right decision.

A lot of people think I'm crusading you see, and I'm not. It doesn't matter to me what kind of a steel guitar you play; what make, how many strings, how many necks, how many pedals.

- ¤ Jerry Byrd ¤ -

It makes no difference to me as long as it's steel guitar and they play music. A lot of people don't understand I guess. They think everybody should sound pretty much alike and I don't agree - especially with steel guitar. It's the most individual instrument in the world. You can take fifty steel guitar players, especially on non-pedal, and they would *all* sound different. Because the least little slur makes you different than the other guy.

So I don't care what they play if it's a steel guitar. I've heard some Dobro players that just flat knock me out - like Josh Graves - he's great. I love it. I would like to see some of the pedal guys get away from the conformity - sounding too much the same tone, the same licks. I know there's more than that can be done with a pedal guitar. A little more melody playing, maybe that's old fashioned - a lot of guys are afraid to sound old fashioned but I think they'd realize, if they just play the melody, play it with some feeling and some coloring here and there that it would be a whole new thing. It'll never be out of style - not ever.

I would like to see that done with pedal steel. A lot of people say, "Why don't you do it?" I say,   "I have too much to do with what I'm doing." Basically, I'm too old to go fight that battle.

You know, a guitar has never played itself. They just stand there or lay there. It's up to you to play 'em. The number of strings and the number of pedals will not make a player - not ever. Sadly enough if it would I'd go buy me one! You still gotta play music. Some people are too caught up in the race: "I'm gonna get one more pedal than the other guy."

Another thing I've never agreed with is making steel guitar a chord instrument. I don't hear it as a chord instrument. I hear it as a lead instrument. You can take a chord on a steel guitar - a 9th, a 7th, what ever you want - and play the same inversion note-for-note on the Spanish guitar and it doesn't sound anything alike. Steel guitar to me is really not a great chord instrument, even with all the possibilities today for pedals, and that was the reason they invented pedals, of course, to get more chord possibilities and to eliminate a lot of work with the left hand as far as slant bar techniques. But they're all too much influenced by what everybody else is playin'.

I played a trade show and some boy came up to me and saw my little ol' black Bakelite Rickenbacher that's in the Hall of Fame. He said, "Is that the guitar you use all the time?" And I said, "Yeah." I was playing in the Rickenbacker guitar company's suite at the show. I said "Why?" He said "Well, you play a lot of stuff so you must play a pedal guitar. I've heard that you've got one at home you keep in a closet and only bring it out for recording sessions." (Laughs). I said "No, this is what I play. I'm not up here sellin' guitars. They pay me to come up and play and that's what I'm doin'." I don't think he ever did believe me.

I did an album called *Admirable Byrd* and I did a lot of pedal sounds in there, not as good as the pedal guys could do it but it was that sound and it was still different. I wrote a lot of the tunes to show what you could do without pedals in an E9th tuning. I got a lot of mail. One of the songs is *I'll be all smiles tonight* and I do a lot of bar slant work, you know, and a lot of people still don't believe I did it without a pedal guitar but I did. To me it's kinda silly. Why would I lie about it if I did play pedals! I'd tell 'em.

If you're a professional musician and you play music for a living, then you've got to play what your employer's going to pay you to play and nine times out of ten they'll want you to play the sounds that they hear today, which are pedal sounds. If you like that and you really dig that style then, why not? But if you want to play something else, you don't feel like pedals are your thing - it might be Dobro guitar; it's just as popular in another field - then really, you've gotta play what you really want to play because that's what you're going to be the best at.

- ¤ Jerry Byrd ¤ -

Of course in my position, having pioneered a lot of this stuff, the C6th tuning and everything, I can always work doin' my thing. If a guy was starting out today, I wouldn't advise him to copy Jerry Byrd or anyone else, really - especially a non-pedal guitar player unless you really love that type of sound. If you do then you'll be good at it and you'll find some work. Looking at it in a cold, hard commercial light, I would advise them to play pedal guitar. I was lucky. Back in the days when I did a lot of recording, they just said, "You take a chorus" or "You do the intro" or "You do a turn around" and nobody told you what to play. But now they do. Everybody gathers around the steel guitar on a session and everybody knows how to play one except the guy playin' it for some reason. It gets to be a little cold blooded and it's more so now. They don't have the warmth and the fun - the real enjoyment of creating in the studio now that they did then. You have big business now. If you're playin' it as a business you've got to produce what they want to buy.

I have two old Rickenbachers. One's an old frypan that I take with me on shows 'cause it was the first electric steel guitar made and they're still the greatest. It's got a sound that's just out of this world. I play it for two reasons, one: to demonstrate what steel guitars looked like originally and number two: because I just love to play it. And I have my old 7-string [Bakelite] Rickenbacher that I used on a lot of recording sessions and a double-neck Sho-Bud that they made for me. It's a beautiful instrument and I use that 95% of the time. It's pretty much a custom built instrument.

When Sho-Bud made me this guitar they had to do some things to it they don't do to their other guitars. One thing I don't like is a tailpiece for steel guitar - I never have, you get a better sound running the strings through the body so they did that for me. It's a matter of taste. Little things like that companies have to do. I've had some other guitars I lend to people and they're using them and keeping them as keepsakes - maybe six in all.

You were one of the people involved in creating the Nashville sound as we now know it. Did you know what you were helping create at the time?

32

- ¤ Jerry Byrd ¤ -

No, and nobody else knew either; it was just something that evolved. At that time for recording sessions, there were only five or six guys doing the majority of 'em, Chet Atkins and myself and a few others. Back in those days, and Nashville still practices this, there's an interest in what the singer is tryin' to do. They'll go to extra lengths to see that they're satisfied. Which is good business. It's always been that way. Back when we started we didn't watch the clock, we were interested in recording four sides, having it good and everybody really pitchin' in.

When the New York singers and all the pop singers started coming to Nashville, that's the thing that impressed them the most - the desire on the part of the musicians to get a good record for them. So that's how Nashville got started and I think that's how they still practice. I hope so.

What I do with my boys - I have them from 11 years old up to college age - what I've found by trial and error and talking about someone who has no knowledge of steel guitar, I start 'em out with 6 strings. The first thing that they learn is the left hand: how to hold the bar, how to move it, how to slant it, forward slant first, reverse slant later. Then we start with a simple A major tuning. You're dealing with new ears and it's easier for them to hear a guitar tuned in thirds.

Then we move to E major, which eliminates some of the slant bar work of A major tuning and makes it a little easier to play - which is really the reason these tunings were discovered. We have six or eight lessons in E tuning, then E7th, then C#m which is a combination of A tuning and E tuning. They're able to get more chords and it starts sounding more like music to them. Then we go into C6th tuning - the final tuning that I teach. There you've got all your chords - at least in triads, major, minor, diminished , augmented, things like that. Then when they're done with that, if they want to get into note reading, they can.

By this time they're able to play pretty good. We then learn chord theory and note reading so they can learn a new tune by going out and buying the sheet music. That's my method.

We've got boys who are only 22 weeks into it playing some pretty advanced stuff. You talk about 22 *weeks* where it took me 22 *years;* I can teach them in 22 weeks 'cause I know the shortcuts. If I was teaching a pedal guitar I wouldn't start 'em out on pedals I don't think because it's too much to learn at once. Steel guitar is, I think, the only instrument in the world where you play position by sight and by ear. So I teach 'em the mechanics so they're relaxed with the playing part and they can then concentrate on what's written down in front of 'em.

It's a privilege to visit with you and your listeners and a privilege to put in another plug for steel guitar having done this for so many years. I'll probably do it until I drop. To me it's the instrument and I think it's just now comin' out of the woods worldwide. The thing I always tried to do was put steel guitar in more than one setting; country music, Hawaiian music, a suite with a symphony orchestra, a Japanese album, and one of the first albums in Nashville with steel guitar and strings: *Satin Strings of Steel* is the name of that album. I don't want it to be called strictly a Hawaiian instrument or a country instrument. I want it to be played in all kinds of musical settings.

[Jerry Byrd plays in many tunings. These are just a few of the more than 15 tunings he uses. His C6th tuning was the inspiration for the standard C6th pedal steel tuning and is very likely the most popular lap steel guitar tuning played today.]

Jerry Byrd's Tunings								
Strings	1	2	3	4	5	6	7	8
A major	E	C#	A	E	C#	A		
E major	E	B	G#	E	B	E		
E 7th	E	B	G#	E	D	B		
C# min	E	C#	G#	E	D	B		
C6th / A7th	E	C	A	G	E	C#	C	A
F# min9th	E	C#	G#	E	A#	F#	C#	G#
C Diatonic	E	C	B	A	G	F	E	
B11th	E	C#	A	F#	D#	C#	A	B

Jerry Byrd on Harmonics

*T*he technique of playing steel guitar harmonics involves picking the strings with the right hand at specific points or nodes to produce a bell-like tone (usually an octave or a 5th above the node point). Many Hawaiian steel guitarists have made extensive use of melodic lines played in harmonics in their music to change mood and texture or "draw in" the listener. Jerry Byrd has been recognized for many years for his remarkable ability at playing harmonics or "chimes" which requires great technical control as the player must keep his picking hand either 12, 5, or 7 frets away from the bar hand at all times. Jerry Byrd shared some of the secrets behind his techniques for playing harmonics on the Steel Guitar Forum:

Most of the time, although I can do three string strums occasionally, where it fits, mostly I do either single or two string harmony. Now, there is one way I do it that the leader of the two strings, like playing the first and second string, the second string would be harmonic and the first string would be open. So you get a different sound then, but the way I do it with my hand when I want both strings to be a harmonic, I just tilt my right hand (picking hand) down a little bit to where I use the thumb pick on those two strings, as the second string is picked first and the top string last. So by moving my hand over a little bit I can get both strings as harmonic if I wish.

On three strings usually you do it on a straight line. A slant depends on the tuning. But I can do it by my picking hand, if I'm doing a forward slant for instance, say first string on the 7th fret, 2nd on 6th and 3rd on 5th, you've got the 5, 6, 7, stair step. So I take my thumb pick and go on an angle, the palm of my hand which makes the harmonic goes on an angle from left to right, the same angle the bar is held in, and that's not easy to do but I do it in some places.

Now, I do another thing that I discovered during a session in Dallas, Texas. I can pick the top string by using my first finger pick (index finger pick) and picking backwards with that pick. The top string is harmonic and the bottom two open; I can pick three strings much easier. The bottom strings are either open or harmonic. I did this on *La Golondrina* on the *Hi-Fi Guitar* album. I just stumbled on it that day during the session, and it came out beautifully.

But the top strings are harmonic and the bottom strings are open, or the other way, the bottom strings are harmonic and the top strings are open. And they are a lot easier to do this way than the other, I can play in real high register as on that record and I can get every one of them just as clear as a bell. So that's the deal on harmonics.

- ¤ -

Greg Sardinha

L to R: Rick Rickard (guitar), Greg Sardinha (steel), Gordon Freitas (bass).

Greg Sardinha is a leading light of the generation of Hawaiian steel players whom Jerry Byrd taught in the 1970's. Greg is active on the Honolulu scene as a steel guitarist, virtuoso ukulele player and producer. His multi-volume CD series, *Made in Hawaii: Hawaiian Steel Guitar*, showcases instrumentals from a sampling of some of the finest players in the islands. In 2001, he was honored to be part of a troupe of Hawaiian musicians invited to perform at a series of concerts at the Kennedy Center in Washington, DC.

How did you come to play the Hawaiian steel guitar and who were your early influences on the instrument?

The first time I laid my eyes on a steel guitar I was right out of high school and playing guitar around town with a dance band. I still play a little guitar or double up on the bass or ukulele.

- ¤ Greg Sardinha ¤ -

Well, the drummer had a steel which I thought was pretty interesting, and I messed around with it for a while. I had a friend, Trip Isaacs, who was Barney Isaacs's son. We used to hang out and when I'd go over to his house I'd mess around with it [*steel guitar*]. Barney was so busy, he didn't really have a chance to teach. His son really didn't get interested 'till I got interested which is strange, because he comes from a musical family.

They had a class that taught Hawaiian instruments and I guess my first lesson was from Bill Palani and then Jerry Byrd had just moved here and he was starting to take on students. He came to this after-hours class and I was one of the guys he picked out along with Alan Akaka.

What was it like to take steel lessons from Jerry Byrd, one of the all-time masters of the instrument?

I didn't know who Jerry Byrd was at the time until I started doing some research and went, "Wow – this guy was big time!" I followed his trail you might say, realized who he was and thought that this was a great honor, especially when I heard his story how he learned from Hawaiians and wanted to give back. There's not really anyone teaching steel. He's pretty much the only one. He's stuck to his guns all this time and there are a lot of guys playing because of him.

What was he like as a teacher? Was he tough on you?

Yeah. He made it known that you had to be dedicated. You had to come every week and show improvement. I was a truck driver so I came in straight from work. I was dirty, stinky and everything when I sat there and plugged away. I really wanted to learn so it wasn't a problem trying to learn the material every week.

He was real tough. I had a problem holding the bar and week after week he would get on my case about it. 'Til this day I don't think I ever got it right (laughs). He's still being the teacher when he bumps into us today. He walks away shaking his head (laughs) I say: "Jerry, leave it alone already!" (Laughs).

What do you feel is the role of the steel guitar in Hawaiian music?

I go into sessions and I'm listening to the tracks and I do all the fills and I'm trying to fill in the spots. By the time I get done they tell me: "Man, that's what the song needed. It just needed the steel guitar to tie it together." I guess the role of the steel is as a lead instrument and a fill-in instrument. It's not really a strum instrument.

What guitars are you playing?

I have a Fender double-8 Stringmaster and Yasu Kamiya, who builds the Canopus steel guitars, gave me three steel guitars. He had me use them for about four months and wanted to know what I thought about it. It's pretty close to a Fender. I had Excels but I'm not really using the Excels anymore. When I do sessions in the studio I bounce back and forth between a Rickenbacher Bakelite and a Jerry Byrd frypan. I also have a Gibson EH-150.

What tunings do you use?

I use C6th [C13th] and B11th and sometimes I mess around with C# minor. I've kind of given up bouncing around with tunings. I have a guitar tuned to Jerry's diatonic tuning.

I got interested in that but I haven't really played it out. I have it here at home and I want to get more proficient on it. The stretches are a little longer.

Do you think tunings can be a kind of trap? Many players seem to try different tunings without really learning any one tuning well.

That's where I'm at; like the E13th tuning: I like the E13th and I've played around on it. It's like the C tuning without the E string. It all resolves back to the C6th. I find myself spending so much time messing around with tunings only to find it all revolves back to the C. I can do the same chords on the C, just in a different position." What used to be on maybe the 1st, 2nd and 3rd strings is now on the 4th, 5th and 6th strings of the other tuning. The voicing, because of the string gauges, actually sounds nicer to me on the C.

What does the B11th tuning allow you to do that you can't get on the C tuning?

I use it because I just like the variety of the sound and the chording. Sometimes I find myself playing pretty much the way I would on the C tuning. You know how you have a certain riff that you do? You just do it on the other tuning.

Greg Sardinha's Tunings								
Strings	1	2	3	4	5	6	7	8
C13th	E	C	A	G	E	C	Bb	C
B11th	E	C	A	F#	D#	C#	A	B
C#m	E	C#	G#	E	D	B		
E13th	E	C#	B	G#	F#	D	G#	E
C diatonic	E	C	B	A	G	F	E	

One of the hallmarks of Hawaiian-style steel is the playing of melodies using harmonics. Do you have any secrets for players who want to improve in that area?

That's a weird one because there are gigs that I do where I can play the heck out of the harmonics and say "Wow. It's a great harmonic night." There can be nights when you play the same song and you get half of 'em. So I just laugh at myself. It's amazing how one night it's great and the next it just doesn't come together. Then I start staring at the frets and wondering, "Okay, I'm playing at the 7th fret so the side of my palm has to be at a certain fret 'cause I'm missing it." Now I'm starting to look at how else I can make myself not miss (laughs). I don't know if there are any secrets. I just feel like I have good days and sometimes, I don't (aughs).

Before I took lessons I listened to Feet Rogers a lot. When I first started out, I was playing with a group and I was playing practically off the neck trying to get this high pitch and thinking "How can they get this thing so clean?" Then the group that was after us was a group called Moana Loa with Cyril Pahinui, Brian Ah See and Eddie Palomo playing steel guitar. I would see Eddie playing like Feet Rogers but he would be playing on the 2nd or 3rd fret. I thought. "How in the world is he getting those high notes - he's not even playing on the 100th fret?" Then I found out what the heck was going on (laughs).

- ¤ Greg Sardinha ¤ -

Who are your favorite players to listen to?

I still like putting on my Jerry Byrd albums once in a while but one of my favorite steel guitar players is Gabby Pahinui. To me, that's the ultimate in Hawaiian-style playing. His feel - oh boy! I listen to him when I get into that state of listening to just steel guitar music. I listen to Jerry 'cause I like his sound. I'm not sure if it sounds Hawaiian anymore like I used to think. Now I know what they mean when they say, "He's too country for Hawaiian and he's too Hawaiian for country." I read that somewhere but it didn't dawn on me 'til I started listening to Gabby.

Jerry found something that works and it's a great sound. I love the sound of it. He has that two-string bend like a pedal would do. I use that too but I think of it more as a kind of a country thing now whereas I didn't think of it that way before. When I listened to how Gabby approached that same thing it sounded more Hawaiian.

I like listening to other styles, like Buddy Emmons. Lately I've been listening to resonator steel guitarists. I listen to Jerry Douglas to get an idea of how to approach the Dobro. Kenny Emerson is really good on the resonator guitar but when he'd play the electric he'd play it the same way he would play the resonator. He would attack it really hard and it didn't sound so good. I played more electric guitar and when I jumped on the Dobro I said, "I've got to attack this harder and learn to play with more with bouncing between open strings and barred notes." Now I try to approach it with kind of a Jerry Douglas mentality but still a Hawaiian song. I don't want to play a country Dobro sound and yet, I want to find an area where I can fit it in and have a different approach to the song. So that's kind of fun.

How did you come to produce the *Made In Hawaii* series of compilation CDs that feature a number of the best steel players in the islands?

I worked at Budweiser for 23 years. The *Made in Hawaii* CD was something I did when I left my job. My wife and I talked it over and I said "Let me give music a try and if it doesn't work out in 3 years I'll look for a new position." So I had a studio and I wanted to do an instrumental CD featuring different steel guitar players. I thought that everybody here was always doing back up work for other local artists and not really getting much recognition. I thought, "I've got to do an album for us – the guys that do all the little back-up work and maybe we'll get recognition that way." The artists on the first CD were Iaukea Bright, Rodney Freedman, Herbert Hanawahine, Bobby Ingano, Fred Lunt, Ed Punua, Casey Olsen and me.

When I did the first one, people really liked it and then I said maybe I'll try to do Volume Two and feature different artists. Time passes so quickly. The third one's out now. A year and a half goes by and it's time to do another one.

In 2001, you had the honor of playing at the Kennedy Center in Washington, DC. How did that series of concerts come about?

I did a steel guitar show in Japan with Casey Olsen, Alan Akaka, Kenny Emerson and Bobby Ingano. While we were in Japan, we did a little traveling. People wanted us to jam so I got stuck on the ukulele as we did some playing here and there, just in the backyards, you know.

Alan said, "Whoa, you play good ukulele." We were just jamming and I was picking and strumming the ukulele. I guess when you see somebody play steel guitar for so long you forget we play other things too. Alan mentioned he was going to the Kennedy Center with his brother Danny Akaka along with George Kuo and Martin Pahinui. He asked me to come and play ukulele. I said sure so that's how I ended up going.

Was it an enjoyable gig?

It was fabulous. I'd never been to Washington. It was really fun and they really took care of us. We played three or four days and every night was packed. They had to bring extra seats. It was nice to play ukulele. I was sitting right by Alan on the steel so I got to poke him with needles (laughs).

What's it like as a musician in Hawaiian these days?

After September 11th [*9/11/01 terrorist attacks in NY & Washington, DC*] it was real bad for a while. We got back from Japan on September 10th and I had been stuffed up with a lot of work and was wondering how I was going to do all these gigs. When that hit everything got cancelled. No work whatsoever. Waikiki was a ghost town. It's fine now; back to normal. I'm working busily. I formed a group called *Po'okela* with some players whom I used to work with.

Do you think the natural beauty that's all around you in Hawaii is an influence on your music?

That's tough. I think I've come to understand where I live. I never used to think twice about it but as you get older you realize more. Other people tell you that you live in a great place and you travel and see other places. I look at the green mountain and the blue oceans and the blue skies now – how clear it is. I really look at what writers write, now. Before, I used to go in the studio and just play the song but now I want to know what the story is about, what they're trying to say so I can put it in perspective when I play steel guitar.

Where do you see steel guitar headed? Is Hawaiian-style steel guitar thriving?

That's the kind of conversation I've been having with Casey [*Olsen*] and Alan [*Akaka*] and a couple of other people because I don't think we have the following that I would want to see. We have a slack key festival here and it draws such a big audience that it's always on TV. Ukulele has been really huge here too. You go to a ukulele festival and you've got 5,000 people and tons of students up there. I remember looking at some old pictures where they used to have 25-30 steel guitar players sitting down taking lessons. When you go to a steel guitar show here you pull in 300 maybe 400 people. I look at that and say what's wrong with the picture here? We're not doing our job if we can't get people interested.

I guess enough time has gone by where there are not many old timers left. I told Alan and Casey, "In another few years, we're going to be those old timers so we've got to step up and get some interest in our instrument and get kids interested." I don't know what it's going to take to spark the instrument in these kids.

Are you doing any teaching?

I've had some kids that were interested but I always see the kids wanting to learn how to play that fast stuff. I started to use a different strategy. "Okay, you want to play fast? Then I'll show what you need to know for picking fast." Then when they get stuck and frustrated I say, "No, you have to go back to basics." What I found out is they don't want to learn songs like *Sand* or *Sweet Lei Lehua* or anything slow – they don't want to go through that stage. They want to play good tomorrow. They're so in a rush that they don't want to take the time to learn the instrument well so they just drop it.

For the time being, I think steel is doing really fine. I hear a lot of it on TV commercials now. We have a lot of steel guitar music on the radio. Still, I'd like to see a steel guitar show where we've got 2500 to 3000 people and a four hour show instead of a two hour show. The future will be what we make out of it for the next generation.

- ¤ -

John Ely

Minnesota native, John Ely is a true master of his instrument. In a succession of albums with *Asleep at the Wheel* in the 1980s & '90s, John perfected a non-pedal steel style that reflected his extensive study of the great western swing players and his growing appreciation for Hawaiian music. He received a Grammy Award in 1988 for his work with *Asleep at the Wheel*. A period of residence in Hawaii allowed him to further develop his trademark warm, burnished tone and command of chord melody technique. John adds a thorough understanding of music theory to his formidable skills on the instrument.

- ¤ John Ely ¤ -

What were your earliest musical experiences?

It was mostly going through a regimen of classical piano instruction. I started playing in fifth grade and all the way through high school. My folks were both avid players – mostly classical music. There was always music in the house and we all played piano. So I was pretty much steeped in music. I was pretty serious about playing piano and I had a great theory teacher.

Do you think reading music and understanding music theory is important for playing steel guitar?

I don't think it is, but it sped the process up for me. I started out playing pedal steel and it seemed pretty abstract. My knowledge of theory helped me sort of figure out what the pedals did and how I could use them. I don't think it's essential, but for certain select studio gigs, it helped being able to read standard notation. But that was just on a handful of occasions.

How did you get from piano to pedal steel and then to non-pedal steel guitar?

Well, piano just about killed my interest in music. I kept asking my teacher to teach me how to improvise, how to compose; I wasn't satisfied just playing the notes. It's certainly a legitimate way to approach music but it just wasn't well suited to me and I actually dropped music for about four years.

In my last couple years of college, hearing steel guitar in pop groups really grabbed my attention. That was in the early '70s when steel guitar was kind of cropping up in other types of music. I've always thought chordally and a lot of pedal steel chord progressions just blew my mind.

A roommate of mine had an old Gibson 6-string—I think his uncle was stationed in Honolulu during World War II—and he was into some of the rock groups that were using steel guitar so he brought it to school one semester. I played around with it and really got sucked into it. I had no idea how to tune it, but a year later managed to get hold of a pedal steel. Basically, from then on, I was just going through the history of steel guitar in reverse (laughs), going from rock stuff to contemporary country music, then going to the older country music, then going to western swing, and finally to Hawaiian music.

How did you get started playing professionally?

I played country gigs in Wisconsin in '73 and '74, but the big key for me was moving down to Austin where I got exposed to the whole western swing thing, which was hard to find in most parts of the country. Starting in '75 through the early '80s I was steeped in western swing and jazzy steel guitar – pretty much playing with pedals. I didn't really shift to non-pedal until just before I joined *Asleep at the Wheel* in 1985.

What aspect of learning to play steel guitar did you find most difficult?

I would say the hardest thing for me was just getting basic right and left hand technique together to where I could stand to listen to myself [laughs]. I have a pretty decent ear and I could barely listen to myself for a couple of years - and that was with practicing 5, 6, 7, 8 hours a day. I bet lessons would really have helped with getting picking and blocking technique down.

43

I think there were some advantages to being self-taught but I could probably have gotten through that period quicker with a teacher.

Had you ever played standard guitar?

I hadn't played guitar that much. I think a lot of people probably go from guitar to steel but I didn't really have much of an idea about picking at all. That added a layer of complexity.

Who were your early influences on the instrument?

My main breakthrough in learning was getting hold of a record called the *Ernest Tubb Story,* a double record set that had mostly Buddy Charleton on steel, I believe. I didn't even know who he was at the time. I wore the grooves out of that record and tried to pretty much learn it lick for lick just to know how to get around on the instrument. He'd have to be a huge influence and then a lot of the Jerry Byrd and Don Helms stuff on Hank Williams records as well as Buddy Emmons and Lloyd Green. Joaquin Murphey was a primary influence - I ate him up.

What about today? Who influences your music?

I think probably David Keli'i is my biggest influence. I got a hold of some transcriptions from the *Hawaii Calls* radio shows and it grabbed me more than anything I'd ever listened to before. I don't know, I just kind of feel his presence when I'm phrasing lines. Probably everybody I've ever listened to is in there too. I have a lot of jazz influences that are kind of peripheral to steel guitar, but I'm sure they're in there – like Bill Evans - the way he approached playing against diminished chords, for example. I tend to like block chords a lot.

A lot of the way I approach single note playing is rooted in the way Joaquin approached it. I remember Johnny Gimble telling me about how Joaquin would stare at the ceiling for twelve hours a day listening to Benny Goodman records. That explains why he had such a clarinet-like sound. I know he listened a lot to Sol Hoopii, too.

As a kid, he apparently hung around the teaching studios in LA meeting people like Dick McIntire and other Hawaiian players.

To me, that's about the most interesting aspect of the history of steel guitar – the interplay between all those different kinds of players around Hollywood. The Hawaiian guys, the western guys; it seemed like they carried on a musical conversation back and forth.

What do you consider some of the highlights of your years with *Asleep at the Wheel*?

Probably some of the recordings, especially the first one I was on, *Asleep at the Wheel Ten,* and the live one where we had a really improvised feel with very little overdubbing. Just to have those come out the way they did was really satisfying. The Grammy recognition for some of that work was nice. A lot of it was just playing the music and doing the better shows and touring overseas. I lived for those kind of things—playing foreign countries where people knew more about the music than we did. I swear, some of the DJs spinning records at our shows were amateur musicologists. It's amazing how knowledgeable Europeans and Japanese are about American music and its history.

- ¤ John Ely ¤ -

How did you get into Hawaiian music and make the decision to move to Hawaii?

That came directly from some of the stuff we did in the Wheel. For one thing, western swing already has kind of a Hawaiian influence. In '87, '88 and '89 we got to play a golf tournament party in Maui—our reward for making it through the grueling state and county fair circuit! So each of those years, I got to hang out in Hawaii for ten days and I had nine days off.

I grabbed the first plane I could to Honolulu and hung out 'cause I'd already heard some stuff that intrigued me. What I heard was a lot of the local steel players and trios and it floored me. The trio with Barney Isaacs on steel, Benny Kalama on bass, and Sol Kamahele just knocked me out—the way they played and sang together. Hawaiian music went through a swing period just as country music did. Going through the whole big band era affected everybody. Hawaii's take on swing just blew me away. It was all so melodic and at the same time so swinging. It just totally grabbed me. Probably that first year I went over I was pushed over the edge, and from then on it was just a question of collecting recordings, learning the material, steeping myself in it, and finding an appropriate time to jump off.

When did you live and work there?

I quit the Wheel in 1992 and moved to Maui in 1995. Jerry Byrd hooked me up with the *Old Lahaina Luau Show,* but after a few months I went through this terrible rotator cuff injury that pretty much took three years out of my music career.

Was the injury a result of playing steel guitar?

Part of it was adjusting to the Hawaiian vibrato, which is a lot more prominent and like many country players, I was lazy about my left hand. When I finally got it in gear I sort of traumatized it, plus I was doing it [*Hawaiian vibrato*] incorrectly, doing it from the shoulder rather than from the whole arm and I just trashed it. I also played with hunched shoulders. So twenty years of playing incorrectly basically caught up with me.

So I found a good physical therapist in Honolulu and hung around Hawaii for a year, and then headed to Minnesota for a couple years doing some computer work for Northwest Airlines. I went back to Honolulu in 2000 to get stuff out of storage and before I knew it gigs were pouring in and I decided to stay. I was really scared about the shoulder, but I powered through it and I realized I'd be able to play again, which was terrific. When you're rehabbing you never know.

September 11 practically wiped out entertainment in Hawaii, and I hung on for two or three months before moving back here to Minnesota. I did most of the 2002 summer tour with the Wheel and have been waiting for the Hawaii economy to improve before taking another crack at it. So I've lived in Hawaii twice. Maybe the third time's the charm!

You mentioned vibrato earlier. What do you feel are the qualities that make the Hawaiian approach to playing steel guitar unique?

To me, the single biggest factor is that most Hawaiian musicians play all the instruments and sing. They just tend to play the steel guitar the way they sing so it has very lyrical quality to it. You never find the left hand faltering. When you listen to good singers hold a note, there's something very steady in the way they hold a note and in the way the vibrato moves. When you hear the Hawaiians play, this singing quality seems to be built into the style. It just grabs me more and has a real emotional quality to it.

- ¤ John Ely ¤ -

Many Hawaiian players also block differently than country or western swing players.

Yes, that has to do with the human voice—the way the Hawaiians do that glottal stop they do—almost like a yodel. A lot of the blocking is done with the left hand and many Hawaiian players perfected this way of moving the bar between strings to imitate the sound of the voice breaking. Right hand blocking is still used, but not as much as in country steel guitar. Also right hand blocking tends to cut off the sound. Hawaiian players can block with the left hand and create continuous sound as a singer would do. This is done by lifting the bar off of one string at the instant you pick another string. When you use your right palm to block, you're actually cutting off the tone slightly. Blocking with the left hand is closer to pick blocking, but really, it's a different kind of a sound.

I understand you took some lessons from Jerry Byrd while you were in Hawaii?

I took three lessons from Jerry, one for every year we did that golf tournament gig. They were powerful because we didn't do that much playing—it was mostly Jerry talking about the phrasing possibilities of the instrument and it just opened up a world of playing options, ways to phrase melodies that I'd never really thought about. His knowledge of the instrument is formidable and it just opened up so much just sitting there, talking to him. That was one of the best things I ever did.

What are the main tunings you're using and what do feel are the advantages or disadvantages of various tunings?

In general, the importance of tunings is overblown. 80% of everything I play I could probably play on any mainstream tuning. That said, I'm still kind of a tuning junkie. My main tuning is a C6th with a low Bb and then a low C below that. It's the most popular version of the C6th in Hawaii, but it's really a C13th. Most mainland C6th tunings don't have the 7th tone in there. To me, it's the best all-around tuning because you get every major chord inversion, every minor inversion, and most of the important 7th chords and there's just a ton of stuff in the slant position.

One glaring omission from the C13th tuning is a real fat 9th chord and the B11th tuning really fills the bill. It's real common to switch between tunings in the middle of a song. Some guys do it in the middle of a solo. Guys like Jules Ah See were known for that.

The Leon McAuliffe E13th is one of my favorites. There's a ton of chord stuff you can get on there but you have to use a fourth fingerpick to select it out. You can get a lot of basic jazz guitar voicings, 4-note chords instead of 3-note chords, that are really, really cool.

Did you ever spend any time with Jerry Byrd's diatonic tuning?

Actually I did, for a little while, and boy, it's a powerful tuning. Whenever I would play it I would just sound like Jerry so I figured, "What's the point?" I don't know when he devised it, but I feel sure that some of its smooth, lush sound carried over to the E9th pedal sound of the '60's and beyond. Another thing about Jerry's diatonic: I like the Hawaiian sound of being able to strum and you can't strum with this tuning. Even with Jerry's C6th, you can't really strum because of that C# note. Jerry generally prefers picking strings individually, but I love the sound of strumming. There are so many variations in texture you can create.

- ¤ John Ely ¤ -

John Ely's Tunings								
Strings	1	2	3	4	5	6	7	8
C13th	E	C	A	G	E	C	Bb	C
B11th #1	E	C#	A	F#	D#	C#	A	B
B11th #2	E	C#	A	F#	D#	B	F#	B
E13th	E	C#	B	G#	F#	D	G#	E
C diatonic	E	C	B	A	G	F	E	

Are you still playing a Fender Stringmaster?

Yeah. I still have my triple neck long-scale from my touring days.

With the 26" scale?

No, it's a 24" scale. The 26", that's the super-long scale. They only made that for a couple of years, '53 and '54, I believe. Boy, they sound great but they're so hard to play. Slant bar work is a lot easier on short-scale instruments (22.5") especially when you're playing below the fifth fret. It can get kind of hairy below the fifth fret anyway, but on a 24" and 26" it's really super hard. Jerry's a proponent of the 22.5" scale. He pioneered a whole way to play in the slant position *and* in tune!
It's easier to manage all of that on a short-scale guitar.

To me, long-scale has a fuller sound. And harmonics on a long-scale sound fatter and they're easier to get. You're less liable to clink one. So I prefer long-scale and I'm willing to sacrifice some of the slants to use it.

What advice would you have for someone who's starting out on steel guitar but getting frustrated in trying to get a good sound?

I'd advise somebody to get a teacher and try to cut down on the time it takes to learn proper technique. Otherwise, it can get discouraging. Anything you can do to avoid the discouraging initial period that probably drives people away from the instrument [laughs]. One thing about being self-taught that's so great is that you force your ear to develop by listening to a phrase and making yourself figure out where to play it on the fretboard. It's a grueling approach at first, but there's no substitute for developing your ear that way.

Jerry Byrd once told me he'd have *Hawaii Calls* on the radio every week and have his steel guitar tuned up and ready to go. And he only had one chance to get it right! I guess everybody kind of learns by imitation starting out. So learning without a teacher has its benefits but short answer: grab a teacher!

Where do you think non-pedal steel is headed?

I think it's on a new wave of popularity. There's a lot going on in all different kinds of music – even Indian music. I think the reason why "straight steel" is here to stay is that it's more accessible than pedal steel and to me, the instruments tend to have a more natural sound with more character due to the interaction between the body and pickup. Pedal steels tend to have a more neutral pickup sound with not as much interaction from the body. This is because of the way the body is reinforced to accommodate the stresses of a pull system. Don't get me wrong, there are great sounding pedal steels out there, but, to me, the Fender and Rickenbacker tone is just sweeter.

Non-pedal steel will always have an appeal because, while there are a lot of hurdles to get over to play it, pedal steel is pretty intimidating by comparison.

A pedal steel is both machine and musical instrument. So the specific challenge as I see it for pedal steel is how do you avoid sounding mechanical and keep those pedals and knee levers from playing you?

Once you saw everybody go to pedals in the late 50's a lot of individuality was lost.

The first wave had it, though. I've always wondered about that. How in the 1960s you could always tell a Lloyd Green solo. You could always tell a Ralph Mooney solo. That's just an enigma to me. Those guys and others played with great flair and their style was unmistakable. In fairness to today's players, I should point out that steel players had a lot more freedom in the old days. And in today's country music, which is kind of a pop amalgam, steel guitar has been forced into a more limited role, providing color and texture but rarely venturing out. To some extent I think modern pedal players have relied on their feet and right hand, and that has tended to limit the stylistic range. The left hand can really add richness and texture to a note or phrase, but it seems to have fallen into neglect.

My theory is that all the people you mention came out of non-pedal playing and had good fundamentals to begin with. Then they used the pedals to augment what they were already doing. The next generation's first instrument – in many cases – was the pedal guitar so their approach was based around the mechanical nature of the instrument.

I think there's some truth to that, although I would never accuse today's best pedal players of not having good fundamentals. In some respects, today's pedal technique is the most advanced ever in terms of speed and proficiency. It's just that for me, there isn't as much variety or as many personalized styles. As I mentioned before I think the nature of music today has had an impact and I think you're right—the mechanical nature of the instrument can dictate style and limit phrasing choices. Keep in mind these are broad generalizations.

I spent so many years on pedal steel trying to get every chord known to man. I probably went through 10,000 index cards over the years trying to get everything in a single tuning. I was more concerned about what kinds of harmony or effects I could get using pedals than about what I was saying musically with even the simplest of licks. I didn't really understand a lot of the fundamentals of playing and articulating notes until I took it back to the '30's, '40's, and '50's. I found out when I simplified my approach to playing steel guitar, it really freed me. For me, less turned out to be more.

Bruce Clarke

Bruce Clarke is one of the living treasures of Australian music. He got his start as a professional steel guitarist during WWII with the *Matariki South Sea Entertainers*. Hawaiian swing was wildly popular in Australia from the late 1930s until about the time commercial television came along in the mid 1950s. Many of the leaders of that music became household names - among them, Bruce, who was active in clubs, radio and on record. Nevertheless, he put his steel guitar away in favor of standard jazz guitar for thirty years, becoming one of Australia's top jazz guitarists, arrangers, and composers, writing and directing over 3000 television and film soundtracks.

After many years in commercial music, Bruce returned to his first love of teaching and performing, establishing the *Guitar Workshop*, Melbourne's premier guitar school. Despite many years away from the instrument, Bruce picked up the steel guitar again in the early 1980s. Finding his steel chops undiminished by time, he wrote new arrangements and released several CDs.

- ¤ Bruce Clarke ¤ -

With the advent of extremely powerful, digital sound editing software Bruce created the Cumquat Records label. Cumquat has developed a world-wide reputation because of Bruce's exquisite restorations of vintage Hawaiian and jazz 78s. These masterful CD transfers benefit from Bruce's understanding of the music and how it should sound. Hawaiian music fans have been thrilled to re-discover lost masterpieces by Dick McIntire, Andy Iona and others greats of the golden era of Hawaiian music.

How did you come to play the steel guitar and what were your first experiences with music?

I came to music when I was 16, in 1941. I was a very self-conscious sort of kid, sort of shy and stuttering, and my mother must have thought, "I'd better do something about this kid." She heard this ad on the radio for the *Hawaiian Club*, a big international organization on the east coast of Australia promoting Hawaiian music. Its heyday had been the 30's and by the time I came along, the war was on and most of the best players had gone on to work in entertainment units.

I had a bit of a problem as a young Australian because the Americans were starting to filter into town and they had more money and more glamour than a 16-year-old gawky kid and I wasn't going to get much nightlife with the girls so I turned to the Hawaiian guitar (laughs). So, I kicked off in a class of about 200 people in a massive hall in the city. They were mostly young people or wives whose husbands were away at the war. I learned to play the *Maori Farewell* on one string in A Major low-bass tuning [*Hi to low: E, C#, A, E, A, E*] and I thought I had it made. The next week, I learned to put in the old *Cha Cha* bass on the open strings.

Alternating bass?

Yeah. Well, after about six weeks the teacher finally got down off the platform – he was a Maori named Tui Hamilton – and he started to walk around the class. I didn't understand this then, but you've got to weed out all the troublemakers, people who are a bit ahead of the others who sit there looking bored and embarrassing the others. So he picked out selected ones and suggested they ought to have private lessons. He said I seemed to have some aptitude for the instrument, though I thought it was probably something they said to everybody to get you to pay a higher fee.

The last lesson I took in the class was *Song of the Islands* in A Major. I practiced and practiced then I went to the first private lesson and played it. He said, "That's pretty good." Then he played exactly what I'd played – no embellishments, nothing – just exactly what I'd played. The difference was unbelievable. I had never been in the presence of someone who could turn notes into music. What he could do that I couldn't yet do was to actually take those dead notes and breathe life into them. When I look back on that it was a fantastic lesson and it took a while before I understood the true significance of it.

How did you move from a kid taking lessons to being a working professional?

I learned from him [*Tui Hamilton*] for about nine months and I eventually got an electric guitar. Because of the war and the shortage of players, one night he said, would I like to come a friends place and do a little playing with them? I didn't realize that they were trying me out to see whether I could do a dance job. I went to this guy's home and he was a red headed Irishman who played rhythm guitar on the Hawaiian guitar.

He played all those crazy rhythms such that in later life I would have described him as a sort of Thelonious Monk of the Hawaiian guitar. He belted into it very enthusiastically and my teacher played Spanish guitar while I played my electric steel guitar. So they booked me for a job at an old people's bowling club and before long we added a bass and we were working as a Hawaiian quartet in nightclubs.

You were playing dance jobs using A Major tuning?

No, by this time I was able to play in C# Minor and a sort of distorted C6th – an A major with two C#s and a C.

The Maori teacher was also an expert on Polynesian dance and he eventually put together a whole troupe of about twenty-four of us. We played a lot of the Army and Air force hospitals and the other circuits around Victoria. There was a ballet of girls – some who were professional dancers and some who were just enthusiastic. I became the musical director writing out the music and chords for the other players.

At this point in time, my whole interest was Hawaiian music. I'd heard all these stories about the wonderful players from before the war. My teacher had a massive record collection so he saturated me in all the tunes and he gave me a tremendous start because he turned me on to the fact that it was no use doing something if you didn't know what you were doing so therefore I should have a total grasp of the theory behind it. He made me into a bit of a theory nut.

I finally ran across one of the steel legends from before the war – a guy called Les Adams, whose records I'd heard. I learned he was going to play a mid-day dance. I went to see them and there was a circular bandstand in the middle of the dancers. I was seated on the edge watching him as closely as I could. I remember he played a tremendous version of *The Carioca,* in G minor. I was amazed at the fluency of his playing. That's a pretty hard tune. In later life, on the records he made, his vibrato was all over the place and he didn't seem to care; he'd lost all the spirit of it.

The war changed music and changed people's taste. It's a terrible thing to say, but here's this guy along with all the others who'd gone away to fight or take part in preserving their country and the things they believe in and they come back and the war has changed what people want. I thought, "I've got something these guys haven't got and maybe I can become a professional."

You're known as being on the finest jazz guitarists in Australia, Bruce. How did your switch to jazz come about?

One day I walked into a record shop and I heard Charlie Christian and that totally blew me away. I didn't know whether it was a steel guitar from Mars or what it was. All I knew was "I've gotta find out about that!" Hot on the heels of that, we were preparing for the biggest show the Hawaiian troupe had ever done. It was right at the end of the war and we were top play in this big military hospital, which had a great theater and a great stage, and it was going to be a big thing. We were all making scenery and painting props and the girls were "planting" grass skirts and there was a radio playing and they announced they were going to play some new music and it was Dizzy Gillespie. That finished me off totally and I knew that's what I've got to try and do.

So I took on the Spanish guitar seriously while I kept playing steel. I played steel until about 1952 but by 1949, I was launched as a jazz guitarist. I went to the right place at the right time in the country with all these young firebrands that were gonna take control of music for the next 20 years.

- ¤ Bruce Clarke ¤ -

I walked in where I wasn't really invited and pushed myself into play and bingo! Within a fortnight, I was making records under my own name flying by the seat of my pants. From that point, I became a jazz musician and I've never been out of work a day in my life. I became one of the biggest arrangers and composers of film music in the country all because of what that Maori teacher had told me about learning about theory.

From 1956 to 1963 I was the assistant musical director of a TV station. In that time, I was getting drawn deeper and deeper into production music. While I was doing the TV job I was also running my own business outside. We did over 3000 jingles and film scores and radio productions. Many of the jazz things we did were done after commercial sessions 'cause I had many of the best players in the land on the staff.

Bruce Clarke (L) with jazz guitar legend Herb Ellis

Did you essentially give up the steel for the jazz guitar?

Well, by 1952, I was playing in nightclubs and the band leader would say, "Okay, now we'll play a Hawaiian waltz." I'd pick it up [*the steel*] and I'd be cold and I felt that I was not doing the instrument justice because it was just an afterthought. I though that the only way out of this is to sell it. So I sold it and I didn't touch a steel again until 1982.

What compelled you to pick up a bar again after thirty years?

I was playing in some jazz joint and a fellow who I had known from those early years came by and said, "There's a steel guitar convention next week. All the guys you grew up with will be there. Why don't you come and see them?" So I went along and here were steel guitar players from all over the country – mostly pedal steel players – and they were all awful. They were terrible! They all played the same song: two bars of C, two bars of F, two bars of G. They all had different titles but basically, were all the same tune. I watched in disbelief. There was only one guy, Jim Jensen, who still had it. The rest of them were mutilating it. They didn't swing, they didn't have any fine expression like the steel playing I'd grown up with. There was a guy on stage playing some Bob Wills stuff and I was sitting there bewildered and an old contemporary of mine walked by who'd also become a jazz player and he said, "How long has it been since you've played one of those?" I said, "Oh, about 35 years." He said, "I bet you could get up there and whip the ass off that bloke right now." (Laughs). So I said, "Yeah, I reckon I could."

- ¤ Bruce Clarke ¤ -

So the next day I went out and foraged among the shops and I found a Rickenbacher Bakelite, just like the one I used to have when I was a kid. So I took it home and waited 'till the house was empty and within about half an hour, everything I'd ever learned came back because I'd learned it properly in the first place. So I was playing all these old transcriptions I used to know, *12ᵗʰ Street Rag* and *Fascinating Rhythm* and my wife walked in and said, "That's the most beautiful thing I've ever heard." So that's where it started.

By this time I'd retired from the profession for teaching so I called my sons and some of my best students who worked for me as teachers and we began to rehearse every Thursday afternoon. I started to write charts to give them the ear training and things that I'd got through playing chords. I wrote about 400 charts sometimes for the steel with two Spanish guitars underneath. The parts were challenging for the people to play. We had 120 students at one point in time so every three months we'd have concerts.

It's kind of unusual for a jazz player to also embrace Hawaiian sounds. I believe Barney Kessel, for example, disliked Hawaiian steel.

I used to invite Barney, Herb Ellis, Joe Pass, and Martin Taylor, and whenever they were in Melbourne, they'd come and do a day's work for me advising students or doing a concert. I remember having an argument with Herb Ellis about it. He said to me he didn't like it [steel guitar]. I said, "Well hang on, I've heard you play a quote and you played it three times - it's a thing called the *Hula Blues*. You play it and you don't even know you're playing it!"

I grew up with the steel as my first love. For thirty years I didn't think about it and then it sort of reared its head and now, with all these records I seem to be where I started out.

How did the Cumquat Records Hawaiian reissues come about?

I ended up with quite a large collection of Hawaiian music. When I sold the guitar back in '52 I gave all those 78's to friends and since this was about the time the LP was coming out, they didn't get played very much. Most of them packaged them up in plastic and put them out in the woodshed or somewhere. So when I rang around about 1982 I suddenly got that whole collection back. That's what became the basis for what I do. [*Noted Hawaiian music collector*] Dirk Vogel supplied me with a massive amount of stuff too.

How did you choose which artist's work you wanted to re-master?

Dick McIntire and Andy Iona were always my favorites, as well as Augie Goupil. One of the big things that affected me was at the end of the war; a whole mess of Tahitians who'd been fighting for the French forces in the Middle East were dropped off in Melbourne for three months for recreational leave. That was amazing. It was almost like party time every night and every day. We played the songs on the Augie Goupil records. That's where I learned all those.

I'm now in process of finishing off Volume 5 of Andy & Dick. The whole thing is sort of a bit of a hole in the head in terms of the massive amount of work it takes for the number of people that are interested. Nobody in their right mind would really do it for the money. I can understand why no major company takes it on because the interest is so small. I don't want to spend the rest of my life doing this But I would like to know that at least I've left this stuff that I thought had value in the best condition I could. What becomes of it then I don't know.

- ¤ Bruce Clarke ¤ -

What do you see as some of the key differences in the styles of Dick McIntire and Andy Iona? Why is their music worthy of the meticulousness of Cumquat's CD reissues?

The music has to have a natural flow and that's what that early Hawaiian stuff had. It was like jazz. It sounded like they were inventing it all on the spot. It's all in their expression. The master steel guitarist from that time was Sol Hoopii and I love what he did but it still didn't move me like Iona and McIntire. There was something about the left hand technique. In the long run, I'd have to say that I prefer Andy Iona's music to Dick McIntire's although it's hard to say why. There's something about the chords in the tunes that just appeal to me more, but it's a pretty fine line; I like them both.

The others I particularly liked were Bobby Nichols and especially, Jack de Toro, who was with Johnny Pineapple. I'll be doing a reissue on him. He had this strange, really beautiful swinging sound and it always sounded – this is only fantasy – like it was coming to you across a short wave radio. It was crystal clear but there was something about it that was different and he could swing like crazy. De Toro made about 12 sides that I know of with Johnny Pineapple. There were a lot of Johnny Pineapple records that had Hal Aloma and different people that were good players but didn't have that magic. I'm also planning two volumes of *Al Perry and the Singing Surfriders* – the ones with David Keli'i.

You've taken a perfectionist attitude to almost the level of obsession in the way in which you've approached reissuing this music.

The Andy Iona and McIntire reissues did take a hell of a lot of work. I went through practically every sound wave checking for distorted waves and resurrecting them. Some tracks I've spent weeks on to get them to where I wanted them only to throw them away and start all over again.

I have access to Cedar software but the main software I'm using is called *Diamond Cut Millennium*, which has got a tremendous amount of good filters that seem to be compatible with this sort of music. Then I usually do the final mastering in *Cool Edit Pro*. I never knew anything about computers 'til one of my sons dropped one in my lap and then the whole thing got out of hand.

You have the unique perspective of having had a foot in two different worlds: that of the traditional Hawaiian lap steel and the world of jazz and commercial music. Why haven't we seen a jazz steel player of the stature of standard jazz guitarists like Joe Pass, Tal Farlow and Barney Kessel?

The instrument itself has every feature that one could want – all the features that the other instruments have. But there were a whole lot of reasons why it didn't get off the ground. It's remained an instrument for enthusiasts or largely confined to one particular type of music.

That record that Buddy Emmons made with John Coltrane's rhythm section gets closer but he was so scared of what he was doing – that was a long time ago – that it became stiff. I've heard him do things that really sound great on a few of his albums, like *Here's That Rainy Day*. He just sounds tremendous. I think some of the things Joaquin Murphey did with Spade Cooley are terrific. It's hard to understand.

Les Adams played for some years in a jazz quartet with a clarinet and a rhythm section. He seemed to be able to improvise quite well – not in the modern jazz sense, but in a conventional jazz sense. I don't think it's the instrument. It's the players. The instrument's only a tool. I've met a few very good single string players but I haven't met anybody that plays advanced chords on it well. I came across this record of Doug Jernigan with Bucky Pizarelli. Pizarelli's a pretty good player but the other guy just gets in the way.

- ¤ Bruce Clarke ¤ -

I don't think that anyone on the steel guitar has reached the point of spontaneous expressiveness and improvisational skills suitable to the music being played as the first great generation of electric players. That would include Sol, Andy, Dick, Bobby Nichols, Jack de Toro, and Sol K. Bright, even though he was of a different ear, there's something magical about his playing.

What about the players since the war ended almost 60 years ago?

I did listen to all of the key figures in post-war music but very few of them have touched me. I might have been impressed with the technical skills of a Jerry Byrd or Buddy Emmons, in particular, but the rest of them quite often sound like a bunch of show-offs, particularly on the pedal steel. Outside of Jerry Byrd and maybe Jules Ah Se, most of the players from the post-war era didn't seem to have the potent individuality that the others had. They didn't seem to be able to project themselves through the instrument. The people I'm talking about pick up the guitar and whatever the tone controls are set for that's what makes the sound. If they moved to a different guitar it would sound like a different player.

I remember one occasion when myself [*jazz guitarists*] Joe Pass and Ted Dunbar spent about five or six hours in Joe's hotel room where there was only one guitar. We were exchanging ideas and passing the guitar around from one man to the other and as that guitar passed from person to person, it sounded like the person who was playing it. The three of us had our own individual sound.

Beyond jazz improvisation, the steel guitar has the same notes available to it as any other instrument so why hasn't the steel guitar found acceptance in mainstream popular music?

It's not the instrument, it's the players. You wouldn't find many steel players that could sit down and have a deep conversation on music with a cellist or a trumpet player. So few steel players can read music. Because of the problem of changing tunings, they've all been brought up on tab. When you get into a real music situation as the world used to be – unlike today where 99% of bands don't read – in that world, the steel didn't fit because the players couldn't read. They couldn't adjust their line of thinking to fit whatever the orchestrator needed. They don't become real musicians; they're sort of fringe dwellers and I think that's what's held the instrument back.

- ¤ -

Cumquat Records:
Sol Hoopii radio
transcriptions

Country Music

Many musicologists would likely trace the genesis of commercial country music to the 1927 field recordings of the Carter Family and "Blue Yodeler", Jimmie Rodgers. The Carter's music reflected the Scotch-Irish musical heritage, while Rodgers' music melded African American and folk traditions into a robust sound that rang true for his core audience of rural, working people.

Lap-style guitar entered the stream of country music via Rodgers' records as well as those of cowboy movie & recording star Hoot Gibson and the seminal acoustic duo, Darby & Tarlton. The emergence of radio in the 1920's expanded the audience for this new music far beyond its previous boundaries.

While the resonator guitar stylings of players like Bashful Brother Oswald and Shot Jackson became a fixture of Nashville's *Grand Ole Opry* for many years, the first comb-and-tissue-paper squeals from Bob Dunn's Volu-tone amplifier in 1934 signified the ascendancy of something entirely new: electric steel guitar.

From the 1940's forward, the "ting-a-ling" style of Little Roy Wiggins, the rich, high-register sound of Don Helms with Hank Williams, and the Hawaiian-influenced runs of Jerry Byrd brought the sound of the electric steel to jukeboxes, radios, and record turntables across America. The popularization of the pedal steel in the 1950's and 60's blossomed thanks to the talents of Bud Isaacs, Buddy Emmons, Jimmy Day, Weldon Myrick, Lloyd Green, Tom Brumley, Paul Franklin and a host of others whose skills on hit recordings contributed to making the steel guitar indelibly linked with country music in the minds of much of the listening public.

Don Helms

Don Helms is a Country music legend. His playing on many of Hank Williams' hit records such as *Your Cheatin' Heart, I Can't Help It If I'm Still in Love With You, Cold, Cold Heart,* and *Why Don't You Love Me,* showcased the steel guitar in a new and dynamike way. In the late 1940's and early 50's, jukeboxes and radio speakers across America resonated with the throbbing, saturated sound of Helms' Gibson Console Grand steel guitar. His rich, close-voiced intros, leads, and fills have been widely imitated for fifty years. Helms scored another career milestone with his playing on Patsy Cline's classic recording of *Walking After Midnight,* and went on to work with most of the biggest stars in country music, including Loretta Lynn, Ferlin Husky, Johnny Cash, the Louvin Brothers, Stonewall

- ¤ Don Helms ¤ -

Jackson, Ray Price, and Hank Williams, Jr. Still an active musician at age 76, Don has played a regular gig with Hank Williams' daughter, Jett Williams, for 13 years. He was inducted into the Steel Guitar Hall of Fame in 1983.

What was your first steel guitar and who were your early influences on the instrument?

I had a little single neck 6-string lap steel and I learned to play it the best I could. I had nobody to teach me, but there were some guys who let me watch them. One was a fellow named Boots Harris, who was at that time playing on the *Grand Old Opry* with a group called *Curly Williams and the Georgia Peach Pickers*. He was from my home town – there's a bunch of steel players from about a 20-mile radius down there [*Alabama*], including Boots Harris, Curly Chalker and Julian Tharpe. I learned a lot from watching Boots Harris. He was good and somebody that I could look up to.

There was another older gentleman down in Florida named Neal McCormack – Pappy Neal. He had a band and he was the steel player. Hank Williams had been a singer in his band at one time. Right after my wife and I got married, Neal said, "Come down to Florida and spend some honeymoon time." By that time, I could play everything that Neal could play. He got the idea that he'd give me a job and he could take off and go fishing for two weeks at a time. I'd see him about every week or two. On a Saturday night I'd see him in the back of the building. We'd be just a playin', people dancin' and he'd just grin and wave his hand and he'd be gone again.

Did you hear Bob Wills' steel players and the Hawaiians on the radio?

I heard some Bob Wills records and I listened to the *Grand Ole Opry* and I heard Brother Oswald play and I was familiar with Little Roy Wiggins. By the early 40's, Jerry Byrd was tearin' it up. It was just warping my mind, all these things that I enjoyed listening to and I said, "I've just gotta learn how to do that."

How did you come to join Hank Williams?

Back in the early 1940s, I was still trying to learn to play. In 1943 four other guys and I put a little ol' band together and we were playin' little clubs down in south Alabama. We would play on a Thursday, Friday and Saturday and most of the time, we'd be off for the first part of the week. One of the guys had met Hank Williams on one of the off days and he said, "I ran into Hank Williams and he's offered us a job." I'd never met Hank. I'd heard him on the radio – just him and his guitar. I said, "Well, it probably won't be any worse than this."

So we met Hank in a music store where musicians hung out. He came down and he said, "Are y'all that group? I'm Hank Williams. Y'all follow me." So we walked out of that music store around the corner into a hock shop and he said, "Jake, have you got any more of them blackjacks back there?" They were clubs, like police officers use. Hank said, "Give me five." So he took 'em and passed 'em out and he said, "Boys, if you're ever gonna work for me, by God you're gonna need these (laughs)!" Playing on weekends in south Alabama toward the end of World War Two just wasn't the safest place to be. So he hired the whole band and that's how I got with him.

- ¤ Don Helms ¤ -

Were you called the Drifting Cowboys at that point?

We didn't call *ourselves* that. When we started to work with Hank he called himself Hank Williams, the Drifting Cowboy" so it was kinda natural for him to call us that because when he was playin' around Montgomery. Once in a while he would make appearances with other people who had bands and sometimes he used their band and he called *them* the *Drifting Cowboys.*

Who else was in the band at that time?

The only one that I think you would recognize was a guy named Sammy Pruitt who played the guitar. After we started playing with Hank, most of the guys went into the service, including myself.

Were you playing your trademark Gibson Console Grande yet?

Not at that point. I didn't get it 'till I came to Nashville. I had already recorded with Hank. I had a double-neck Fender that I used on one session with Hank that had *Long Gone Lonesome Blues* and *Why Don't You Love Me Like You Used To Do, They'll Never Take Her Love From Me and Why Should We Try Anymore.*

We were doing a week-long show in Baltimore and this guy came to a show and he said, "I want to trade guitars with you." I said, "Well, I don't know whether I do or not. What have you got in mind?" He said, "I got a brand new guitar that I want to swap you for the one you're playin'." He took me out into the hallway and he opened it up and it was a brand, spankin' new Gibson double-neck. You know how a new guitar smells? The lacquer or whatever it is? It smelled like a new guitar. I asked the guy if he was sure that was what he wanted to do. He said, "Yeah, I want the sound that you're getting on Hank Williams records. That's the guitar I want." He waited 'round 'till the show was over and he took the Fender and I took the Gibson and I've been playin' it ever since.

Your use of a Gibson stood out because most professionals at the time, especially on the west coast, were using Fender guitars. Do you feel your tone on Hank's records was markedly different because of the Gibson?

I was a little more proud of this guitar 'cause it was pretty. I was sort of the only one around who had one. A lot of people were getting' Fenders back then – including me – but I felt better about the Gibson 'cause everybody was sayin', "Man! What a sound!" You like to hear stuff like that but I can listen back to what I played with the Fender and there was not that much difference. You listen to (sings) *Why Don't You Love Me Like You Used To Do?* and if I played it today on the Gibson it'd sound pretty much like the Fender.

You ran the guitar through a Fender Pro amp?

Yeah. It had a 15" Jensen speaker.

What were the main tunings you used at that time?

E6th and B11th - the same tunings that I use today. Everything that you've ever heard me play was on those tunings. On the outside neck it's E6th. The other one is B11th. I keep both necks hot all the time and I switch around. When I'm not playin' lead, sometimes I'll just pad it with some chords and stuff. With that B tuning, by skipping strings, I could play a lot of chords without moving my bar an awful lot, kind of like they do today with pedals – just play pads under the lead instrument.

59

- ¤ Don Helms ¤ -

Don Helms' Tunings								
Strings	1	2	3	4	5	6	7	8
E6th	G#	E	C#	B	G#	E	C#	A
B11th	E	C#	A	F#	D#	B	A	F#

Do you do much slant bar playing?

I never was real good at slants. Of course, I had to play some and still do. When Jerry Byrd played you knew who it was. He was good at what he did and I admire him so much. He is the granddaddy of playin' slants.

You were one of the first steel players in country music to start playing really high up the neck in the upper register.

Yeah. [*Producer & publisher*] Fred Rose had me doin' that. Some of the songs were so high up the neck and the frets were so close I couldn't see 'em. My hands covered up the whole area and I didn't like that because I could not be totally accurate so I missed a lot of stuff. But that's what they wanted and everything that Hank did became a hit so I didn't argue with it. I just got as far up the neck as I could.

Hank Williams had a wide vocal range. Did you have any trouble staying out of his register?

Not really. If he sang at the 12th fret, I'd play at the first fret. I could play pert near all the time and not get in his way.

Did you see a difference in the way the players in Nashville approached steel guitar versus the way the west coast players approached the instrument?

Yeah. They were a little more commercial around Nashville. They weren't afraid to play the tune. The guys on the west coast were already past that and they were in the jazz stage of it. They had long learned how to play the melody, now they were foolin' around! Little Roy played pretty close to the melody and so did Jerry Byrd and on the slower songs, I played pretty close to the melody. On the up-tempo songs I hopped it up a little bit similar to what Joaquin Murphey and some of them guys would play.

Do you think that Hawaiian music had much influence on early country music?

Yeah. I think Joaquin Murphey was a good example of that. If you took what he played and slowed it down, you would have what Sol Hoopii and some of them guys played. Joaquin was just playing a lot of the same notes faster. I met Joaquin once and it was one of the highlights of my life. I got to talk with him a little bit. He didn't talk a whole lot but he was somebody that I admired greatly. I never could play like him, but neither could anybody else.

Many of the intros you played with Hank have become part of the language of country steel guitar playing. Did you plan them out or generally play them off the top of your head?

To give you an idea, after he'd taken his leave of absence to go get his head on straight and then come back to Nashville, he came back to do a record session. We went through several tunes and he said,

- ¤ Don Helms ¤ -

"This next one goes like this." He sung about two lines. He said, "Don give me – hell, you know what to give me." So I gave him an intro and we went all the way through it and believe it or not, nobody made a mistake where we had to do it again. They said, "That's a take." I played that song with him that *one* time and I never saw him again. It was *Your Cheatin' Heart*.

Another very familiar intro that I did was with Patsy Cline on *Walkin' After Midnight*. That was a very similar thing. She just came in the studio and said, "Somebody give me an intro to this." She had sung enough of it that we kinda knew how it went. I thought, "Heck, I will." And I did. I did a lot of recording for Decca back then. I was fortunate to be part of that A-Team, they called it, of Grady Martin, Tommy Jackson, myself, Harold Bradley, Floyd Cramer, Buddy Harmon and Bob Moore. She wasn't even on Decca Records then, she was on Four Star, I believe. She came in and did four or five songs. That, by far, was the best known of the songs I recorded with her.

I understand the studio musicians had great respect for Patsy.

Oh yes. I had met Patsy when she was still appearing on the Arthur Godfrey show, before she ever recorded. I was playin' for the Wilburn Brothers and we were up in Virgina and she and her husband Charlie invited us to dinner at her house. Everybody loved Patsy Cline. She was just very forward and open and a lot of fun.

You've played with many of the all-time greats in country music. What do you recall as some of the highlights?

I did a thing one time with the Louvin Brothers. I did a solo record with Charlie Louvin then I turned around and did a solo with Ira Louvin and Ira recorded a song called *Cash on the Barrelhead*. I didn't record anything with them as a duet.

I recorded all the early Ray Price songs: *Release Me, I'll Be there, Don't Let the Stars Get In Your Eyes*. The last song I recorded with Ray was *I've Got a New Heartache*. I also recorded all of the early stuff with Loretta Lynn like *Coal Miner's Daughter, Blue Kentucky Girl, Don't Come Home A Drinkin' with Lovin' On Your Mind* and some of those. Also Bobby Helms' *You Are My Special Angel*; (Sings) *Jingle Bell, Jingle Bell, Jingle Bell Rock; Fraulein*. I did an album with Johnny Cash called *Now There Was a Song*. We did famous songs by several different artists like George Jones, Roy Acuff and all. I recorded albums with Web Pierce and Jim Reeves and Red Sovine and gosh, I can't remember 'em all.

Did any of these artists ask you to play differently for them than you had with Hank?

I don't recall that they did. That's probably the only reason they were usin' me anyway – 'cause I'd played with Hank. That opened more doors for me than anything in my life. They knew what I played and there were other steel players available like Buddy Emmons and Jimmy Day – all of the top great players were around - so the ones that I played on, it was by their choice.

When you or Jerry Byrd or Noel Boggs played an intro you were instantly identifiable. That's not the case with most of today's pedal steel players.

It's anybody's guess, isn't it? Buddy Emmons and Jimmy Day – Buddy especially, in my opinion, was the forerunner in the pedal movement. When he would play something, all the guys like me would say, "God! That's what I wanted to play!" Therefore it seemed to me, for a long time everything was sounding like Buddy. Whatever Buddy played, everybody'd learn how to play *that*. But now, it's not *all* that way. For instance, there's nobody more identifiable than John Hughey.

- ¤ Don Helms ¤ -

You're still playing the same Console Grand today?

I played pedal steel for thirty-something years and I just started back a little over two years ago on the Gibson. I retired it in 1959, got a Sho-Bud and put the Gibson under the bed. Somewhere along the way, my wife was cleaning under the bed and she kicked it and said, "Honey, why don't you get rid of that?" I said, "I can't, baby, that's our retirement."

Alan Jackson knew about the guitar and he wanted to borrow it 'cause he was doing a TV show with a Hank Williams segment. So I sent it to him and when he sent it back, I opened it up and their was a check in there – a real nice check. I told my wife, "I've got this thing figured out. I'm gonna retire and start booking that guitar."

One day I was home puttin' some strings on it and sat down behind it and it just felt good. As long as I'm in this business, I'm gonna do this. I've got a garage full of pedal steels if you need one (laughs). I never was real good at playin' pedals. Everybody else was several years ahead of me to start with and it wasn't a competition, but I just didn't feel adequate. I never was real proud of it. But when I took that old Gibson out and played it, the very first day people said, "Man, that's what you need to be doin' all the time." And I said, "Well, okay, that's what I'll do" and I'm still at it.

I understand you've compiled a CD of some of your instrumental steel work with the *Drifting Cowboys*.

I took some cuts from old radio shows or portions of stage shows, put all that together and titled that CD, *Fifty Years of Legendary Steel Guitar*. I've even got some cuts on there where Hank introduces me to play – that was 1950 & '51. It took me 50 years to put that together (laughs).

What are you doing musically these days?

John Hughey has helped me a lot. I would like to start playing more of the steel guitar shows. I've been with Jett Williams for 13 years and I've turned down a lot of steel guitar shows because I was afraid I might be booked. Jett has slowed down to only about 20 dates a year. She's Hank's daughter and really a nice person. She sings a lot of Hank's songs and I play 'em just as I did for Hank. She's been good to me and I never go on stage without sometime in the performance having her turn to me and say, "I love you." I say, "I've played with all the Williams and she's the only one that tells me that (laughs)."

- ¤ Don Helms ¤ -

You can certainly look back on an exceptional career, Don, as one of the most imitated steel players ever to record.

It's been a very interesting life. I hear some of my licks on the radio today. Some guys will throw in a little lick I played. I don't try to hide my tunings or any of the licks I play. I'm glad to show 'em to people. Steel players are a clannish group – we stick together pretty close. You see a bunch of steel players, you see a bunch of guys having *fun!*

- ¤ -

Gibson catalog, 1940

Billy Robinson

Billy Robinson is the Houdini of the lap steel guitar. His abilities in seamlessly executing bar slants coupled with various combinations of behind-the-bar string pulls enable him to imitate a pedal steel guitar with uncanny accuracy.

One of the founders of the Nashville steel guitar dynasty, Billy played on hit country records by Red Foley, Webb Pierce, Carl Smith, George Morgan and many others on radio, tours, record and the *Grand Ole Opry*. His ability to mimike the styles of other players was legendary. Despite many years of pedal steel playing, Billy returned to the non-pedal guitar full time after retiring from his parallel career in the graphic arts. He was inducted into the Steel Guitar Hall of Fame in 1996 and is a fixture today at steel guitar conventions, where he dazzles new generations of listeners with his astoundingly fluent bar work. His CD, *Lap Steel Guitar Instrumentals* was released in 2002.

- ¤ Billy Robinson ¤ -

How did you and the lap steel guitar first get together?

When I was ten years old, my mother bought me a steel guitar. We had a neighbor who played and I kinda enjoyed his playing. I didn't want to practice on it 'til I moved into another neighborhood where the kids had a little band. So I learned to play the guitar so I could get into the band, which I did. I played steel guitar on up until I was 18 years old and got the job with Red Foley in 1948.

Jerry Byrd, Zeke Turner and Louie Innes, who was on the Prince Albert show, which was the NBC coast-to-coast show on the *Grand Ole Opry,* all left to go to Cincinnati, Ohio. I had been listening to Byrd, and of course before then to Roy Wiggins so I could copy both their styles. At 18 years old, anything that Foley had recorded with Byrd on it, I could pretty much do it just about like Byrd. Maybe not quite as well, but I was closer than anybody else in Nashville.

So I auditioned, got the job and quit high school. It was myself, Grady Martin, the great guitar player, Ernie Douglas and Zeb Turner. At that time, that particular job was like being on staff at WSM so anytime anybody new came to the *Grand Ole Opry,* we were the staff band that worked with them. WSM paid us a salary to work with these people until they got their bands.

Who were some of the people you played with?

When George Morgan first came, were with his backup band. I got the chance to do *Candy Kisses, Please Don't Let Me Love You* and a bunch of tunes with him until he hired Don Davis as

his steel guitar player. I did get to record with him on his first tunes.

Carl Smith came and we were his band until he hired Johnny Siebert to play steel. *Overlooking an Orchid* was the first tune I recorded with Carl. When he got Johnny Siebert, of course Johnny played on the rest of the things Carl did.

With Web Pierce I did *Wanderin',* and *Silver Bells.* We were his band until he hired his own band.

And of course, I recorded on everything Red Foley did from 1948 to 1952 when I got drafted in the Army … *Chatanooga Shoe Shine Boy, Tennessee Border,* and on and on. After *Chattanooga Shoe Shine Boy* was a tremendous hit for Foley, everybody wanted to use us.

- ¤ Billy Robinson ¤ -

You also worked briefly with Hank Williams?

I say I worked *with* Hank Williams but never *for* him. I was never in his band where he paid me a salary, but I did go to Germany with him. I did early morning radio programs with him and some traveling' shows in 1949 before he got his regular band and Don Helms came on. Jerry Rivers who played fiddle with Hank Williams was in our little kid band.

You got to revisit your roots for a Clint Eastwood movie?

Yes. Do you remember *Honky Tonk Man?* I played the Dobro behind him. In the movie, he goes to the *Grand Ole Opry* – the Ryman auditorium. The Ryman was set up the way it looked when I worked on it from 1948-52. It really gave me a thrill. Here I was standing with Clint Eastwood on the same stage I stood on with Hank Williams, Red Foley and everybody else.

What brand of steel were you playing then?

When I first started I had a single-neck Bigsby 8-string. That's what I did most of my recording with.

What tunings were you using?

I was using a C6th tuning at that point in time with an E on top. I did a little thing in the bass. To get a 9th chord, I'd tune to an F# in the bass.

Billy Robinson's Tuning (1940s)							
Strings	1	2	3	4	5	6	7	8
C6th/9th	E	C	A	G	E	C	A	F#

Did you have to come up with creative licks for intros, outros and turn arounds all off the top of your head?

Yes, right off the top of our heads. I don't read music. We'd get into the studio, which was at the Tulane Hotel for most of the recordings. That was the first studio in Nashville. We'd try one thing or another thing and just do it off the top of our heads.

Tell me about the record you made on which you imitated the styles of a number of famous steel players?

That was with Smilin' Eddie Hill. The mandolin player was a fabulous player – Paul Buskirk. Hank Garland was on it. I played like Jerry Byrd, and then I did a thing like Oswald. Somebody did a chorus like Chet Atkins, and Hank Garland, Grady Martin – I forget how many people.

In those days the people were friendlier. Now, it's all spit and polish. Everything's gotta be just perfect. In those days, we just wandered all over the stage and had a good time. When I started, I was only 18 years old so I was quite a bit younger than most of the people I was workin' with and most of them are now dead. I have great, great memories of all those people who were on the Opry.

- ¤ Billy Robinson ¤ -

Who were some of steel players who influenced you when you were starting out?

Roy Wiggins, I guess, was my first influence. There was a little girl named Becky Barfield who was with Pee Wee King and the Golden West Cowboys. My mother had a rooming house at one time and Becky had a room at my mother's. Roy Wiggins was dating her and he came over one night to pick her up for a date and heard me trying to figure out how to play *Steel Guitar Rag*. He showed me how to play it. He was a good friend and my first influence.

Of course, when Jerry Byrd came to Nashville, I started listening to him and he was a great influence. I really enjoyed both those players and tried to copy what they were doing. I would buy those old 78 records and wear out the part of the record where the steel guitar came in (laughs)."

Did you listen to any of the Hawaiian players on the radio, like Dick McIntire?

There was a program I used to listen to called *Hawaii Calls* with Johnny Pineapple playing steel and he was an influence on my playing, but not as much as Jerry Byrd.

Did you ever work with Hank Garland?

Sure. Of course Hank Garland was on the *Sugarfoot Rag* that Red Foley did and Hank was a good personal friend of mine.

Where you surprised when he went so far into modern jazz later on in his career?

No, as a matter of fact. When I started on the Opry in 1948 he was working with Cowboy Copas. Bob Foster was playing steel and Hank was on guitar. Gosh, he was playin' jazz in 1948. I wasn't a jazz player, but one of the things we used to love to do was to go into a club where they were playing jazz music and would let him sit in. They'd say, "Here's a guy from the *Grand Ole Opry*" and sort of make fun of it. Then he'd get up there and play jazz and just blow their minds (laughs). He's a fabulous musician.

Did you switch over to pedal steel, as so many players did, after Bud Isaacs' recording of *Slowly* came out?

I did get involved with pedals on and off for 20 years and I absolutely sounded like everybody else and got tired of it. So I started back on a little 6-string non-pedal guitar, then I went to a 7-string guitar, an 8-string, then a 9-string and then a 10-string guitar with a D-string on Top. That's been something I've really enjoyed doing. At age 71 I'm still learnin' guitar and haven't even begun to do all the stuff that can be done on it.

Billy Robinson's 10-string Lap Steel Tuning										
Strings	1	2	3	4	5	6	7	8	9	10
C6th/9th	D	G	E	C	A	G	E	C	A	F

- ¤ Billy Robinson ¤ -

What's your main guitar these days for that tuning?

It's a special made for me by Derby, the people in Louisville, Kentucky. I wanted the strings to be perfectly parallel and I had a 10-string guitar spaced out on a 12-string neck so that I'd have more space between the strings. I use a large bar and this allows me to get bar slants all the way down the neck pretty well evenly. As the frets get closer your slants get closer and as you go down the neck toward the keys, the slants are more dramatic. A lot of the steel guitars are not parallel. They slant toward the tuning keys. This Derby guitar works great.

I've heard it said that one of the best pedal steel players out there is Billy Robinson – the joke being that you play without pedals. You're well known for your advanced pull string technique - sharpening the pitch of a string by pulling the string behind the bar with your left hand.

Billy on WSM radio broadcast with Red Foley

Absolutely! I pull every string on the guitar except the small G string. I pull strings the most with the finger next to the pinky. I pull strings a half tone, sometimes a full tone and I also pull a string with a bar slant - a back bar slant where there's a 4-note chord that I'm hitting. I love for people to watch me play because my bar hand is backwards, forwards, sideways, string pulling and all. That's what makes it fun.

A lot of people say, "You sound like a pedal steel." Well, anything that I can get out of that guitar I'm gonna get out of it. I don't care if it sounds like a pedal or whatever else it sounds like. It doesn't *all* sound like that. Some of it I do just for the fun of it.

On the steel guitar shows I do a thing where I tell, people, "Here's the difference between this guitar and a pedal guitar: you can do certain things like this." Then I do some Roy Wiggins things and some Jerry Byrd stuff. Then I say, "A pedal guitar can do some stuff like this…" Then I do some things pulling strings that sound just like a pedal guitar. Then I end up saying, "It's absolutely impossible to do what I just did on this guitar (laughs)." So I have a lot of fun with it.

Do you ever drop the bar?

I sure do! As a matter of fact, I dropped it the first or second night I played the Opry and it rolled all the way across the stage and everybody got a good kick out of it except me. I was nervous and my hands were perspiring. I still drop the bar every now and then!

- ¤ Billy Robinson ¤ -

Do you have any advice for folks who want to improve their pull string technique?

My advice is to get a guitar with parallel strings spaced far apart. If you want to pull strings, don't use tight strings. The diameter of the string needs to be slightly smaller than normal in string pulls. You'll find that pulling the wound strings is a little more difficult. I'll occasionally pull more than one string at a time but not too often. That's very difficult to do. So do all this and then practice a heck of a lot (laughs)!"

Do you think about things like pick blocking and palm blocking? People today seem to be obsessed with technique in a way that wasn't talked about 30 or 40 years ago.

I don't really think about it, I just do it. Most of it is the palm although I do some with the bar. It's a feelin'. You just do what you have to do and I can't really describe any particular technique that I use except when I do the Les Paul stuff, that's all done with the palm.

Who's your favorite steel player?

Tom Morrell. I've know him for several years. Every two years I play the Dallas steel show. He's a great player. He can play western swing as good as I have ever heard in my life, bar none. I don't know his tuning but he gets some of the wildest chords on it. He's a good friend and a heck of a player. He loves those old tunes like anything Sinatra ever did and plays the fire out of it. His technique is fabulous. He used to play pedals too but he just quit.

Back when you started playing, when a song came on the radio you knew in just a few bars whether it was Billy Robinson, or Jerry Byrd, or Noel Boggs, or Joaquin Murphey. Now, it seems like everybody sounds the same.

Absolutely! Pedals contributed to that because they're all doing the same thing. That's the reason I quit playing' 'em. I love the way some people play pedals, but from my personal standpoint, it's a mechanical monster. I have a Sho-Bud Pro III that Shot Jackson made for me but I just don't play it anymore.

Today you can't tell one steel player from another and a lot of the singers are the same way. They all have the same sound. The music is sort of an electronic drone. If you've ever heard a Bagpipe you know what a drone is (laughs).

So anyway, if I do a slant, my ear tells me if it's sharp or flat or right on. If you push a pedal, it's gonna be right on only if your guitar's in tune. That takes away some of the feeling. I love the technique, the beauty and the feel of having to do it with your hands.

Do you think the steel has been typecast as a country music instrument?

The steel guitar is *not* for just playing' country music, it's for playing all kinds of music. To give you an example, some of the tunes on my latest CD are *Moonglow, Theme From Picnic, Tico Tico, Mumbo Jumbo* and *Body and Soul.* You can play tangos and rhumbas or anything. That's always been my philosophy.

You did a great version of *How High the Moon* on your album, *Lap Steel Guitar Instrumentals* that paid homage to Les Paul by including a lot of his classic licks.

- ¤ Billy Robinson ¤ -

Right. Ernie Newton who played bass with us played with the Les Paul Trio. He was the first guy I'd ever seen that played bass fiddle with a snare drum mounted right on the side of the bass. He would play snare drum with a brush while he was playing the bass fiddle. He played the bass with his thumb and held the brush with his other fingers. Chet Atkins' brother Jim played rhythm guitar with Les.

You took a kind of retirement from music for a while in the middle of your career.

I went into the Army in 1952 and when I got out, I used music as a sideline and went back to school and into the commercial art business. I was Art Director for a manufacturing company for 27 years. I was the one who designed the Sho-Bud logo and the panel on the Sho-Bud Christmas Tree amp. I told Shot Jackson, "We'll just light up these knobs so people can read them." I also did all his early literature and photography. I'd do all his design, printing and layout work and he would give me a guitar. Shot and I were good friends.

You don't make the most money in the world, I can tell you, playing steel guitar as a sideman. I always continued to play music on the side 'cause I just love to play. I play every day. It's like taking an aspirin in the way it relaxes you. If you can keep up the learnin' process it makes it fun. So I made my living as a commercial artist until I retired at age 65 and now I do a lot of oil paintings, most of them related to music. I'm 71 and I'm still learning every day. That's what keeps me young.

- ¤ -

Marian Hall

Marian Hall on stage with Tex Williams, 1960

In the 1940's & 50's, the style of country music played by musicians based in and around greater Los Angeles was much different than its Nashville counterpart. It was often faster, more experimental and favored loose arrangements and hot, improvised solos. Players like Joe Maphis, Merle Travis, Speedy West, Jimmy Bryant, Joaquin Murphey and other Spade Cooley alumnai set the tone for the inclusiveness of the West Coast country style that would evolve into country-rock and the Bakersfield sound in the 1960's.

This is the fast company in which Marian Hall found herself when she began her career-making stint on regular television broadcasts of Town Hall Party, a Los Angeles musical variety program that featured the best West Coast country musicians, as well as nationally-renowned weekly guest performers. Marian's trademark Bigsby steel served her well for a long and rewarding career in music.

- ¤ Marian Hall ¤ -

How did you come to play the steel guitar and what was your first instrument?

When I was about three I studied tap dancing. Then my mom decided that I should take music lessons from a Hawaiian who taught at a music store down the street from us. So I learned from a Hawaiian, which had a lot to do with my technique and ultimately, the sound that would come out of my guitar. He even taught me to sing in Hawaiian, which is a very phonetic language and it's pretty easy once you get the hang of it. I had a little 6-string Oahu lap steel with a fake mother-of-pearl plastic finish and there was an itty bitty little Oahu amplifier that matched the guitar. That's how I started.

How did you move from student steel player to working professionally?

My sister played standard guitar – that's what she learned at the music store. We started singing together and made up the name of *The Saddle Sweethearts.* We were pretty outrageous (laughs). I think we were twelve and fourteen at the time we ended up on TV.

What was it like in the early days of television?

At that time, TV was very primitive. There were antennas only on every fourth house. The director was also the janitor. The make-up was very dark, sort of orangey; things like that. There was a little variety show and we auditioned for the show and actually got on it. From there, we sang at different places with different people and eventually my sister wanted to go off on her own. My folks helped me get a Bigsby guitar and I started down the road of being a sideman.

How did you come to play a Bigsby, a high-end custom instrument?

At the time, that was the ultimate. If you really wanted the best, that was it. They were all custom made and somehow or another I got one of the appointments. He would build one a month. One person would have January, one person February, and so on and the only records Bigsby had were little cards on his wall. He would just devote the entire month to making your instrument, no matter how complicated it was or how simple. He made my first guitar which was a double-8. At some point, I got the bright idea that I wanted a 13th tuning. I mainly used an E6th tuning with a high G# on top. I decided I wanted a 13th tuning and an A6th tuning. I don't remember who invented this: it was a little lever attached to my A6th tuning and when you threw the lever, it changed it to an E13th. I think Paul Bigsby probably invented that at some point to satisfy one of my notions. I lived in Downey where his shop was, and we got to be good friends. He would change the strings on my guitar, which is something he didn't do for other people.

You were playing pedals pretty early on?

Well, I had my guitar and started playing around. When Bud Isaacs came out with that sound I ended up getting a couple of pedals put on my guitar and then I got more pedals and eventually, I decided I wanted a new guitar and Paul made me one with an 8-string neck and a ten-string neck. I took the E6th tuning and ran it all the way down from a G# to a big E string. I had all my pedals on that neck and eventually, I even took the other neck off and put a pad on it because I was controlling everything with the pedals at that point. I could get all the chord changes so I didn't need another tuning.

Did you actually play a pedal guitar while standing up?

I had the guitar in a standing position. I had a Bigsby volume pedal too. If you use a volume pedal with your right foot and all the tuning pedals with your left foot you'd have both feet in the air. You can't do that standing up, so I would just kind of sit back on a tall stool. So I sat on the stool and the effect was the same as standing up. I had a big board across the front that Paul made for me.

Do you still have that Bigsby guitar?

Yes I do. I sold my first one and I wish I knew where it was. If one only knew in life what's going to be valuable later on! I've talked to many people who are trying to trace the history of all the Bigsbys. It's very difficult because there were no serious records kept. He really did work off the top of his head.

Who were your early influences on the instrument?

Joaquin Murphey, Jerry Byrd, Remington and Boggs. I stole from all of them. I really liked Jerry Byrd. I thought he was exceptional. He could kind of bridge the gap between Hawaiian and country - just a unique style. Today no mater how great it is, you can't tell who's playing. In the old days, everybody had such a distinctive sound that you always knew whether it was Noel Boggs, or Jerry Byrd, or Joaquin Murphey.

Did you know Joaquin at all?

I didn't know him personally. It was very difficult to know him personally but I used to go and drool in front of his steel like everybody else. I thought he was wonderful. He was kind of eccentric but incredibly talented. When there was a break, he would detune his steel as if somebody was going to come up out of the audience and steal his tuning. The absurdity of that is the thought that somebody else could take that tuning and play like he did. It's not in the *tuning*, it's in the *brain*! (Laughs).

Do you think the widespread use of pedals has contributed to the homogenization of steel playing?

Well, I think that's an interesting point. I hadn't thought of that but it makes all kinds of sense because that [*pedals*] is the thing that determines what you sound like. With people like Jerry Byrd and Noel Boggs, they had to get the effect they wanted with a set of strings in a certain confirmation. And now, you can get anything you want by pressing a pedal.

How did you happen to get the job on the Town Hall Party Show?

I was on the show for four years. I got it because the guy who was playing steel wanted the night off. The truth is that Noel Boggs wanted the job at Town Hall. For some reason, I guess because he felt like Noel Boggs could take his job, the guy called me to sub. I think he thought that I was probably the least threatening person he could have called (laughs). The funny part about it was that very shortly after I subbed, they decided to replace him and they called *me*.

Did you think, "I've really got to pull out some hot licks to keep this gig?"

My philosophy was to make the singer sound good. I wasn't there to show off. I was there to make the singer sound good. That always appealed to singers, naturally. A lot of guys would just play all over the singer – show off. That's not a good move. So, for some reason, they called me and I was there for the next four years and did *everything* including the *Tex Ritter Ranch Party*, which was a film series for Screen Gems. It was basically the Town Hall cast and Tex Ritter was the MC. They filmed these shows and they're now circulating on tape all over the country.

- ¤ **Marian Hall** ¤ -

Town Hall Party All-Stars, mid-1950's. Marian Hall is 3rd from the right.

Spade Cooley's All-Girl Orchestra, circa 1957/1958. Marian Hall is seated behind Spade Cooley (standing).

How often were you on the air?

We were on in the afternoon two hours a day. And then we were on three hours on Saturday night – live – and then on Sunday, we would broadcast for two hours from a park. We were busy. We were *really* busy.

Did you do recording sessions too?

We recorded for Columbia. There are a lot of singles and at least one album that I know of that was with the Town Hall Band. I did one Freddie Hart session on Capital and the rest were all independent recordings.

Let's talk about some of the people you worked with at Town Hall, starting with Merle Travis.

Merle was a genius. He had an incredible IQ. He was very, very bright but he never let it show too much unless he was talking to someone with whom he could have a serious conversation about philosophy or physics. I enjoyed that part of him very much and besides that, he was just a fabulous guitar player. He and Paul Bigsby had worked on designing the solid body guitar. That's where Fender got the idea.

How about the *Collins Kids*? Did you find them exceptionally talented?

No, they were just cute. Joe Maphis tutored Larry [*Collins*] and he learned all of Joe's licks. They were very much the favorites of the producers of the show. They were always featured on *Tex Ritter's Ranch Party*. There were always at least two songs by the *Collins Kids* on every episode.

Joe Maphis was a flashy guitar player. Did you ever feel any pressure to keep up when you played with Joe?

No, he was a wonderful guy. Joe and Rose both. I have no complaints about anybody on that show. There were no major egos or problems like that. Joe was technically the bandleader. He always looked out for the band and he'd always make sure that I got some face time, you know, a solo here and there. We never had any rehearsal at all and the show was three hours long. We had a typed-out list of songs that were going to be on the show and the keys of the songs. We would pencil in who does the intro, who does the turn around, who does sixteen bars here and there. That was the way we did the whole thing.

How did you learn to improvise the kinds of hot solos required on a lot of the tunes?

A lot of it was listening to guys and stealing from 'em! That's how you learn. Even taking from horns or big band sounds; it wasn't just from other steel players. I learned the most from standard guitar players early on in my career, even before Town Hall. I was lucky enough to work with Dickie Phillips and people like that. He played a standard guitar flat on his lap and squashed his fingers down. He was an amazing musician.

Did you ever drop the bar on live TV?

No, but we were playing a show one time and I had a stool with this rod up the center, which was how I disassembled it, and that rod broke in the middle of a song and I fell backward. I pulled the guitar in on top of me and the mic was connected to me and I never missed a note (laughs).

- ¤ Marian Hall ¤ -

The guys were laughing so hard. It's, funny, but it never occurred to me to stop. I just kept singing.

With Merle Travis & Joe Maphis

That's what you call professionalism!

Or stupidity, I'm not sure which (laughs).

What did you do after leaving Town Hall?

I worked with Spade Cooley for one season. He had an all-girl band. In the far reaches of television's early days there was a show that was very popular called the Ina Rae Hutton Show. She had an all-girl orchestra. So Spade Cooley decided he was going to do the same. I played steel and there were horns and harps, fancy silk uniforms, and just everything in the world.

The part that I'm proudest of is that when that show closed, he asked me to do a TV show with the *guys* in his band. I always feel like it's more of an honor to be with the guys than with the gals – not because they're not good musicians – but because it's not regarded the same somehow. As the one female musician in a bunch of males you're held in higher regard than in a bunch of really good female musicians.

Did you feel like you had to work harder as a woman?

Yeah. My strongest suit was that I was reliable. I played well. I wasn't a genius, but I played well and you knew that I would come in at a certain level and stay there. A lot of guys who are absolutely brilliant are either coming in drunk or don't show or have other problems. I was incredibly reliable.

How did you get the gig with Tex Williams?

Tex Williams always had a good band. Billy Armstrong was the bandleader. He was a fiddle player, an absolutely brilliant musician. He knew I was on Town Hall, but for some reason, Billy just wouldn't take me seriously. Well, the very same guy that had had the job on Town Hall called me to sub again (Laughs). I knew that I had one shot at that band. They had a lot of very intricate big band arrangements with the guitar, the fiddle and the steel. I went to the guitar player and this guy was so wonderful to me. I said, "I want to learn every band arrangement that you've got so that when I come in there to sub this weekend, I'll know all the arrangements." He thought it was funny and he didn't want to have to play the whole weekend without being able to do their arrangements. So we sat in his den and I learned them all. I got to the job and Billy said, "Well, we can't do the arrangements so we'll have to substitute something for the instrumentals." The guitar player said, "Let's just give it a try." Well, I hit *every* lick. Never after that was I *that* perfect. You never saw an expression like the one on Billy Armstrong's face because they were intricate arrangements and all in your head. So, I got the job.

I was on TV with Tex Williams the day my son was due to be born. They couldn't find anybody to take my place so they just kept me behind my guitar. On the day he was supposed to be born, Billy

- ¤ Marian Hall ¤ -

Armstrong said, "You are making me so nervous! You'd better go home." (Laughs). We didn't get paid a lot of money but we had a lot of fun in that band.

Later on, you had a regular gig traveling with the stars of TV Westerns?

Right. The stars of the *Virginian, Bonanza, and Gunsmoke*. Hal Southern from the Frontiersmen formed his own group, which I joined. The stars would appear as their character at fairs and rodeos but then they had to have some sort of an act. A few of them could sing enough to do okay but others had to recite a poem or whatever and then we'd have to tap dance. Whatever it took to make a show out of it. They'd fly us out on the weekends and fly us back. It was a very interesting time for me.

Then you became a musical director for Disneyland?

At one point I was working in Tomorrow Land with a big band and they'd also have this big country and western night and I was one of the bandleaders, usually in the New Orleans area. We would just play all night long on a flat bed thing with horses dragging it around. If you don't think *that* is precarious - bouncing up and down trying to connect your guitar (laughs). So it's been an interesting life.

I went through a time when I was just singing and released some records but they didn't do very much 'cause they were on independent labels. I wrote some songs and Glen Campbell recorded one of my songs but then his career dropped off and I decided it wasn't worth chasing *that* anymore.

I joined the *Frontiersmen and Joannie* and we did cowboy music. We did four-part harmony. It was High Pockets on accordion, Wayne West on bass, my sister Joannie on guitar, and me. I didn't hang it up until about fifteen years ago when I got rheumatoid arthritis. I don't know how I lucked out. I did get a lot of breaks and I'm very grateful. It was so all so *interesting*. I was fortunate in working with good people who were very good to me. They were patient enough to let me survive long enough to learn!

With Randy Price & the Jubilaires, 1970

- ¤ -

Marian (seated behind Spade Cooley), Circa '57/'58

Kayton Roberts

Florida native, Kayton Roberts started his musical career in his father's band. He spent his early years as a professional musician doing gigs around North Florida with Toby Dowdy and others, as well as appearing on *The McDuff Hayride* television program. In 1951, he purchased the double-neck Fender guitar that has been his trademark ever since.

In 1967, Kayton joined the band of Canadian country star Hank Snow as a rhythm guitarist. When pedal steel guitarist, Jimmy Crawford left to join Faron Young, Snow learned that his guitar player doubled on steel and could emulate the sound of Joe Talbert, the steeler on his early hit records. Kayton moved over to the steel guitar chair, becoming a fixture on Snow's recordings and the stage of the *Grand Ole Opry*.

- ¤ Kayton Roberts ¤ -

Kayton Roberts has an awe-inspiring command of the instrument. In his hands, behind-the-bar string pulls, marimba effects and swinging country licks seem to tumble from his amplifier without effort. Kayton credits Jerry Byrd and Joe Talbert as his inspirations. He can often be found performing today along with his talented keyboardist spouse, Iva Lee Roberts.

[This interview was conducted for the CBC {Canadian Broadcasting Corporation] in the early 1970's by radio veteran Laurie Mills and is transcribed here with his permission.]

Kayton, how long have you and the steel guitar been together?

(Laughs) About all my life … and I'm 46.

Who did you hear that turned you on to the instrument?

I don't know. I guess it goes back probably to the days of Boots Harris, a fellow who used to play steel guitar with *Curly Williams and the Georgia Peach Pickers,* and also a fellow named Slim Idaho. There were a lot of great steel pickers back when I was a real small kid - before I could even play the instrument. About the time I started learning it, Roy Wiggins was my inspiration. That was during the time Eddy Arnold had all those great songs. Roy was my inspiration right there, and later on down the road, I really attached myself to Jerry Byrd and his style. I guess I followed that more than any, although not leavin' out Joe Talbert 'cause his style is what I'm followin' playing behind Hank now - of course addin' my own thing but basically, it's the Talbert style that he put behind Hank Snow.

Did you listen to any of the Hawaiians like Sol Hoopii or Dick McIntire?

No I didn't. For some strange reason, I wasn't that interested in Hawaiian music for many years. I was just too tied up in country music but now, it's completely flip-flopped. The way the set up is now, I just don't really care that much for country music and I *love* Hawaiian music. I'm a Hawaiian music nut!

What is there that a steel player like you doesn't like about today's country music?

Well, I like it but I just feel there's too many people playing that sound too much alike. You know, what has happened is that the instrument has become so mechanical that the instrument is playin' the man and the man's not playin' the instrument. Now, you do have to have a lot of talent to do what a lot of the guys do - like someone like Buddy Emmons and Weldon Myrick. There are some great steel players but to me, they have a tendency to sound a whole lot alike. Used to be you could listen to a particular artist and in just like a minute you'd know who it was. Let's say like … Hank Williams. If he were to kick off a song, Don Helms was his old steel player and why, just the minute that Don Helms hit that song, before Hank ever opened his mouth, you knew who it was. Joe Talbert with Hank Snow was the same way. You knew exactly who was fixin' to come out even if you'd never heard the song before.

Do you think, the pedal steel is allowed to become too gimmicky, past the stage where it's no longer a musical instrument but maybe a sound effects machine?

Well, that's pretty well put. That's what I think about it. You must have put some thought in that. It is too mechanical and they do a lot of things with it. On the Opry, those boys do a good job there. They take those fuzz tones on there then they play parts and it sounds just like a violin section.

And when you've got that on some of your records, unless you listen close you'd think that was violins but it's a steel guitar usin' a fuzz tone.

The sound effects you create on stage are without a whole bunch of little electronic boxes that sell for $89.95. It's just you and a volume foot pedal and muted strings. When did you start doing this? It's just so beautiful and so effective to hear someone who can play the instrument.

Well, I don't know. I've always looked for somethin' different. This sounds strange and I guess I've never even said this to anyone before, but Les Paul, he played some very tasteful music and I have transferred a lot of what I used to hear Les Paul do over to the steel guitar. Nobody else does it that much [*manual sound effects*] they do it of course, but not to the extent probably that I do. Of course,

the basic reason I do it more so behind Hank in my playin' is to keep somethin' different coming. In other words, I'm the only lead instrument that plays behind Hank. Therefore, I will play full chords then I will chime with a little finger chime and then a kind of a muffed, kind of a marimba sound which is just a muffed string with a lot of bass on it, really. And just anything that I can think of that will fit the taste of that particular song. Some things you could do just don't fit.

How many steel guitars have you had since you started playing?

Let's see, the first one I ever learned on was a little ol' Rickenbacher that my Daddy had; just happened to have it layin' around the house and I learned to play a little bit on it. And then our house burned and we had another little ol' guitar, an old 6-string and I learned on it 'til I bought this one here and I've had it ever since. It's 29 years old. [*Fender Dual Professional*] I bought it in 1951 and I'm still playing the same instrument.

Fender doesn't have much competition for non-pedal steels these days, do they?

No (laughs). You know, I don't know if Fender's aware that I even exist. A lot of people use the instrument that they play as a kind of a commercial thing towards the company they represent. But that's not the case with me. I don't know if Fender just doesn't care or I don't care, but we never got together on it.

Mentioning the good non-pedal steel players is something you can do on one hand. There's Jerry Byrd, Little Roy Wiggins, Don Helms has gone to pedals now, there's Leon McAuliffe, of course, then you - Kayton Roberts. Do you think it's still possible for "Clyde Schwartz" who starts taking steel guitar lessons and wants to learn non-pedal steel because he likes the instrument to do something with it? Or is it, as a musical instrument, on its way out?

You may get arguments on this. This is my own opinion about this, but playin' the guitar like I play it, nothin' comes cheap. Everything that you get out of the instrument, you've got to get out yourself. It can be done, but what you need to do is get around people that are doin' it. Like a kid that hangs around a garage, that kid'll be a great mechanic one day - if he's interested.

In other words, if you were around me a lot, and learned things and I showed you how I do it, if I was somewhat of an inspiration to you - like Jerry Byrd was to me - well, then you get down and hunt and search, and you work it and perfect it and you just hear somethin' you just love and just go home and just try to do it. Singers even do it. A lot of times singers almost train themselves to sing like other people.

Have you ever spent much time playing around on the pedal steel?

No, I never have (laughs) because, to tell you the truth (laughs) I'm afraid I'd like it! You know (laughs) I believe I'd like it because you could get fuller chords and stuff like that. As you hear pretty chords - you know, I like the guy who's playin' tonight behind Kitty Wells. This guy is fine! It's really pretty! You can get real beautiful chords with it and if I were to do it and find it that easy then I might like it and want a change.

Well, you leave pedals alone then! (laughs) I like what you're doin' now.

Well, I'm gonna stay like I am really because, right off, I'm unique. I have gone in places to play - even other musicians - and they've walked by and said, "Man, what do you play?" "What is that!?" "What's that you've got there?" After you sit down and play it awhile you have them scratchin' their heads - they find out what it was and it's unique in it's own sense.

What do you do with yourself when you're not doing music - not touring with Hank?

Well, I have another job in Nashville, TN …music has almost gotten to be a part-time thing for me now because we don't really work the road that much with Hank, only about 20 days a year so that leaves me a lot of time to do other things. My son's in the business. He's a singer and sometimes I play some jobs with him.

Well, I mean it quite seriously, don't play around with pedals cause I'd like to continue hearing Kayton Roberts playing that good steel guitar "properly".

Don't worry (laughs) I won't go to pedals! (big laugh).

Kayton Roberts' Tunings								
Strings	1	2	3	4	5	6	7	8
C6th / A7th	E	C	A	G	E	C#	A	A Octave
F13th	F	D	A	F	G	Eb	C	F

- ¤ -

Jeremy Wakefield

He got *really* good, *really* fast - that's the general consensus among Jeremy Wakefield's peers. One of the best of the crop of young steel players inspired by the great non-pedal players of the Bob Wills band and early electrified country music, Jeremy combines an aptitude for hot improvisation, an encyclopedic interest in players of earlier generations, and a silky-smooth singing voice. His CD with Dave Biller, *The Flaming Guitars of Biller and Wakefield*, brings to mind the fireworks generated fifty years earlier by the duo of Speedy West and Jimmy Bryant. On a classic Bigsby guitar, his outstanding touch is instantly recognizable.

- ¤ Jeremy Wakefield ¤ -

How did you first come to play the steel guitar and who were your early influences?

When I got into college, I started listening to a lot of country music and started hearing Lloyd Green and Pete Drake and stuff like that. Initially, I was interested in pedal steel and managed to get hold of an MSA single-10 with 3 pedals and 1 knee lever. I started figuring stuff out – or trying to – just on my own. I didn't really know of anyone to take lessons from.

Did you have any experience playing music before acquiring the MSA guitar?

I played guitar in church growing up and my dad kind of taught me to play guitar. I had played in a couple bands in junior high and high school – rock & roll bands, basically. I went to college for art at Cooper Union, in New York, and kept playing a little bit, but music didn't start to be my main interest 'til after I graduated from college.

How did you take the next steps toward playing music professionally?

When I first heard that stuff – like Tammy Wynette records and Lloyd Green – I didn't really know what a pedal steel was. Like most people, I hadn't really ever seen one. I mean, I'd seen it on television, but I didn't really have any idea what was goin' on there. So I had to find out. I guess about a year into it, I started realizing that a lot of the stuff I was trying to play wasn't pedal steel. I'd find myself pressing both pedals down and pressing the knee lever to get that 6th chord sound. Pretty soon I figured out that I should be playing some sort of a C6th deal. Then I moved to California and met people who turned me on to stuff like Joaquin Murphey and Vance Terry and Herb Remington and all that. I felt like I had my work cut out for me.

What do you think is the most difficult aspect of learning to play steel guitar?

I remember thinking in the first two years, the one thing that would have made me throw the thing in the trash was trying to figure out the right hand technique, all around. I kind of thought it would be an easier transition from guitar to steel but yeah, using the finger picks and playing clean, blocked single notes was definitely something that demanded a lot of discipline.

When did you move to a non-pedal steel guitar and what was your first instrument?

An old 6-string Fender Champ was the first non-pedal guitar I had. I had a Guild electric hollow body bass that I traded to a friend for it. After not too long, I bought a double-neck Rickenbacker – probably a 50's Rickenbacker – and I still play that quite a bit. The solid body one. I like the scale on that. I've also got a 1954 Bigsby that I play with this band, *The Lucky Stars*, which is sort of a western swing/country kind of group. I do like the 22.5" scale of the Rickenbacker better. I do some slant work and I think it's better too 'cause you can put a lot heavier strings on a short scale guitar which has a big impact on your tone.

Because of the tighter action?

Exactly. You can have them really cranked up; nice fat strings. I like that better.

Who are some of your favorite steel players?

Well, Lloyd Green was definitely the first guy who caught my attention, but when I started trying to figure out non-pedal stuff, it was Don Helms and also Vance Terry that I listened to.

- ¤ Jeremy Wakefield ¤ -

I went crazy trying to figure out Vance Terry's stuff. He was something else. He was a real swing musician. Joaquin Murphey is my favorite of all those guys.

Have you heard his last recordings on pedal steel that Mike Johnstone produced?

Yeah. It's great. I've talked to a lot of guys who say, "Oh, it doesn't sound like Murphey. It sounds like he's trying to do something totally different than what he was doin' in the 40's and 50's." I think there are plenty of similarities with his close-voiced chords and his phrasing and his *tone*. I met a guy who was friends with Murphey and made some recordings with him, he said, in the early 50's in his house and I tend to believe him judging from the kind of stuff that Murphey's playing and by the tuning as well. But it's just him and a steel and it's all chords. He plays *Moonlight in Vermont, Night and Day, Body and Soul* – all tunes like that. It's not that far off from the last CD.

I understand that you play without a volume pedal.

Sometimes I do. It kind of depends. When I'm playing the Bigsby on western swing kind of stuff I'll tend to use a volume pedal, but a lot of times when I'm playing the Rickenbacker and sitting down, I haven't been using it recently.

Do you play acoustic steel?

I picked up one that's a Weissenborn but has a round neck – like a Spanish guitar. I've never seen another one. The headstock is slotted and it's got a nut extender on it. The guy whose grandmother played it said she bought it and played it as a Hawaiian guitar so it was never played as a Spanish guitar. It's a beautiful sounding instrument.

How did you hook up with Dave Biller to record *The Hot Guitars of Biller & Wakefield*?

I had the honor of playing with Biller in Wayne Hancock's band. I felt like that was a good break for me as a player 'cause that was a gig where I really got to stretch out whether I liked it or not. Playing in Wayne's band, you have to be ready to play four choruses in a row and not repeat yourself too much, although I did. We did several tours with Wayne to Europe and around the states. I learned a lot about steel from Biller about how to play tastefully.

Jeremy Wakefield's Tunings								
Strings	1	2	3	4	5	6	7	8
C6th	G	E	C	A	G	E	C	B (High)
C# minor 11th	E	C#	G#	E	C#	Bb	Eb	F# (High)

What tunings are you using?

I've got a C6th with the 5th on the top – a high G. Instead of an A on the bottom, I've got a high B so it's like a major 7th. On the other neck on my Rickenbacker, I've got a C# minor 11th that Murphey used. Herb Remington used something similar. Speedy West used it too or something real close to it on his *"I'll Never Be Free"* solo.

- ¤ Jeremy Wakefield ¤ -

Have you ever tried any of the Hawaiian tunings like the B11th?

I've fiddled around with it but I guess it hasn't sunk in. I'm often just trying to settle on a good 6-string Hawaiian tuning. I've been using C6th with a high E, but I like the sound so much of a major tuning, like low bass A, or those tunings where you don't always hear that 6th note in there.

Do you pick block or palm block?

I palm block but, now that I think about it, I guess it just depends on the order of notes and the order of strings I'm playing. On a single string, I'll tend to pick block.

You're playing these days in a jazz standards band with a vibes player?

Yeah, D.J. Bonebreak plays vibes. He played drums with X, which was an LA punk rock band – they still play. He's been playing vibes for at least ten years and he's great. We have Wally Hersom on upright bass, [*former Big Sandy bassist*] T.K. Smith plays guitar. It's pretty much jazz. We're shooting for a 1940's era, small group sound.

That's challenging stuff to play on non-pedal steel.

(Laughs). I'm not even in the ballpark. It's sounds a lot better when there are five of us doubling the lines (laughs). We play standards like *Three Little Words, Honeysuckle Rose,* and we do some Hot Club of France material like *Swing Guitars, On the Alamo, China Boy* and *Love Song to a Chambermaid,* which is a Fats Waller tune. We do a couple of bop tunes like *Ornithology, Straight No Chaser* and *Yardbird Suite.*

Have you ever played any of the steel guitar shows or conventions?

I've only been to one up in Walnut Creek, California that Tom Bradsaw did. Ralph Mooney and Bobby Black played. That was real inspiring to see Bobby Black because it was the first time I'd really seen someone play lap steel like that. It was incredible. Ralph Mooney was great too.

Let me ask *you* a question: do you know anything about Rico Turchetti? I've got one 45 rpm record where he's playing with Archie Bleyer's Orchestra and it sounds like a combination of Alvino Rey and Roy Smeck. It's got pedals, and it's real sophisticated but it also has a little bit of a comical side to it. *Limehouse Blues* is on one side and *St. Louis Blues* on the other.

According to Jody Carver, "Rico Turchetti played a homemade pedal steel on the Arthur Godfrey Talent Scouts show back in about 1950. Rico's guitar was custom made by a friend in Rhode Island and he actually used chain that was used for toilet tanks. He could raise some of the strings but not lower anything on his single neck steel. He tuned to an E6th Tuning with an E on the top. He played a bit like Alvino, using mostly sweeping chords and very few if any individual finger grips."

After your initial experiences with your MSA do you still play pedal steel?

My Bigsby has nine pedals and I've got a couple of them set up to do the Bud Isaacs change on the middle neck, but I don't ever really use 'em. Over the years I've kind of gone in and out of using them a little bit. I used them a little bit on that *Biller and Wakefiled* record. Those are not the strongest songs on that album; definitely (laughs).

It's not that I don't like using them, I just haven't concentrated on it.

How do you approach improvising on non-pedal steel? Do you tend to go out of the chord forms or do you take a more scale-based plan of attack?

Well, I do try to think about the chord forms while I'm improvising, but I also try to keep in mind some kind of a melody that I might not otherwise be able to get by just staying in the chord forms. My knowledge of all the modes isn't really conscious enough to really know exactly what I'm doing all the time. When I improvise, it's mostly by ear, I guess.

What advice would you give to people who want to learn to improvise on the instrument?

Well, I'm not sure if I read this or Vance told me this: learn the major scale everywhere all the way up and down on the neck on every string in every possible configuration. That was really helpful to me, especially in learning how to hear intervals and learning where they lie on the fingerboard.

That's what Herb Remington taught Vance when he took lessons from him as a teenager. Vance's playing with Jimmy Rivers is mind boggling.

It really is. I've never heard anything even close to that as far as a steel player playing chords and chord melody.

What steel-related activities are you involved in these days?

I have a day job now. I work as a scenery painter currently for a Disney subcontractor painting scenery for rides for Tokyo Disney and Disney here in California. They've been real flexible in letting me go on tour over the years. Sometimes it's too flexible but that's been one of the benefits. Outside of playing with the *Lucky Stars,* I've done a few weeks of touring the west coast with *Asleep At the Wheel* while they were looking for a permanent steel person.

And with the jazz band, we have a weekly gig at a coffee shop where we basically play for tips and sandwiches and coffee. It's great (laughs). I feel like a real musician; I've got a weekly gig for the first time!

Junior Brown

As the only world–renowned virtuoso of the *Guit-Steel,* Junior Brown is king of a kingdom in which he is the only subject. The Austin, Texas native turned professional as a teenager, spending years as a sideman to groups such as *Asleep At the Wheel* before becoming a solo artist. He has since played diverse venues, including the *Grand Ole Opry*, rock clubs, and the soundstages of network television programs.

Junior Brown's music and deep baritone voice recall the honky tonk heroes who inspired him, especially Ernest Tubb. Junior invented his own guitar, which combines a standard 6-string Telecaster-style guitar with a lap steel guitar. In both his lyrics and flat-out astonishing guitar and steel improvisations, Brown combines sly humor with a freewheeling imagination that draws equally from honky tonk, western swing, surf guitar and even Jimi Hendrix. In 1994, *Guitar Player Magazine's* annual readers' poll named him best lap steel player, best country artist, as well as the winner for best country album.

- ¤ -

WESTERN SWING

The Carter Family epitomized the old world values of hearth and home. Listeners could imagine them singing harmony on their front porch. Milton Brown and his Musical Brownies, on the other hand, epitomized all that was new and exciting in the first third of the 20th century: jazz, nightclubs, fast cars, and hot, improvised solos that owed as much to Louis Armstrong or Joé Venuti as to the breakdown fiddle tradition.

Western swing, as Brown's innovative new music came to be called, successfully incorporated a crazy quilt of American music that included New Orleans jazz, Memphis blues, fiddle breakdowns, cowboy songs, the conjuntos of the Tex-Mex border, big band and even rhythm & blues. While often mentioned as a branch of country music, western swing, with its tight ensemble playing and instrumental solos is closer in spirit to jazz.

Thanks to the recordings of Leon McAuliffe, Herb Remington, Noel Boggs, Joaquin Murphey and Vance Terry, the steel guitar became indelibly linked with western swing. Fine players like Maurice Anderson, Tom Morrell, John Ely, Cindy Cashdollar, and bands like *Asleep at the Wheel* have continued to keep the torch of western swing burning bright.

Bob Dunn

Bob Dunn

The sound of Bob Dunn's revolutionary steel guitar playing had an almost visceral effect on musicians and listeners all over the southwest during the mid-1930s.

Born in 1908 in Fort Gibson, Oklahoma, Dunn was the oldest of four children. After hearing a touring Hawaiian troupe as a boy, he became fascinated by Hawaiian guitar, eventually taking correspondence lessons from Walter Kolomoku. He quit school by the eighth grade and was playing professionally by his mid-teens with a number of touring outfits including Paul Perkins's band, the *Panhandle Cowboys and Indians*, and *California Curly and his Cowboy Band.*

According to Kevin Coffey, writing in the *Journal of Country Music,* "It was a chance encounter that occurred while Dunn was in New York working pickup gigs on Coney Island that first alerted him to the amazing possibilities of electrical amplification of the guitar." Fiddler Jimmy Thomason told the story that Dunn "… ran into this black guy who was playing a steel guitar with a homemade pickup attached to it. He has this thing hooked up through an old radio or something and was playing these blues licks. Well, this just knocked Bob out and he got this guy to show him how he was doing it."

- ¤ Bob Dunn ¤ -

According to Thomason, Dunn was so obsessed with the man's concept that he "... followed him all the way to New Orleans" to learn more.

Dunn joined *Milton Brown and His Musical Brownies* in late 1934 and began a two-year recording career that would change the sound of both western swing and country music forever. The *Brownies* introduced many concepts that would become standard for western swing bands: jazz-inflected singing, jazz piano, hot fiddle and steel soloing, and a wide ranging repertoire that cross-pollinated numerous regional musical styles.

Though he had been exposed to the breakdown fiddle tradition as a youngster, Dunn – a trombonist himself – was heavily influenced by the hot, staccato phrasing of jazz of players like Jack Teagarden and Louis Armstrong. His virtuoso, horn-like soloing in a simple A major tuning was unprecedented for a steel guitar player at that time. Like Django Reinhardt on guitar, or Louis Armstrong on trumpet, there was simply nobody else who could do what Dunn could do on his instrument. His imprint on musicians of the time, as well as on subsequent generations of steel players, remains indelible.

While the stories surrounding his drinking are legendary, Dunn apparently gained control after a three-year stint in the Navy. After WWII, Dunn the high school dropout, earned a degree in music from the Southern College of Fine Arts and opened a music store in Houston, where he taught, and virtually retired from playing gigs. Bob Dunn died in 1971.

The author is indebted to Kevin Coffey for his fine article on Dunn, titled "Steel Colossus", which appeared in The Country Reader: Twenty Five Years of the Journal of Country Music, (Vanderbilt Univ. Press, 2000).

When Milton Brown and his Musical Brownies were on tour in 1935, Milton's younger brother Roy Lee Brown, then 14-years old, was with them. The following are Roy's recollections of Bob Dunn.

When did you first hear Bob Dunn play?

In late 1934, *Milton Brown and the Musical Brownies* had a daily radio broadcast from 12 o'clock until sometimes 2 o'clock on KTAT in Fort Worth, Texas. Wanna Coffman, who played the bass fiddle, had one of these National all-metal guitars. During the program, he'd play at least one, sometimes two, Hawaiian tunes. They'd lower the mike and he would play that National.

Bob Dunn was traveling with the *Oklahoma Cowboys & Indians* and they were just a country band – they did these shows in theaters. They didn't play dances. So Bob Dunn came up to the studio. The studio was on the mezzanine of the Texas Hotel. They had chairs there and there was always a big crowd and sometimes they would even string out onto the mezzanine.

Wanna would always tune up his guitar before the program and just stand it over in the corner. Well, Bob Dunn came in and I guess he introduced himself – I wasn't there – I'm getting this from my brother Derwood and the other members of the *Brownies* – and he saw Wanna's guitar over there and picked it up. Wanna told Derwood, "He's gonna get my guitar out of tune." Then Bob started fooling around on it and when they saw what he could do, man, everybody's eyes bugged out! He was playing jazz on that steel guitar! Milton put him on the program and he did three numbers: *Old Water Mill, Ida Sweet as Apple Cider,* and *Moonlit Waters.*

- ¤ Bob Dunn ¤ -

How did Dunn come to play an amplified guitar?

At that time, late 1934, some of the orchestras had amplifiers. A lot of them carried a rhythm guitar but rarely ever did they play lead - maybe only a little bit, but they really couldn't be heard. The amplifiers were just coming out.

Bob Dunn ran across this colored fella on Coney Island. This fella had a guitar or a steel guitar with some kind of a pickup hooked up to it that he ran into an old radio as an amplifier. Bob found out how that guy could do it and then Milton found out where there was an amplifier for sale in a music store in Mineral Wells, Texas.

Milton went over and got that amplifier and Bob Dunn borrowed one of Derwood's Martin guitars. You could get these steel extenders that you could put up at the nut to raise those strings. He then took that V-magnet and magnetized them. So the first electric guitar in a western swing guitar wasn't a solid body, it was a Martin.

Bob Dunn had a big guitar that he had played with the Oklahoma Cowboys and Indians. He had played "take-off"[*single note lead guitar*] guitar with them. He was a great standard guitar player as well as a steel player. He also played trombone and he copied what he did on the trombone on the steel guitar.

Bob Dunn's Tuning						
Strings	1	2	3	4	5	6
A major (high-bass)	E	C#	A	E	C#	A

What was it like to hear him for the first time?

Nobody knew what it was. They couldn't tell whether it was a horn or what it was. I soon saw him in person because I traveled with the Brownies in the summer of 1935. I went out to Crystal Springs every weekend. It was a dance hall called Crystal Springs Dance Pavilion. I didn't hear him that first time he played on the air, but that Saturday night I heard him out at Crystal Springs 'cause Milton had hired him immediately.

It must have been wild to hear him because nobody else sounded remotely like him.

That's right. People would write in, 'cause phones weren't available. We had one phone in our block. They wrote letters. They would make up the programs by the requests from the mail that came in. People would write in, "What's that sound we're hearing? Is that horn or what is it?" (Laughs) It was a sound not heard before, I'll say that!

How did he come to use a magnet on the strings?

Guitar pickups now all have their magnets built in. I guess maybe that guy on Coney Island taught him. I've seen him use it before a radio program; before a dance. He'd run that magnet up and down those strings and it gave it a better sound.

- ¤ Bob Dunn ¤ -

Did he use the old flat style steel guitar bars?

I'm pretty sure he used a round bar and I don't believe it had a finger groove on top of it.

Was Bob's drinking a problem?

I never did see him get too much. I knew he drank and most of the musicians of the day drank. They had bootleggers all over the country then.

What was your role with the band?

I was fixin' strings for [*standard guitarist*] Derwood. Derwood broke so many strings, he played so hard. He played down near the pin bridge on a Martin guitar. The only thing that was amplified at that time was the PA system and Bob Dunn's steel guitar. He broke a lot of strings so he always carried two or three guitars with him and he always had a young person to fix strings. I was there when he'd broke strings on both of them and hollering at me "Hurry up! Hurry up!"

Sounds like you were one of the first roadies.

Yeah (laughs) I was one of 'em. In the summertime of 1935 & '36 I traveled with the Brownies because I was out of school. I was 14 years old when I started traveling with them. Then Milton got killed in '36.

Did steel players crowd the bandstand to see what Bob was doing?

Once in a while. Ever hear of Lefty Perkins? Milton was playing at the Oak View Inn in Dennison,

- ¤ Bob Dunn ¤ -

Texas, and Bob Dunn was, of course, playing steel and this guy came in and was watching him and Bob knew him. After a while Bob said, "C'mon, get up here. Sit in". He got up there and turned the guitar completely around – it was strung up right-handed. He played left handed and he came close to playing like Bob. Later on he played with Derwood and the *Brownies*.

Did the *Brownies* rehearse very much?

They did at first then in later years they didn't 'cause everybody knew exactly what everybody else was doin'. When they recorded for RCA Bluebird they'd all stand around one mike and they'd put the banjo maybe out in the hall. The fiddles and the vocals had to stand close. Derwood stood close to the mikerophone because he sang harmony with Milton. They just put 'em in different positions to try to get a balance. They told them, "If you make a mistake, just keep going." That's why on those early records, you'll hear mistakes in there. They didn't stop and do 'em over (laughs).

The first time Bob came into the studio and Milton was gonna hire him, he had to play over in Dallas with the *Cowboys & Indians* and he asked Wanna could he borrow that National steel guitar so he could play it over there at a show that night. They couldn't hear that guitar out at Crystal Springs unless they lowered that mike. The fiddles played right up into the mike and the vocals were right into the mike and Milton – before the PA system came in – Milton sang into a megaphone like Rudy Valle. There was so much laughin' and hollerin' and kickin' the floor that you wasn't gonna hear anything unless it was amplified.

Bob's amp must have been way back from the mikerophone.

On those records you can hear a little feedback. They didn't know how to handle that amplifier. It was a volu-tone amp. It was about 12" or 14" inches, something like that. They were just getting on the market.

Did Bob stay with the band after Milton's death?

Bob stayed a while but then he left and Cecil Brower and Cliff Bruner left. They were makin' more money than any other band at that time. They were the most popular band in the southwest. This was during the depression but everybody was driving a brand new car. Then in 1937, the band disbanded. Bob went down to Houston and Beaumont, Texas and recorded with Cliff Bruner and his group called the *Vagabonds* – they were mainly Bruner's band. Then he ran a music store in Houston. He could play as much standard guitar as he could steel. He really ate it up.

- ¤ -

Leon McAuliffe

Like Humphrey Bogart's famous instruction to "Play it, Sam", in the classic film *Casablanca*, Bob Will's "Take it away, " became a legendary American catchphrase. In addition to his talent, Will's habit of calling out the names of his musicians prior to their solos at dances and on record, helped make Leon McAuliffe one of the most recognized steel guitarists in the world. Even though he is most associated with the *Texas Playboys*, McAuliffe also enjoyed a long and fruitful solo career as a band leader and radio station owner.

- ¤ Leon McAuliffe ¤ -

Born in Houston in 1917, McAuliffe began playing professionally by age fifteen. After a stint with Lee O'Daniel's *Light Crust Doughboys*, McAuliffe joined Will's *Texas Playboys* in 1935. With the *Playboys*, McAuliffe recorded many songs that have become western swing classics and influenced a generation of players to take up the non-pedal steel guitar. *Steel Guitar Rag*, McAuliffe's adaptation of an earlier tune by Sylvester Weaver became a huge hit, and a later composition called *Panhandle Rag* became a Top Ten hit in 1949. Both tunes have become steel guitar standards.

After serving as a flight instructor during World War II, McAuliffe founded a big band called the *Cimarron Boys*. By the 1960s, as western swing's popularity had eroded due to the pervasive influence of rock & roll, McAuliffe played music only sporadically and devoted his time to ownership of a radio station, KAMO in Rogers, Arkansas. With the western swing revival of 1970s, McAuliffe staged reunion concerts with former members of the *Texas Playboys* and recorded a few solo albums. He is remembered as a pioneer of the instrument and a legend of American show business.

The following interview was conducted for the CBC in the early 1970s by veteran Canadian broadcaster, Laurie Mills, and is transcribed here with his permission.

How did you get your start in music?

Well, my dad played a guitar. He and my mother separated and divorced when I was about seven years old. Prior to that time he had been on the road travelin'. I remember, as a little boy, quite young, under seven, when he would come home, he would have friends over and they would sit and play. And Dad played a fingerpicking – what they call a Chet Atkins-style guitar today - and he also had a mandolin and had several friends who played instruments. I remember as a little boy sittin' down on the floor at his feet and listening to him and there was somethin' about the sound of a guitar that stayed with me.

When I was going to be fourteen, in January – that Christmas – my mother asked me what I wanted for Christmas and I said, "I want a guitar." She worked at a bank in Houston and she said, "Have you got a guitar picked out?" And I said, "Yes, Ma'am" and she said, "Where is it?" I said, "It's around the corner in a pawn shop." I used to meet her at the bank and sit down there, you know, and wait for her. It was a $7 Stella acoustic guitar. So she got it for me for Christmas.

Well, then I decided I wanted to learn to play it and I'd better get me a teacher. I used to listen to everybody that played guitar of any kind on radio in Houston. There were three or four people who had little programs, usually a steel guitar, standard guitar and a ukulele. They were teachers and they would advertise their schools on the radio. This one fella I liked a little better than the others and I went to see him. His name was Lattés Merrick – he was a Bohemian fella and he had a studio there in town. I went to see him and I took my guitar along. He said, well it'll cost you a dollar a lesson and I said, "Fine." He asked if I wanted to play steel or standard. I said, "I don't know." He said, "Well, I'll give you lessons on both."

Of course, this was during the depression and I imagine students were not too plentiful so he was anxious to get one. So with the diagram method that he used, he gave me lessons on both standard and steel guitar. I took about twelve to fifteen lessons. In each lesson he would give me a song but he wasn't givin' me enough songs fast enough to suit me (laughs). I was learning my song that he gave me to play for him when I got back the next week and I was listening on radio to everybody *else* that I could hear. I was trying to play other songs that I heard.

- ¤ Leon McAuliffe ¤ -

So after about ten or twelve lessons I figured I guess I can learn 'em about as fast as he can teach 'em to me and it's cheaper to quit takin' lessons. So I did.

Let's skip a lot of years and talk about when you got into playing as a professional, rather than just playing at home.

Well, it was actually pretty quick because I lived with that guitar. In fact, and I am not overly proud of the fact, but the schoolwork just dropped out of site – I didn't crack a book, man, I hate to say it, (laughs) but I didn't crack a book from the time I got that guitar and I finally wound up quittin' school in my junior year.

I began to look for other musicians to play with. Whenever I'd hear of a guitar player somewhere I'd contact them and see if they wanted to sit down and play. I met quite a few people this way. I think one reason I stayed more with the steel than the standard guitar was 'cause nearly everybody else played standard guitar but there weren't many steel players.

Have you anywhere along the way learned to read music?

Oh yes, I taught myself to read after I had been playing for a couple years. The first thing, Lattés never did tell me what key I was playing in and his diagram system didn't really explain it because it was numbers instead of notes. I met a fella who played good standard guitar and he was much more progressed than I was and he and I started playing regularly – we'd rehearse together – and he could tell me what key we were in. In other words, he'd hit an F chord and I'd find it on my steel guitar and then I knew where F was. So then I bought books and learned about it. I figured it out on my fingers, you know, if E was an open string then it's only a half tone up to F then F sharp and so on. I figured it out that way and the same way for the chords.

Anyway, to make a long story short, this boy's name was Freddie Rollins. He got us some little parties – house parties – and dances to play for where we made a little bit of money. So then we decided we were good enough to play on radio so we went down and auditioned. A popular thing to do in those days - there were Triple-X and A&W root beer stands all over town - and they would build a little bandstand out in the parking lot and musicians would get out there and play and then they'd pass the hat around for tips. We played some of those and it kinda went from there. To tell you how quick it was, I got a job on network radio with the *Lightcrust Doughboys*, on the Texas Quality Network, in Ft. Worth, when I was sixteen years old.

How longer were you a member of that group?

I was there a year and a half. Bob Wills had started that group, [*Lightcrust Doughboys*] then he left to form the *Texas Playboys* and went to Oklahoma and they hired a new band. That's how I got the job. So the man who ran the show, who was president of the mill there that made the flour, he liked the sound of a steel guitar and he didn't find one around Ft. Worth after Bob left and the whole band went with him. So he called his sales manager in Houston who went to the radio station where I was playin'. He sent me to audition and I got the job. I stayed there until I was eighteen, in January of '35, when I went to work with Bob Wills – in March of '35. He heard me on the radio and offered me a job.

How long were you a Texas Playboy?

From March of 1935 until I got my draft notice in December of 1942.

Did Bob allow you to be Leon McAuliffe or was he pretty restrictive in what he wanted his boys to play?

- ¤ Leon McAuliffe ¤ -

Oh, no. He gave you absolute, total freedom. The only thing he wanted you to do was play what you felt and smile and have good stage presence, be friendly with people, and enjoy yourself so that they would enjoy themselves. He told me, "Whenever I point to you, you smile at me." "You acknowledge the fact that I have given you the chorus, give me a smile and then just play whatever you want to play, but go. When you get through, turn around and smile back at me and I'll give it to somebody else."

Quite a few people, including Merle Haggard, who has an abiding love for the music of Bob Wills, have said, "Bob was not a great fiddler but he's so greatly important because of what he did in music."

Well, there's all kinda ways to determine how great somebody is. If you were gonna say "As a schooled musician" no, he was not great. But as a musician who had creative, innovative ideas, who set his own style, did his own thing, did what millions of people loved, and made much money at it, made many friends, was a tremendous personality – one of the biggest names in show business - Bob Wills was one of the greatest fiddle players that ever lived. If you use that as a yardstick.

After you got out of the Navy, is that when the *Cimarron Boys* were formed?

Well, yeah. I got out of the Navy in December of '45, I guess it was, when the war was over. January of '46 I started my band. I didn't call them the *Cimarron Boys* right at first; I just called it *Leon McAuliffe and his Western Swing Band.* When we opened the Cimarron Ballroom in May of 1950 - I don't know if you're familiar with any Oklahoma history, but it was called the Cimarron Country. There's a Cimarron River; there was a land run on the Cimarron Country at one time, so Cimarron is an Oklahoma name. It was a western name; it had a good ring to it, so we called our ballroom the Cimarron.

About that time we decided we couldn't get along with Columbia Records and we set up our own label, Cimarron Records. So we became the *Cimarron Boys* (laughs) *everything* was Cimarron, including my publishing company.

How long were the *Cimarron Boys* together?

They were together until May of 1965.

I would guess it makes you pretty happy to note the continuing interest in western swing that got the *Texas Playboys* back together?

Right. That, to us, is a very gratifying thing because, you know, we had reached an age for a time where the music was not so popular. I mean, it *died* in the middle '50's & '60's because young people set the trends and young people went to rock & roll and different sounds. And then, it stayed kinda that way and I was glad to be out of it, really, because it got tougher on the road, you know, when you don't have the leading thing or somethin' that's really current. It stayed that way until about 1973 when we made this record with Bob Wills when he was dying and wanted to do one last record. He picked eight men of all the *Texas Playboys* that had ever been in forty years and I was fortunate to be one of 'em.

We made this record, it was a hit, Merle had the tribute album, Waylon Jennings sang "Bob Wills is still the king" and it just seemed like it caught fire. *Asleep at the Wheel* and Commander Cody and Charlie Daniels and a bunch of the bands started diggin' this up.

They were playin' rock music and they said, "Hey, we want somethin' different" so they went back and dug this up and the kids loved it. So the young people grabbed hold of it again and that's why it came back.

I'm happy you're still playing the non-pedal steel but at the same time I wonder why you didn't switch as so many of your contemporaries have?

All right – it's real simple. I played a pedal steel guitar in 1941. Gibson came out with a guitar called the Electraharp. Somebody else came out with one with some pedals, I can't remember the name of it but it had about four pedals at an angle across one side. The problem was that when you depressed pedals, stretched or lowered strings, and then let 'em back, they weren't good enough quality to come back in tune. So you were fightin' tuning all the time. I didn't like that. I was having to spend too much time tuning. So I tried it out and I didn't like it.

Now, then came along World War II and I carried my guitar all through the Navy and they didn't do much improving on pedals and metallurgy and all these things 'til after the war. I started my band and I had *Steel Guitar Rag, Panhandle Rag*, several hit songs, my band established on records, and my sound on the steel guitar established. And I was standing up, fronting my band. Now, there's no way you can play a pedal steel guitar and stand up. And there's no way that you can successfully front a band sittin' down. So I had two reasons: frontin' a band and a style already established. So I stayed with the four-neck guitar.

I have a very beautiful Sho-Bud guitar that Shot Jackson made for me specially and gave to me about 1963 and I wouldn't take $20,000 for it. But I don't play it. I don't want to get involved in anything that is different than what I am known by.

When did you write the *Steel Guitar Rag*?

Well, I wrote that thing back when I was still taking lessons from my teacher. Because he taught me to tune my guitar to an A major chord, with an E on top … E, C#, A and then E, C# A – you know, just octaves. I was listening on the radio, as I said, to just about everybody else. And there were a couple Hawaiian groups … there was a group from Houston called the *Palm Islanders* that were very, very good. They had a fine steel player. Anyway, I said "The Hawaiians sound different. What are they doin' that we're not doin'?" Lattes' said "Well most of the Hawaiians play in the key of E, they tune their guitar to an E." I said, "Well, how do you do it?" And he showed me.

Okay, so I'd play my guitar in A for a while and then I'd tune it to an E, just trying to find positions on the E neck, which were different than the A neck. Running an arpeggio (sings major arpeggio) that's all it is, just runnin' down the chord. But I liked that sound; it stuck with me and I wanted to put a little beat to it and it just came from there.

You couldn't possibly have known then that you were writing a classic?

Oh, no. I had no idea at all, you know. When I went to audition for the *Light Crust Doughboys*, they gave me a job and were going to put me on the noon program that day. They said, "What do you wanna play" and I said "Well, here's one I wrote. If you like it, well, we'll try it." I played it for 'em and they said "Yeah, we like that." So we put it on the air. And then when I went to work with Bob Wills, it was the first thing that I had played with Bob. So Bob wanted to record it so we made our first session for Columbia in 1935.

This is the one where, very early in the recording session, Mr. Art Satherly, the Recording Director, stopped and came into the studio. He said, "Bob, you're hollering and talking and you're covering up the musicians." (Laughs). This is funny because Bob was a very determined and high-spirited man and he did what he thought was right. Bob said, "Oh is that right?" "Yes", said Mr. Satherly. "We can't hear them for you." Bob said, "Okay" and he turned around to the band and said "Pack up, Boys, we're goin' home." (Big laugh). And Uncle Art, as we called him, said, "Oh no, Bob, I don't want you to go home!" Bob said, "Look, you hired Bob Wills and the Texas Playboys. Now get somethin' straight – Bob Wills talks, hollers, says whatever he wants to anytime he wants to. Now, if you want to record it that way, we will. If you don't, we'll go home." Art said, "All right."

Bob wanted to do *Steel Guitar Rag*. And Art said, "Bob, I'd rather not do that song. We have a fella named Roy Smeck on the label who plays steel guitar instrumentals and we just don't need more of that kinda thing." Well, Bob accepted that at that time. In the meantime, another year went by before we recorded again. You must remember also that you didn't just record three or four tunes, you went into the studio and you recorded for a week. We did as much as forty-eight tunes on a recording session. We'd go to Dallas, or Chicago, or wherever and record all week long!

Anyway, a year went by and we went to Chicago to make records. In the meantime, we had played this song (*Steel Guitar Rag*) at the dances every night and on the radio show and Bob knew it was a hit because the people asked for it all the time. And they just danced the stuffing out of it. So, when we got up to the second recording session, Bob said, "Now look – I'm gonna record this song." Well, he had sold enough records in that year's time that they said, "Yes, Bob, whatever you want to do." (Big laugh). So that's how it happened.

When we got ready to do it, Bob said "Leon, I want to do this a little differently. You hit a chord, let me say somethin', and then you start." That's when he came up with "Take it away, Leon."

What is your instrument these days?

I still play a four-neck – eight strings on each neck – Fender steel guitar. No pedals.

How are the necks tuned?

I still basically use an A tuning on one and an E tuning on the other one, with eight strings, of course, I added the sixth note. I have an A6th instead of an A major. The E chord has a sixth, a seventh, a ninth and a thirteenth. So we basically call it an E13th chord – still with an E on top.

Now, when I got the third neck, I had to come up with a new tuning. I could not get diminished chords, I couldn't get augmented chords and I couldn't get major seventh chords. So I sat down and devised one that still had the E on top, but by using four picks and stretching my fingers and picking different groups of strings, I could get the chords that I couldn't get on the other two necks - a major seventh, for example. I can get a flatted fifth, I can get an augmented ninth, I can get full diminished chords and, by having the E on top, I use it in conjunction with the other two necks and whenever I jump from one neck to the other, I usually jump straight across. So, I can get at least one inversion of most any chord – a great many of them at least - not as many as you can do on pedals but that was my answer to the pedal thing – to get more chords.

- ¤ Leon McAuliffe ¤ -

Leon McAuliffe's Tunings								
Strings	1	2	3	4	5	6	7	8
A6th	E	C#	A	F#	E	C#	A	F#
E13th	E	C#	B#	G#	F#	D	G#	E
Diminished	E	C#	A	F#	F	Eb	Ab	D
Bass tuning	D	B	G	E	D	C	B	A
The Ab string in the diminished tuning is tuned 1/2 step below the third string. The low A in the bass tuning is tuned to the same pitch as a bass guitar.								

How old a guitar is it?

I got it in 1950. In about 1940, I got my Rickenbacher double-neck guitar and then about '47, I switched to a Fender double neck. I don't know when they came out with a triple neck, but they sent me one. They came up with the idea because Leo was very innovative. Boy, he was always in there workin' tryin' to do somethin' new and better. When they came up with the four-neck, Don Randall called me up and said, "Why don't you come out here; got somethin' for you." I got one of the very first – Noel Boggs, me and Joaquin Murphey got about the first three. They were both on the west coast and I was back in Oklahoma. I went out there and he showed it to me. I said, "What are you doin' with that other (fourth) neck?" Don said, "Got bass strings on it!" (Laughs) I said, (shakily) "Okay, how do you want me to tune it?" He said, "tune it any way you want to." So I came up with a tuning.

With the bass strings, I have a lot of low notes I would not have had before – that's how I use it. When you reach that far – for that neck – you're really a little out of position, you know. It's a little awkward. You have to lean way over and get back.

So, you don't use it a whole lot but it's a very good effect and for playin' parts with a band. If I had the front line playin' a whole bunch of notes, I could get bass notes on the bottom and really fill it up.

How active in music now are you and the Texas Playboys? Are you together forever or just on occasion?

Well, of course not forever. I'll be 63 in January. The bass player, Joe Ferguesson, is 65. Smokey Dacus, the drummer, is already 68 and Al Strickland, the piano player, will be 73. When you reach those ages, no matter what your heart tells you and your soul feels, your body tells you somethin' else.

As you know, on that last Bob Wills recording, Bob went into a coma that night and he lived a year and a half but never knew anybody. The record went on to be a hit and Mrs. Wills was getting call after call …would the *Texas Playboys* perform? They wanted us to do a show down at the educational TV network, in Austin, Texas called "Austin City Limits." Well, that thing showed internationally and the calls just flooded in from there.

Now, Bob was gone and I had been the one that had had my own band so Mrs. Wills said, "Leon, will you take this group and front it and play some dates?" So, we all got together and talked to her and decided we would play a maximum of twelve dates a year and that we would only play if we got our price and she'd get a share, just like the rest of us. We won't drive anywhere because we can't drive

- ¤ Leon McAuliffe ¤ -

to a job, play two or four hours then get in the car and drive home anymore. So we make sure we get airfare and everybody gets a good sum for it. We just got together and set our own rules.

And we love to play! When we get started, the music itself starts our adrenaline and this starts the people's adrenaline goin'. We can't just get up there and poke through a song – there's no way we can do that – we've gotta throw ourselves completely into it. Well, when you throw a seventy-year-old frame into it for that long a time, (laughs) it takes you a few days to get completely over it. So we do play and we've made three albums since the last one with Bob.

One last question for you, Leon. In light of today's music and all the pedal steel guitars there are around, is the non-pedal steel guitar a dead creature?

I would say that yes, if you are going to be a steel guitar player playing for somebody else because your competition can do so many more things, technically - play faster, more chords, more weird sounds, more things. As a sideman, with the pedal guitar, it doesn't demand that you stand up in front and entertain, you just sit there and play your guitar. So all your concentration can be on it.

If I were trying to get a job with somebody else today, I would have to play a pedal steel guitar to keep up with the competition. I'm very fortunate that I was able to set a style of my own back then because there weren't that many steel guitar players. Gosh, when I went to work with Bob Wills, me and Bob Dunn and Noel Boggs were about the only three steel guitar players that I knew of playing in Western bands. They had just started usin' them. So we didn't have the competition you have today. If you had to compete with Buddy Emmons, Curley Chalker, and Lloyd Green and the other two thousand players on records and on the road, you'd have a tough time doin' it (laughs).

- ¤ -

Joaquin Murphey

When Earl "Joaquin" Murphey arrived on the Los Angeles music scene in the early 1940s, listeners were captivated by the effortless fluidity, drive, and creativity of his improvised solos. Steel players were dumbfounded. He was so far ahead of his contemporaries, it was twenty years before any other steel guitarists came close to matching him.

The technical aplomb of Sol Hoopii, the guitar arpeggios of Django Reinhardt, the block piano chords of George Shearing and most importantly, the fluid clarinet runs of Benny Goodman, all found voice in the western swing music Murphey played with Spade Cooley, Tex Williams, Roy Rogers, *Andy Parker and the Plainsmen*, and a host of other Los Angeles–based groups. A jazz musician disguised as a cowboy, his picking on solo features like *Three Way Boogie* and *Oklahoma Stomp* had a huge influence on steel guitar greats such as Buddy Emmons and Speedy West, who wore out the grooves of their 78 rpm records in an effort to copy Murphey's licks.

- ¤ Joaquin Murphey ¤ -

His solos on *Honeysuckle Rose* and *Sweet Georgia Brown,* recorded with *Andy Parker and the Plainsmen,* became legendary. In lieu of pursuing a career on the road, Murphey spent most of his professional career playing with dance bands in Southern California. He stayed with the non-pedal steel long after his contemporaries had moved to pedal steel and remained with his signature C^{6th} tuning, feeling that the Nashville-standard E9th tuning used in country music was merely a gimmikek. Despite sliding out of the spotlight in the late 50's, Murphey's profile remained high with steel players and he was inducted into the Steel Guitar Hall of Fame in 1980.

The stories surrounding Joaquin are legion. He'd de-tune his steel guitar when he left the bandstand so others couldn't learn his tunings. He'd simply walk off stage if the music wasn't to his liking. He was seen lying face down in the street talking lovingly to his car. In sorting out the truth of this lonely and mysterious man, one thing stands clear: the recorded evidence unquestionably supports Joaquin Murphey's place as a towering giant of the steel guitar.

During the last years of his life, Joaquin was befreinded by Los Angeles steel player and producer, Michael Johnstone, of *Class Act Records*. Dissipated by alcohol abuse and down on his luck, Joaquin hadn't touched a steel guitar in years. Along with musician and steel builder, Chas Smith, Johnstone helped him clean up. *Murph*, his first solo recording in 20 years, features a master swing musician in the twilight of his life revisiting the lush harmonies of the big band era. Fifty years after his heyday, his playing continues to enrich and astonish listeners. Joaquin Murphey died of cancer in 1999.

The author is indebted to Mikehael Johnstone for making available his 1995 interview with Joaquin Murphey.

- ¤ Joaquin Murphey ¤ -

You recorded a solo album back in the 70's with Buddy Emmons playing bass and Leon Rhodes on guitar. I understand you weren't happy with the way it came out.

That piano player we had on that album, this guy was drunk the whole time and he was just pounding. Of course, I blame the engineer. He should have brought him down in my phones or Scotty [*Producer, Dewitt Scott, Sr.*] should have really just got rid of him cause he was constantly playing in the same register I was.

Buddy Emmons was playing bass on that record. Gosh, when I played one song for him he picked it right up, and of course Leon Rhodes, boy, he'd pick it up too. One introduction I remember we threw together in a couple minutes.

Of course Buddy, everything he played came out real good but the drums were playin' just a little bit behind, you know, so I couldn't play on the backside without makin' him drag even more. It was all wrong. I was tired and it was raining outside and there was moisture in the air and I couldn't stay in tune. These guys never rehearsed so we'd be trying to work things out on the spot right there and Scotty's saying, "Well, you guys about ready? Let's go!" Scotty of course, he put up the money. I was broke. It was humiliating. I had a dollar and a half in my pocket and that was it. I had no control.

What are your goals for this new record?

Boy! This is really something. It's hard for me to believe this is actually happening 'cause I figured I'm done - finished years ago - and now I'm gonna make a new record! What I want to do now is perfect what style I do have and if I put a new record out, maybe they'll say, "Hey man – Joaquin is playin' better now than he ever played." Of course it don't compare with what you modern guys can do but at least I can still do this! [*Play fast steel guitar runs*].

The kind of songs I'm gonna do on this record - jazz instrumentals - it shouldn't be all that complicated. One good piano player that really knows what's happening - knows the bag - once he hears a few of my songs and the way I play, he should adapt to it real quick.

And this time, I'll pick my own songs - I'll be in control of that. I want to do some of my compositions. That's what I've always wanted. You just get me some good musicians – hell, all the ones I know are dead. I'll take care of the rest.

Did you have the luxury of rehearsals with the *Spade Cooley Band*?

With Spade we used to rehearse for hours before we'd go in and do a recording. Boy, it was polished, and you could tell. I want to get back into it but I couldn't stand that routine like I did with Spade, workin' nights and the next day we'd have to be at Universal [*movie studio*] even though you'd have to sit around for four or five hours and do nothing.

You hear stories about Paul Franklin, Buddy Emmons and those guys - all they do is play the guitar. They get up in the morning and play their guitars until it's time to go somewhere else and play their guitars. I've played long enough to know they'd have to practice that much to play like they do.

- ¤ Joaquin Murphey ¤ -

Well, that reminds me of Curly Chalker. He used to do that. For a couple weeks he wouldn't come out of the room 'cause he was working on something. He told his wife, "I don't want to be bothered - just set the food there by the door 'till I have time 'cause I'm gonna stay in here till I get it." Two weeks he stayed in his room one time!

When you practice something - I did this all my life - you're trying to get it a certain speed so you practice it at that speed and you flub and so you're practicing flubbing. So you slow it down - however slow it has to be - where you don't make any mistakes; get it clean and then speed it up a little. But then, some days, this hand won't work you know. But I'm not gonna worry about it.

Buddy Emmons, back when he was a young man and wasn't playing pedals yet, would actually take his Fender or Bigsby to bed and lie there playing it across his stomach.

Hell, I did that too. I'd stay up all night. That's what it takes.

How do you like your guitars set up?

The string spacing is gonna be 3/8ths at the nut and all the way up to the tailpiece – the strings will be perfectly parallel all the way down so I can synchronize myself better, especially with the tip of the bar on single strings around the first two frets.

I like to try and comp block chords like Shearing did on piano and that should be even easier with that new pedal guitar cause I won't have to jump around so much. I like an amp that don't sound too bright in the high register – that's good from say, the tenth fret on down. It should be pretty mellow, you know, a little more body.

Do you regret not going to the E9th sound?

I just try to do what I do and play as tasty as I can with what little I know. I just play C6th. I can't do all that fancy Nashville stuff and I hate it anyhow – it's so gimmikeky. When I got into steel, I started out with F#9th. Then on the other neck I used a C6th with E on top. Then I got the idea ... well, I'm gonna move everything over and have a G on top and I'm gonna put on that C# like Jerry Byrd and then the high B which I thought up and I've had that for years. Guys used to ask me, "How do you get all those modern chords with no pedals?"

Joaquin Murphey's Tuning								
Strings	1	2	3	4	5	6	7	8
C6th/C major 7th	G	E	C	A	G	E	C#	B
The 8th string B is a .020 gauge plain string.								

You know for a while there, everybody was scheming on my tunings so on gigs, I'd have to detune it during intermission when I'd go have a drink or else all the other steel players would sneak up and write down my tunings. Those were trade secrets man! (Laughs). So now, I don't want to change it, I just want to add pedals to it - that's all.

On the other neck I had that F#9th - that's what I did *Oklahoma Stomp* with. You know I had that high string down there.

You had an out-of-sequence high string on that neck, too?

Yeah, even then. I was about maybe 17 or 18. At first it was an F#9 with a low string and I figured no, I didn't like the sound, it was real muddy. So I put the high string on. It was the last string. But instead of a wrapped string, it was a plain string - It was a 3rd string gauge actually that I used. Boy! It really changed it! It sounded modern then. I got the idea from listening to Django and I wanted those intervals to be handier. But when I listened to Sol Hoopii and I figured hell, he's not getting it either so I'm gonna add a high 9th to it. And like I said, I also used that concept on the C6th neck. I had three necks eventually. Why not use 'em all?

Are you talking about your triple-8 Bigsby?

Yeah. God! Best guitar I ever had. But hell, Mike, you could sit there on your guitar [*12 string universal pedal steel*] and get ten times more chords than I ever could.

Don't bet on it! How important is a good drummer to helping you pull off a good steel guitar solo?

Well, I've had some drummers where they would, if I'm playing a little behind the beat, they're dropping back – trying to stay with me and Jesus, it drives me nuts. You say, "Man you're draggin'" and they say, "No, *you're* draggin'." They just get mad. I don't want to fight with anybody. I want a certain type of competency and if you can't cut it then just say so. I'm easy to get along with.

- ¤ Joaquin Murphey ¤ -

I used to work with Muddy Berry with Spade Cooley. God, that guy could really play. He knew my style and hell - he'd lay down a beat and I could just lay back and blow. I never had to wonder if this drummer's gonna drop me in the shit 'cause that can break the spell. If they play the wrong shit, I can't play at all. My mind blanks out and I get mad. I just want to take the guitar and smash it over their head.

- ¤ -

Cindy Cashdollar

Variety, consistent quality, and unerring taste have been the hallmarks of Cindy Cashdollar's career as a professional steel guitar and Dobro player. Her five Grammy Awards are testament to both her wide-ranging musicality and her status as a first-call sideperson for leading country, folk, rock, blues, western swing, and American roots music artists such as Bob Dylan, The Dixie Chicks, BeauSoleil, Dwight Yoakam, Grahm Parker, Lyle Lovett, George Straight, Reba McIntire, and Rosie Flores, to name just a few.

A native of upstate New York, Cindy's early career was spent playing Dobro with John Herald, *The Band's* Levon Helm and Rick Danko, and touring with Leon Redbone. She spent eight years contributing swinging solos to six albums and logging thousands of miles on the road with the acclaimed western swing band, *Asleep at the Wheel*.

Since leaving *Asleep at the Wheel*, Cindy has been a key addition to Austin's vibrant musical scene, appeared on Garrison Keillor's *A Prairie Home Companion* radio program, and freelanced with

- ¤ Cindy Cashdollar ¤ -

BeauSoleil, Tony Rice, Jorma Kaukonen, Peter Rowan, Sonny Landreth and others. She has also produced four instructional videos on traditional western swing steel and Dobro for *Homespun Tapes*.

How did you come to play the steel guitar and what was your first instrument?

I started on guitar when I was twelve years old. I took the regulation folk guitar lessons and I got into Delta-style blues picking on a standard guitar. Then a few years later – I was in high school at that point – I heard a John Fahey record, his only record done on a major label, called *Rivers and Religion*. It had him doing bottleneck style in open tunings and so that was pretty much my first introduction to slide.

I was fiddling around with that on regular guitar and then I heard someone playing Dobro and thought, what a great instrument for covering both the things I loved at the time – country & blues. So I started taking Dobro lessons. I did that for quite a long time and it wasn't until about a year before I joined *Asleep at the Wheel* that I got a steel guitar. Mike Auldridge's *Eight String Swing* record came out on 8-string Dobro and I think that's the first thing that got me into the swing tuning – the 6th tuning.

Then from there, I thought this was great but I want more strings and a fatter sound so I got a double-neck Fender and just started fooling around with it. I was touring with Leon Redbone at the time that I got the steel but there wasn't really a lot of room for it in his show. So the steel was just a hobby. But then, when I got hired by *Asleep At the Wheel*, it was kind of sink or swim - either you learn the instrument or forget the gig.

How did you get the gig with *Asleep At The Wheel***?**

I had moved from Woodstock, New York to Nashville because Leon wasn't touring that much and, living in Nashville, I'd hear who needed a Dobro player a lot quicker than in Woodstock. I heard that AATW was looking for a steel player and they happened to be coming in to Nashville to do a show on TNN. I had my promo pack with me and when the bus pulled up in front of the TV station – I didn't know anybody – I just asked if I could speak to John Ely and John came out and sure enough he was giving his notice so I gave them a demo and then they called. The demo had just one steel song on it. The rest was bluesy lap steel and Dobro. Ray Benson said, "I know you're not yet a steel player but you have potential so we'll give you six months."

How long did you stay?

Eight and a half years (laughs).

Did you have to alter your technique moving from acoustic to electric?

When I started that gig I had a double-neck Fender and I had one neck in G6th tuning and that wasn't working out too great. I moved to Austin and John Ely and Herbie Remington gave me a few lessons. It really helped. I worked so hard. I had never worked that hard before in my life. At that point, it just became a challenge.

I loved AATW and had listened to them for years and years and I had seen them live and thought, "What a great gig. Either you learn how to play this thing or you're not gonna have this gig." I used to wake up at night yelling out string gauges – literally. I was just driving myself crazy trying to figure out the tunings and what gauges worked (laughs). Going from Dobro to lap steel was like going from a manual typewriter to an electric typewriter.

Because of the increased sustain?

Yeah - and the attack. I was still digging in to that steel like it was an acoustic guitar! I had to change my whole approach and it was extremely difficult to change mid-stream like that. It's just a totally different animal. You're dealing with more strings and they're closer together. So I had a lot of work cut out for me but somehow (laughs) - and I still can't figure out how to this day - I was able to overcome all these obstacles.

It's certainly clear that you did!

Thanks. I just think it was total determination. Plus it was so new. At that point, I had been playing for years and I was in my early 30's and I think I was ripe for something new.

How would you describe the role of the steel guitar in a western swing band?

Well, because of the richness of the instrument, it serves as part of a section - like saxophone, fiddle and steel - or it can simulate the sounds of a horn section by itself. It's great for all those horn-like hits and pads. The other role is the musical colorizing that it can do. And as far as lead playing, it's like any other instrument. So steel guitar has got a sound that, for western swing, seems to lend itself to all three roles perfectly.

What steel guitars are you using these days?

I have a Remington Steel triple-neck and a Fender triple and double-neck. I also have a little Rickenbacher 6-string lap steel, a custom Frank Campbell lap steel, and - I'll admit it - a Flying-V Melobar.

What about acoustic guitars?

I have a Paul Beard resophonic guitar, a Gibson Dobro and a 1937 round-neck Dobro that was converted for lap playing. That was my first Dobro that my dad bought me. I have a Weissenborn Style-1, a newer John Pierce Weissenborn, an old National Tricone Style-1, and my favorite little guitar I've been using a lot is a little square-neck Stella.

- ¤ Cindy Cashdollar ¤ -

I also have a Danelectro baritone guitar that I had converted for slide. The baritone sounds great and I'm having so much fun with it. I keep it in a low A tuning. I just had the bridge raised and a nut built for it and it plays great. I also use a Danelectro tremolo pedal because I found I had a lot more control with it than anything else.

What tunings do you use?

I use C6th, E6th, and E13th – the first tunings John Ely showed me and I stuck with these. My E6th has the 3rd on top. On Dobro, I usually keep it in G tuning but I use many different tunings depending on whom I'm playing with. There are so many tunings.

Cindy Cashdollar's Tunings								
Strings	1	2	3	4	5	6	7	8
C6th	G	E	C	A	G	E	C	A
E13th	E	C#	B#	G#	F#	D	G#	E
E6th	G#	E	C#	B	G#	E	C#	B
G major	D	B	G	D	B	G		
G6th	D	B	G	E	B	G		
D major	D	A	F#	D	A	D		

How do you keep track of so many tunings without going crazy?

I have a book and I write *everything* down.

How much affect do you feel equipment has on a steel player's sound and how much of your sound is in your hands?

That is such a good question; I'm still trying to figure that out. I think it's really in the player's hands. I truly believe there are some people who can play through the worst amp in the world and still sound amazing. Particularly for non-pedal steel, I favor a 15" speaker and a tube amp and those are a combination you really can't buy (laughs). If you're playing in a loud band, I think you unfortunately need the power of a transistor amp. I think having a good amp clearly helps, but all those players with Bob Wills' band weren't playing through anything sophisticated and yet they made it sound amazing. I really think there was a different breed of players then because of what they had to deal with in terms of lacking what we think of as sophisticated sound recording equipment. I also think they listened to each other a lot more closely because of that.

What's your take on some of the steel greats like Joaquin Murphey, Herb Remington and Noel Boggs? What do you think sets them apart from one another?

They're so different from each other and it's interesting to listen and after a while, after you've been playing steel for a while and you're really steeped in their styles, you can almost hear how they're thinking. What sets them apart is how they think in their approach to their instrument.

Was there any one western swing player who was a particular influence on what you played with *AATW*?

I don't think there was one more than another, but because I was wood-shedding so much when I joined the band, I was influenced greatly by John Ely and Lucky Oceans. For the old recordings, mostly Herbie Remington, Vance Terry and Noel Boggs were my main influences. Herbie was very jazz oriented and Vance and Noel seemed to do all those chordal things so beautifully. Even their chord stuff sounded like single note stuff. I loved Joaquin Murphey but his style was so far removed from the way that I was approaching the instrument that I didn't try to assimilate much of what he did into what I was doing at that time. His style was just so different. He was like the Steve Vai of steel guitar (laughs). I've never heard another player sound like him. I always think of Speedy West as the Jimi Hendrix of steel guitar and Joaquin as Steve Vai.

Listening to all those recordings – especially when I listened to the beginning of a solo - I would listen to how those players would approach a solo and that, I think, is what influenced me on style.

How does your playing change when you play Cajun music with *BeauSoliel*?

In joining that band, I kind of split up duties between Dobro and steel. After all those years with the Wheel, here I was getting acquainted with the Dobro again. I was trying to figure out how to fit the steel into the music. They keep their traditional style but they also have a very contemporary edge. I tried not to play like a western swing player with them. I really tried to get into their rhythm and stay out of the way of the interplay between the accordion and the fiddle.

That's an amazing band because they have drums and percussion so there's a lot of stuff going on. It was a great experience to adapt to a totally different style and it worked well even without my trying to copy any of the Cajun players.

You've also been playing with a band intriguingly named *Hen House*.

That was just for fun. It was one of those bands done in everybody's spare time. It was a group of women: singer/songwriter/guitar player Rosie Flores, Sarah Brown played bass – she's played with Albert Collins and a lot of other blues players – and Marcia Ball or Becky Hobbs played piano. It was strictly roadhouse-type music. That was just for fun. I was playing more overdriven lap steel with them than anything else.

Who else have you played with recently?

Since leaving *The Wheel* it's been this incredible journey of freelance. It's the first time I've been on my own and it's a whole different ball game. Lately, I've done some work with Peter Rowan and also Jorma Kaukonen. I've done *Prairie Home Companion* a few times, traveled with Kelly Willis – she's a wonderful singer/songwriter - and I also do a lot of jingle work here in Austin. I'm even going back to do a tour with Leon Redbone, whom I haven't worked with in about twelve years. I'm getting to use non-pedal steel in so many areas where people just don't expect it. So it's been great doing these shows with all these different artists. Their audiences have either never seen a non-pedal steel or they're just really surprised it's there in the show. So getting to do that plus play all the tours I've done has really been fun.

Tell me about your new CD project.

- ¤ Cindy Cashdollar ¤ -

I've been working on my own CD that's made up of duets with all different slide players. Sonny Landreth is on one cut with his band. There are duets with Herbie Remington and Lucky Oceans. Red Volkaret is on there, Steve James, and Mary Cutrafello. I'm doing a track with Jorma this fall.

It's like a spectrum of slide guitar - kind of like a potluck dinner. I just called up all these people and asked them what they wanted to do. I've also licensed a song of mine for a new CD called *Masters of the Incredible Lap Steel Guitar.* It has Greg Leisz, Bobbie Seymour and lots of other people on it.

How did you come to do your instructional videos for Homespun Tapes? Do you enjoy teaching?

I love teaching. When I went on the road I couldn't take students anymore. I knew Happy Traum from growing up in Woodstock, NY. It's really an honor to do the tapes and it's great to know that you can help a lot of people who, like me in the beginning, had a hard time finding a teacher. I've got two Dobro videos out: *Learning Bluegrass Dobro* – which came out in '89 - and a new video called *Dobro Variations* which covers the G6th and open E tunings, as well as a whole section on minor playing, because that's kind of a stone in the road when you're delving into Dobro. *Minor Swing* is the song covered to show all the different things you can do.

Then of course there are the two western swing non-pedal steel videos and those are taught using C6th tuning. I also do workshops and some of the people at the workshops have the videos and are familiar with me.

Is non-pedal steel obsolete or is it on a new wave of popularity?

I think it's definitely on a new wave of popularity. Even though it's still not as widely recognized as the pedal steel, I think it's on a whole new level of recognition and I really think that the rediscovery of older music has helped it. I hear it on a lot more jingles, I'm hired to use it on a lot more jingle work, and there are a lot of bands that are utilizing it again. It's a very versatile instrument.

What kind of music do you listen to for pleasure and what kind would you like to play that you haven't yet tackled on the instrument?

Well … Bossa Nova. I love that music so much. It's just so melodic. It would take a little work but then again (laughs) what's more work than learning steel to begin with? I think that the voicings and the sustain of the steel would color that music so nicely and the flow that you get from the steel would fit very well with those lilting, sustaining melodies. It would be a real challenge, mentally, because it's a whole new style of thinking and musical approach. So that's definitely something I'd like to tackle.

- ¤ -

Herb Remington

Herb Remington

Herb Remington is one of the most famous of the steel guitar alumnai of Bob Wills' *Texas Playboys.* His playing on the late 1940's *Tiffany Transcriptions* is notable for the way it combines traditional Hawaiian stylings with hot, swing-based soloing. With the *Playboys,* Herb wrote and recorded the steel guitar standard *Boot Heel Drag* which appeared on the flip side of Wills' famous recording of *Faded Love.* After leaving Wills, Herb joined Hank Penny's band, recording another steel guitar standard, 1949's *Remington Ride.*

In the 1950s, Herb settled in Houston where he spent many years recording and playing in a Hawaiian group along with his wife, Mel. In 1978, Herb began over-the-counter retail sales of steel guitars. In 1986, he started building his own line of pedal and non-pedal steel guitars, known respectively as the *Sustainmaster* and the *Steelmaster.* Herb continues as an active musician recording and playing gigs with *Playboys II*, whose members are all former sideman for various incarnations of *Bob Wills' Texas Playboys*.

What were your earliest musical experiences?

My mother gave me piano lessons when I was about five and I stayed with that 'til I was about eight or nine years old when I heard a Spanish guitar. Every now and then I heard a recording with a guitar. That fascinated me and I wanted to do that and was able to take lessons for $1.25 a week, which was pretty expensive - this was during the depression - but my mother managed that. I learned how to play guitar much like Merle Travis or Chet Atkins - with your fingers instead of a pick. I was able to read and had a good teacher.

Then, I went to some movies where I heard Hawaiian music. This was back in South Bend, Indiana where the winters are cold and the palm trees look awfully inviting, as well as those hula girls and all that. The sound of that steel guitar was just more than I could handle. I *had* to do that. So the Oahu Company enlisted kids by the dozens and hundreds and I took sixty lessons on the number system. You don't learn notes but if you have an ear, you can take off from there. They would gather from a three or four-state area a whole bunch of players to play at Chicago's Soldiers Field. We had 1500 steel guitars at Soldiers Field one time and we played two tunes: *Stars and Stripes Forever* and I can't remember the other one (laughs).

That must have been something to hear.

(Laughs). I'd hate to hear it today but it sounded wonderful to me then.

How did you move from amateur to professional?

I formed a little trio. We called ourselves the *Honolulu Serenaders of South Bend Indiana* (laughs). We played a few little clubs and I played my way through high school. As soon as I got out of high school, I knew where I had to go: California. I was going to get in a Hawaiian band. All the jobs were filled up. Sam Koki was playing at a place called the Seven Seas in Hollywood and they weren't about to fire Sam, he was one of the famous guys in those days.

So those jobs were all taken and the only thing left to me was to get a job playing something – any kind of music, anywhere. I played what they called Skid Row in Los Angeles. It was a series of little, shadowy dives, maybe a dozen to a block, in downtown Los Angeles. Each little place had music. I played in a trio with an accordion player and his son playing bass. We played from 7pm until 3am – a long, long job. I would come home with $150 to $200 in my pocket every night.

That was great money for those days.

Oh my gosh! That didn't last long 'cause we were a terrible sounding trio even if I was part of it (laughs). So, I auditioned for Ray Whitley's band. He was holding forth at the Riverside Ranch – the place to hear western swing in those days. I think he had ten or twelve pieces. Merle Travis was in the band. Doggone if they didn't hire me! I stayed about 3 weeks and the union caught up with me. They had a 3-month waiting period in those days. You had to belong to the union for 3 months before you could get a union job, which that was. Ray Whitley said, "When you get through with your waiting period come back and I'll hire you again." So I went back to Skid Row and then got my greetings from the Army – this was in '44.

I carried a little single-neck 6-string Oahu and a tiny little Oahu amp in my barracks bag the whole time I was in the service and played in the camps where I was stationed. I met a few guys that I've known all my life since.

How did you become a member of the *Texas Playboys*?

When I got out of the service I went back to California and I heard that Bob Wills was auditioning for his brother, Luke Wills, who was forming a band. Roy Honeycutt played steel with Bob at the time. I auditioned with Bob and a few of the Playboys at Jay's Motel in Hollywood. They all gathered in this room and I sat on the bed and Bob said, "What do you play of my music?" I said, "Well, I know *Steel Guitar Rag*," and I played that for him. Junior Barnard was on rhythm guitar. He said, "Anything else?" I said, "I know an old tune called *Dream Train.*" Bob said, "Let's keep the kid and send Roy to Luke's band."

What was your first gig with the band?

Well, the next night we were playing at Santa Monica pier and they lent me a pair of boots three sizes too big and a cowboy hat that came down over my ears. We played that huge Santa Monica Pier ballroom with Spade Cooley's band. There were 5,000 people there that night. Noel Boggs was playing steel with Spade that evening. He'd already been with Bob and got off the road to play with Spade. Both bands were set up on that monstrous stage for a national, coast-to-coast broadcast.

Now, Bob's theme song was of course, *San Antonio Rose,* which has a steel guitar part. That was a steel part I knew, fortunately, but when it was my turn to play my tone bar slipped out of my hand and went down amongst the feet of all these people and they all went scrambling for it. Noel happened to be standing at his steel on the opposite side of the bandstand and picked it up exactly where I left off and finished the break while I was still struggling to get that bar back.

I thought,"For sure, this is my last night – first and last." Evidently, Bob said, "Well, we'll keep the kid. It could happen to anybody." We left on tour the next day and I stayed with him until 1950, playing one-nighters from 1946 to 1950.

What guitar were you playing then?

I had a double-neck Rickenbacher – the old stair step model. When you took your hands off one neck it went out of tune when you played the other neck. I was constantly tuning the thing. They made some fine guitars but that particular model was made out of some kind of aluminum alloy and it was just too responsive to temperature.

I was constantly battling that sucker until Fender got me on one of his guitars. We made a lot of recordings; made all those *Tiffany Transcriptions*. I wrote *Boot Hill Drag a*nd a couple other things.

Your playing in those days seems like a mix of swing and Hawaiian style playing. You played some hot solos with the *Playboys.* Did improvising come naturally to you or did you have to work at it?

Well, I had a Hawaiian touch. I had to work at it. It was not easy for me.

Fortunately, I had a good sense of meter and pitch, and some of that's born in you. Of course I had a background in music. The ad-lib choruses that we played were off the cuff; sometimes they fit and sometimes they didn't. Bob was an inspiring individual and you always felt like you had to work hard to please him. He was a fair guy and we were making good money and you felt you had to do everything you could to get as good as you possibly could in a short length of time. Do your best at all times, that was the feeling - and if you didn't *feel* that feeling, Bob would get rid of you.

There have been so many bands that were popular in their time but are now virtually forgotten. Bob's music is still widely available on CD, books have been written about the *Playboys,* and many of his sidemen like you have become revered figures. What do think are the special qualities that have made the music of Bob Wills and the *Texas Playboy*s endure?

Well, Bob knew what he wanted or at least knew it when he heard it. He would try to enlist the services of the best men he could get to travel, pay 'em well and get everything he could get out of them. He took a chance on me not knowing if I would develop at all. People like Jimmy Wyble, Joe Holley - the left-handed fiddle player, Johnny Gimble, Junior Barnard – all those guys got their start with Bob.

Junior Barnard had an almost rock & roll attitude in his guitar solos. In that sense, in the tone and aggressiveness of his playing, he was kind of ahead of his time.

Yes he was, and I was lucky to work with him. The beat was there just like rock music. Bob liked a good heavy beat and the syncopation off that beat was what Bob lived for.

Who were some your early influences on the instrument?

I was basically influenced by the west coast steel guitar players: Noel Boggs, Joaquin Murphey, Speedy West and there was a whole clutch of 'em out there that I enjoyed. I listened to Alvino Rey who was a chord man and not much of a technician, but as far as feeling is concerned, he was a master musician. I'd give anything to have his theory knowledge. He was good at harmonics. He was good at chords and he had the first [Gibson] Electraharp where the pedals were off on one leg of the steel. You could change every string either up or down with one pedal. He had some monstrous pedal changes to play the chords that he did back in those days. I've got a recording he arranged with the band and the *King Sisters* doing Hawaiian melodies and the arranging of that thing was just fantastic. A lot of the youngsters today have never heard of him and it's tragic. He still lives in Ogden, Utah.

Did you listen to Dick McIntire and the other Hawaiian players?

Of course. Dick McIntire, Sol Hoopii, Ray Kinney – I can go on and on. Dick McIntire was my inspiration from that angle. When I was in high school, instead of having lunch at school, I would run home as fast as I could to listen to a 15-minute broadcast called *Trade Winds Tavern*. It was Dick, and I think, a Hammond B3 organ and a rhythm section. There was very little singing; it was mostly instrumental. He played an E7th tuning which I loved in those days and he was in his prime. I would listen to him and dash back to school every day.

Two of your original tunes have become steel guitar standards: *Remington Ride* and *Boot Hill Drag.* How did you come to write them?

Bob came to me one time when *Panhandle Rag* had just come out by Leon McAuliffe and they were kind of in competition with one another. *Panhandle Rag* was a big hit and Bob said, "We're gonna record in Hollywood next week and I want you to write something that'll compete with that thing." I had never written anything before in my life. I thought, "Well, I've got to do something commercial that sounds like a steel guitar and not something else." So I did a lot of sliding in it, named it a crazy name, [*Boot Hill Drag*] hoped for the best and Bob liked it.

Remington Ride Bob heard but he didn't like it. He didn't consider it a dance tune and he considered the band a dance band. I finally recorded it with Hank Penny after I left Bob.

What were your main tunings with the Playboys?

It was either A6th or I had a tuning I put together I called an F#13th. I had little strings on the bottom instead of the big strings. The 8th string on that 8-string guitar was tuned to a higher note than the first string. The 7th string was tuned to Eb or D# - which is a half tone lower than the 1st string.

You had to be careful of how you played them. I could get everything – I could get a diminished chord, 6th, minors, I could even get 10ths on it. But I could not play a major triad and that used to worry me to death. I couldn't get G major, C major or any of the vanilla major chord sounds. I could get root and 5th or root and 3rd but I couldn't get all three of them. The A6th on the other neck, there's where I got my major chords. Usually, I had a triple-neck with an E13th on the third neck.

Speedy West took that F#13th tuning and used it on *I'll Never Be Free* with Tennessee Ernie Ford and Kay Starr. It was a monster hit across the country and in the steel break you can hear that F#13th just as plain as day. Speedy used it differently than I did. He said, "Herb, it was that tuning that gave me my Capitol contract. That tuning did more for me than anything I ever did." I was glad to give it to him, though back in those days, steel players were very possessive of their tunings. Joaquin Murphey would tune his guitar out when he left the bandstand.

Herb Remington's Tunings								
Strings	1	2	3	4	5	6	7	8
A6th	E	C#	A	F#	E	C#	A	F#
E13th	E	C#	B#	G#	F#	D	G#	E
F#13th	E	C#	G#	E	Bb	F#	D#	F#
The 8th string F# is a plain string 1 whole step *above* the 1st string. The 7th string D# is 1/2 step *lower* than the first string.								

Tell me about your career after leaving Bob Wills and how you happened to work with Leo Fender.

That came from Bob. Every time Bob came to town, Leo would supply everybody in the band with new amplifiers. When they came back after a three or four month tour, he'd show up with all brand new models and take back the old ones. Then he got into building steel guitars and he sent me out with the first double-neck that he ever made. It had stovepipe legs that weren't even adjustable and there was no height difference between one neck to the other. It was real awkward. I took that one out on a three-week tour with Bob and came back and Leo's desk was just loaded with these orders from steel players around the country who saw my guitar.

- ¤ Herb Remington ¤ -

I would give him little things I thought he should incorporate in his guitars and they were very meaningful to him. For the length of time I was with Leo, anytime he had a new model of anything, I got it. He didn't even want the old ones back. He said, "More power to you. I blame you for everything. I'm doing well out here and it's your fault (laughs)." For years, I didn't have to buy a thing until he died.

Did you move to a Fender pedal steel when Leo began building one?

I tried to play pedal steel more like Alvino Rey, where you make chords with it. Leo's first pedal steels didn't flat strings, they raised strings. I needed something that would also flat strings, like the old Gibson Electraharp did. Leo never made a changer that would do what anybody wanted. The Fender pedal steel guitar was pushed aside when Sho-Bud, Emmons and MSA came along because they did all those things. They flatted strings and raised them and you could have all kinds of combinations.

When I took Leo's, I tried hard and there's a couple of early recordings where I used a chord or two [*on the Fender*]. It wasn't the crying, Nashville E9th sound that they're using today. I just tried to make chord changes. I still don't care for the Nashville sound. It's not as versatile a tuning as 6th tuning whereby you can get chords if you want and still play a melody line. E9th is pretty much for sound effects, backing up singers or playing country music with three or four chords. There are those who've done much more like Emmons – he can play anything he wants to on it – he's just that kind of guy.

The whole attitude towards steel guitar in Texas seems to be worlds apart from Nashville.

Well, you're right. I say that all the time and nobody listens to me. I say it's the Mississippi river. Anything west of the Mississippi is western swing and 6th tunings and anything east of the Mississippi is E9th, Nashville style, a different concept completely.

You've stuck with one or two tunings and their variations for your entire professional career. Do you feel that attempting to play in many tunings can be a trap that can impede a player's progress?

You might call it that. I had enough sense to realize that if I try to learn everything that's on one tuning I've got my hands full. I experimented with one tuning or the other to find out what it was that I wanted. I didn't want to play what somebody else played. I wanted to play what I like to hear and I never got really wild with it; major chords, major 9*ths*, 13ths, diminished 7ths - the standard chords that are used in pop and big band music. That's what I still play when I play a pedal steel. If I'm going to play country, I'll use my bar to acquire that sound. I know how to make those crying sounds that they demand sometimes. If I play what I want to play, I'm doing things like *Canadian Sunset* and Glenn Miller arrangements.

What do you feel is the most difficult aspect of learning to play steel guitar?

Execution. I guess it's true with all instruments, but there are habits that you must learn at the beginning of playing steel. If you do not learn correctly you can never conquer bad habits that develop. Blocking with the right hand, getting a clean note with no noise and good tone was terribly important for me. I never was a fanatic about amplifiers. I would take an amp and work with it 'til I got the best out of that amp and never worried about it again. A lot of guys keep trading guitars, trading amplifiers in order to get the sound that's mostly in the way you play and how you adjust what you've got.

- ¤ Herb Remington ¤ -

Players today seem to be obsessed with gear and with techniques, like speed picking, that seem intended more to impress other steel players than listeners.

Speed didn't seem to really enter into it until the 60's. Even Curly Chalker was not a speed demon. People like Buddy Emmons worked out this pick blocking technique where you could play just as fast as you'd ever want to play, but it was never incorporated in recordings except as a blur. Someone might have written a chorus to show off the technique, but it was admired by other steel players and not by the general public. That's why you've never heard it much and never will, I don't think, on commercial recordings unless they're made for other steel players.

In the 1940s through roughly the 1960s, steel players all had very individual styles. You knew whom you were hearing in just a few bars. Now everybody sounds the same. Do you have any thoughts as to why?

The guitar's playin' them; they're not playing the guitar. The pedal steel contributed because it's a machine and they all have the same tunings. The only difference would be in the touch and my ear's not that discerning. I can hardly tell one E9th player from another unless it's an excellent player like Buddy Emmons. His signature is in his fingers. Back then, you could tell youwere hearing Noel [*Boggs*] or whoever it was in just a phrase. That's because they were playing the steel. It's their hands. The bar is being moved. A lot of your pedal men, they don't move the bar hardly at all. If you can learn how to manipulate that bar where you can make it talk – literally talk – then you usually have a signature that's recognizable.

The steel is an instrument that most people would say you need to play by sight but I understand you taught a blind person to play.

Yeah, a man by the name of Ernie Bumstead. I'll never forget him. There's nothing to feel. You don't feel any frets go by. The middle finger protrudes further out from the bar than the rest of the fingers. I designed a little thing that went off in front of the strings whereby the man's middle finger would hit these nail heads I put there so he would know where the frets were as his hand went up and down the strings. He could tell by listening and also by feel where his chords were. He played for twenty years over in Louisiana; made a living at it. The nail head thing worked fine and I went to *Lighthouse of the Blind* to try to convince them they needed something like this but it just never did catch on.

How did you become a guitar builder? As a master of the instrument, what design aspects did you feel were mandatory for your line of Remington Steel pedal and non-pedal guitars? And, What would you like people to know about your non-pedal instruments?

That they're much better than any guitar in the past because I use stainless steel instead of chrome plate. Stainless steel is a hard material and lets the strings sustain. I use ash like Fender did. If you play my guitar at the 1st fret you have plenty of finger room. With the old Fenders, you would bump into the tuning keys as you played at the 1st fret. Little things that mean a lot. There's an area, where you play with your right hand, carved into the wood to allow you to have more space between the necks without making the guitar any bigger. It just gives you more space without bumping into the neck ahead of you.

There were guitars I didn't think were built correctly and also there was an element of ego that went into it. "You've done everything else, Herb, so why don't you just build your own steel?" I did and I've got one of the better ones on the market. The big hullabaloo, the excitement around pedal steel has waned. It's not like it was in the 50's, 60's and 70's. Even the recording industry doesn't use steel as much as they did. It was a business I wanted to get into and I accomplished it and now I wish I was out of it 'cause I'm playing now more than I've ever played.

It's not generally known that you're actually the steel player behind Buddy Emmons's famous intro to Willie Nelson's song, *Night Life*.

I played the original steel part with Paul Buskirk and Willie Nelson here in Houston in 1955. We worked up the intro that everybody's familiar with on *Night Life*; that came from me and Paul. That thing was released as a 45 but it just didn't go anywhere until Ray Price recorded it. Emmons took that intro and everybody thought that's where it came from. Not that it makes all that much difference but we were kind of proud of the sound we got on that album. I went to the studio yesterday as a matter of fact – this is the same studio 30 years later – and I played it and knocked 'em out.

You recorded albums in the 1990s with both Jimmy Day and Kayton Roberts. What were those experiences like?

The album with Kayton was non-pedal. We had a great time and we sounded different enough from one another that somebody listening should find it interesting to hear the contrasting styles. Same with Jimmy - I played pedal steel with him. We're in the same boat together but he's fishing with a different rod.

You also made a record called *Texas Swings* with jazz guitar legend, Herb Ellis. I understand that what should have been a great experience turned out to be not so hot.

Herb had a case of the "red butt" that day and we just happened to fall on the wrong day. It was a downer for him to do western swing and it was obvious he was not happy. He frowns on it as beneath him.

That's funny, because he grew up in Texas and western swing is part of his roots.

He was just not happy and everybody was uptight. What tickled the rest of us is it's one of the best selling things he's done in years. We had fun doing it but his tempos were real quick. He was still fast at his age. We all had to "hub it" to stay up with some of his ideas.

You mentioned that you're playing more today than ever before. What musical pursuits are you involved with these days?

I play in a number of western swing bands, all in the Houston area. I'm playing tonight in a place called Cat Springs (laughs). We gotta *find* the place. I've ordered a new Polytone amp and I've fallen in love with the tone of those things. This little guy only weighs 35 lbs. There's also the 8-piece *Playboys II* band. I have Johnny Gimble and Leon Rausch and all the good guys that were there with me in the 40's. If they want a smaller job, I called it *Playboys I* (laughs).

Do you think the non-pedal steel guitar has a bright future?

Yes I do. There's resurgence ofn interest in the instrument but somebody's going to have to make a recording and get it out front. Junior Brown's using it. Cindy [*Cashdollar*] played that guitar I built for her around the world. It's going to have to take another *Sleepwalk* or *Steel Guitar Rag* – something to make these kids say, "What in the devil is that!?" That's what it's going to take to keep it going.

- ¤ Herb Remington ¤ -

Good musicians have taken it into another realm where it's just too much. Some of them play the steel like a jazz clarinet player and they're appealing only to other musicians. We've gotta get back to simplicity again, I guess.

I'll never forget when Hank Williams came out with *Lovesick Blues*. I was with Bob and we had all these Glenn Miller arrangements worked up for strings and we were proud of what we were doin'. Then here comes Hank Williams. I couldn't stand his voice, I thought it was awful. Today it sounds pretty good (laughs). All the people who went to our dances turned their backs on western swing and went to the Hank Williams crowd – basic country. It told me something: we left those people when we started doing big band arrangements. It wasn't *Steel Guitar Rag* anymore and it wasn't *San Antonio Rose.* They just didn't get thrilled with it the way they did when we kept it simple. That's what Nashville did. They cut it way down to basics, three chord songs and there are bands today that are doing the same thing and they're bringing it back.

Kids have lost melody and harmony. I've got kids that have played bottleneck on a standard guitar and after two or three years of that, they hear a steel guitar play harmony. They come in my store and I play something for them they've never heard before and they just go berserk – they love it. But they're not being exposed to it like they should be.

- ¤ -

Tom Morrell

Before he finally got around to doing an album of his own in 1995, Tom "Wolf" Morrell had toured with some of the greatest western swing of the 1950s & '60s, helped to establish a pedal steel company, [*MSA*] and had been inducted into the *Steel Guitar Hall of Fame*.

Born in Texas, Tom was playing guitar, steel guitar, and Dobro by his teens. In the 1950s, he toured with Ray Price, Tex Williams, Wade Ray, the *Texas Playboys*, and the *Western Starlighters*. In 1995, Tom hung up his pedal steel in favor of a Bigsby triple neck non-pedal guitar and began a series of western swing recordings under the name *Tom Morrell and the Time-Warp Top Hands* that fuse the best aspects of the genre with Morrell's love of jazz.

- ¤ Tom Morrell ¤ -

On twelve classic CDs, Morrell's liquid steel guitar melds with the stylings of top-flight western swing veterans, like guitarists Benny Garcia and Rich O'Brien, fiddler Bobby Boatright, trumpeter Rodney Booth, and accordionist Tim Alexander, to create a tapestry of American music. As an improvising, swing steel guitarist, Morrell is almost without peer as single notes and double stops pour from his instrument with the fluidity of a jazz guitarist.

A terse Texan, Tom Morrell is a man of deep musicality but few words. The author was however, able to pry the following interview from him.

What was your first steel guitar?

Well, I took lessons for a little while when I was a kid until they kicked me out 'cause I bought an Alamo guitar instead of buyin' one from them. I bought the Alamo from Sears or somewhere like that.

It was like the Oahu Company; they wanted to sell you the course and the instruments?

Yeah. They were sellin' cheap brands – Magnatone or something like that. I forget exactly what. So I went and bought this real nice wooden one.

How did you move from being a kid learning the instrument to playing with professional musicians?

There were some people who lived behind me that played so I went back and started playin' with them instead of taking lessons. Every once in a while they'd come up with a job. It just kinda evolved from there.

Who were some of your early influences on the steel?

Back then, you could hear just about everybody that played. Nowadays, there's thousands. I listened to everybody. I listened to Joaquin, Noel Boggs, Bob White, Herb Remington, Alvino Rey, Ricco Turchetti, Johnny Bonavillion out of New Orleans - he was really good. I just bought everything by steel players I could and put 'em on the record player and listened to 'em.

Johnny Bonavillion never received the recognition he deserved.

No. He never left New Orleans to my knowledge.

In the 40's and 50's, all the steel players sounded so original. In just a couple bars you knew who was playing. Now, steel players sound so alike it's next to impossible to tell one from another. Do you agree?

Without question. It's true with everything. Hell, just look at the cars going down the street – they all look alike. You get up close and can find a few little deals that look different but basically, they all look alike. You didn't have much input back then. Nowadays you're just overwhelmed with input. Joaquin Murphey, when he was learning, probably could only listen to five or six steel players. Nowadays, you can listen to five or six hundred.

- ¤ Tom Morrell ¤ -

You got all these mail order steel guitar courses that say do this and do that. The originality is missing. It's just inevitable, I guess. Too bad.

Have you heard the last recordings that Joaquin made?

Yeah. He played with no pedals for so long I guess he wanted to play pedals to get some chords but without question, his best stuff was when he was playin' non-pedal.

You had the opportunity to play with some of the greatest players at the tail end of the golden age of western swing. What were some of those experiences like?

What was it like? It was good. I liked it. Back then, you didn't have any of this goddamn country shit. So it was all good.

You were one of the early founders of the MSA Pedal Steel guitar. What brought you back full circle to playing the non-pedal instrument?

It's what I started off on. For western swing, you didn't have to have all the pedals. Why lug all that crap around? I played pedals for a long time – probably forty years.

So you finally decided to go back to your roots?

That's a writer's way of sayin' it. It wasn't, "Let's go back to my roots." I just said, "Screw it. Why carry around somethin' that weighs seven thousand pounds that you gotta tune for ten hours and crap like that when you can just pull your little ol' guitar out and play it?"

What is your main guitar these days? Did you retire your triple-neck Bigsby?

I'm not playin' the Bigsby. I have a little single-neck. I can put it in the overhead bin of the airplane and not have to worry about freight, checking it. It's real compact. It's called C&W and was made by a guy named Carson Wells. He does it kind of as a hobby. He doesn't have a production line or anything like that. It's kind of like the artwork on my records. I told him what I wanted done and he built it. I set it up here and modified it a little bit. It's made out of mesquite. That was the main thing that he did that I didn't come up with. I said, "Nah, let's not do mesquite. Let's use birdseye maple." He talked me in to it and man, it's really good. If you don't like my playing, we'll burn the son of a bitch and I'll cook you a steak on it!

What tuning are you using?

A ten string E13th.

Tom Morrell's 10-string Lap Steel Tuning										
Strings	1	2	3	4	5	6	7	8	9	10
E13th	G#	F#	E	C#	B	G#	F#	E	D	E

You can get everything you need out of that one tuning?

I get enough.

- ¤ Tom Morrell ¤ -

How much does equipment matter? Is it all in your hands?

No, everything affects it, but your hands are the most important.

Do you pick block? Palm block? Never even think about it?

I never think about that stuff.

How did the *Time Warp Top Hands* come about – you're now on your 12ᵗʰ CD?

A piano player named Johnny Case who put out some real good albums on his own – got his own little label – called and wanted me to do an album. So we sat around and talked and he said, "You can do whatever you want, a country album, a western swing album, or a jazz album." There wasn't a whole heck of a lot being done in western swing at that time so I said, "Let's do a western swing album, which is kinda like jazz anyway." So we did a western swing record and it was different enough that everybody seemed to like it and it caught on a little bit – not like Garth Brooks – but okay. It just went from there.

Tom (seated) with Curly Lewis, Randy Elmore, Mac MacRae, Tony Ramsey, Leon Chambers, & Roy Rosetta

You've done all the producing and arranging for the series?

I've done almost all of it. When Jerry Byrd came in he did his arrangement of *La Golindrina*, but basically, I did all the arrangements. There's where my pedal playing comes in, that background. Sometimes you don't tell 'em *what* to play, you tell 'em *when* to play.

You've worked with some great players and singers on the series.

Is Benny Garcia [*legendary western swing standard guitarist*] still playing?

Yeah. Every once and a while we'll play a *Texas Playboy* gig together. Now Tommy Alsup's doing a lot of the Playboy stuff so I don't see Benny much on that deal. The drummer, Tommy Perkins, and Benny have a little jazz trio up in Oklahoma City.

What was it like to work with steel legend Bobby Koeffer? In the old clips of him playing with Bob Wills he just smiles out at the audience as he solos and never looks down at the neck of his steel. Did you ever catch him looking at his guitar?

126

He looks at it every once in a while but he doesn't have to. He's a showman, but he's also a good player.

On *Pterodactyl Ptales-Volume IV*, you trade solos with ex-Merle Haggard guitarist, Clint Strong. He came out of the gate like a racehorse on most of those tunes.

I wanted him to play an acoustic guitar and he brought in a Les Paul and he was just ready to go. Every song on that album we did a little bit faster than I wanted to do it. It just ended up that way.

Tell me about your latest CD *Stylin'*.

I don't know what to say about it. We just recorded a bunch of songs that I like. It's a little jazzier but I consider it to be western swing. One of the reasons I like western swing is because you can play jazz.

Western swing is a melting pot of practically every kind of American music except maybe rock & roll.

Not every kind, but I can remember back in the old days when there was some rock & roll – wasn't any heavy metal, but it rocked. There's a lot of rockabilly bands nowadays who say they're western swing players but they really ain't. They're just rockabilly.

Do you have any advice for players who are just starting out and trying to learn to play creative solos?

None that they'd listen to.

Did you go through all the rudiments of music, practicing scales and such?

No, and I probably should have.

You get a very personal sound on Dobro. Do you view it as a different instrument from the electric steel?

Oh yeah, completely different. I use a G major tuning: D-B-G-D-B-G. I don't recall recording with any other tuning. Every once in a while I'll tune it to E major.

So you play jazz tunes like *Sweet Lorraine* out of G tuning?

Yep, that was in G major tuning. I took lessons from this guy named Don McCord. He was a great Dobro player. Too bad he never recorded. He was really good. Don played balls to the wall.

Did you ever listen to the Hawaiian players like Jerry Byrd?

Yeah. Jerry's probably one of the five best steel players that ever lived. He's still alive and still playin'.

He's got a new book coming out.

I'll buy it.

Other than steel guitar music, what kind of music do you enjoy listening to for pleasure?

I don't listen to much steel guitar music. I listen to mostly jazz, big band stuff like Basie, Kenton, and Sinatra.

You've done a lot of the graphic art for your record covers. Is that very satisfying to do?

Yeah. I haven't done the last few. I call him [*artist*] and say draw this and draw that. He's a commercial artist; I'm just a steel player.

- ¤ -

American Roots Music

The widespread availability today of previously regionalized music, distributed via new and reissued digital recordings, alternative radio programming, and the pervasive world wide web, has served to bolster a trend that has been in evidence for forty years: the cross-pollination of musical styles and genres. It's not completely out of the realm of possibility today to find a Hawaiian-bluegrass-swing band. While many musicians would prefer to be beyond category, it's nevertheless a reality of the marketplace (and probably the human genome) to need a way to categorize musicians whose work reflects multiple genres.

The term American Roots Music serves as a convenient metaphor for the work of artists whose music contains elements of blues, folk, country, rock and various regional traditions. The steel guitar has been an integral ingredient in the roots music stew since practically the beginning of recorded sound.

The musicians whose interviews follow stay true stylistically and creatively to the genres they embrace while simultaneously re-imagining the language of American popular music.

Ed Gerhard

Philadelphia native Ed Gerhard, moved to New England in 1977 where he has carved out a career as an acoustic guitar soloist of poetic sensibilities and impeccable musicianship. On both originals and traditional songs, Ed's ability to play melodically while paring a song down to its essentials serves to communicate a deep understanding of the intent of the song.

Ed has released seven CDs on his own Virtue Records label that have received wide critical acclaim for both the quality of the music and the exceptional sonic aspects of the engineering. He has also collaborated with Breedlove Guitars on an *Ed Gerhard Signature Model* guitar. The guitar became a best seller for Breedlove and won the *Player's Choice Award* in 2000 from *Acoustic Guitar Magazine*.

- ¤ Ed Gerhard ¤ -

Increasingly, Ed has used lap steel guitars in his music. His 2002 release, *House of Guitars* was based upon locating forgotten instruments in pawnshops and used guitar dealerships and recording them with the same care and meticulous attention to sonic detail that he uses on his high-end custom instruments. The results are stunning. If you're lucky enough to see Ed in concert, you'll likely see him with his beloved Weissenborn guitars which he plays with exceptional attention to tone color.

How did you come to play the guitar and who were some of your early influences?

I think I was about ten years old when I heard Segovia on TV. That was the first time I'd ever heard a guitar played all by itself. You'd always hear rock & roll or folk records or pop or whatever's on the radio but never the guitar by itself. Even at ten years old I knew something profound was taking place. It wasn't 'til I was fourteen that I finally convinced my father that I was serious about the guitar. He got me a guitar for my birthday and it was all over from there.

A friend turned me on to the *Blues at Newport 1963* album. I heard great players like Mississippi John Hurt, Dave Van Ronk and John Hammond and that just totally changed my direction. Very early on, I was playing slide guitar and I guess my steel and Weissenborn playing is really an extension of my slide guitar playing, not really from hearing Hawaiian music or anything like that.

What guitars are you playing and in what tunings?

My first steel was a National Dynamic, which is just a gorgeous, really sweet sounding steel. I've got two Oahu electric steels: a Tonemaster and a Diana, as well as a Supro double-neck - all 6-string guitars.

I have a Weissenborn Style-1 and Style-2. The Weissenborn copy that I tour with was made by a company called K&S. It basically serves to hold the strings and pickups; it's useless beyond that (laughs). Acoustically, it doesn't sound like much but for some reason, it's just like magic with a Sunrise or a Rare Earth pickup. The Rare Earth is a really nice, high output pickup. I use a Humbucker Rare Earth in the Weissenborns but sometimes I'll put a single coil in if I'm recording and I want to get a slightly rounder sound out of it.

I'm not going too far afield with tunings though I'm starting to experiment more - like with the C#minor tuning and D6th. DADGAD is a nice tuning for steel guitar. [*D suspended tuning is comonly called DADGAD, low to high, the reverse of this book's format*] The Weissenborn that I tour with is in open D tuning but harmonically, it's pitched to B or sometimes to C.

Ed Gerhard's Tunings						
Strings	1	2	3	4	5	6
D major	D	A	F#	D	A	D
D suspended	D	A	G	D	A	D

- ¤ Ed Gerhard ¤ -

What bar and picks do you use?

With the Weissenborn, I'll use a thumb pick but I don't use any fingerpicks. I use a Shubb SP2 bar. They have an SP1 and an SP2; the one I'm using is the shorter one. The first bar I tried was a bullet bar and it was really fun but playin' on stage when my hands were getting sweaty, the thing would just go sailing off (laughs). It flies around like an armor-piercing missile so you gotta move all your other guitars away.

I don't think there's a steel player alive who hasn't dropped the bar.

You look at an old Weissenborn and you see plenty of evidence of that!

You're well known for the lush beauty of your tone and the sonic richness of all your recordings. How much effect do you think equipment has and how much of your tone is in your hands?

In my approach, the equipment is just there to relay what you're putting into it, not to modify or screw with it at all. So you've just gotta play through stuff that's either gonna enhance it or not kill it. When I hear other players playing my Weissenborn, it doesn't sound at *all* like the sounds that I make on it. So I'd have to say that 99% of your tone is in your hands.

What's the most difficult aspect of playing melodies on a steel guitar?

With any style of guitar, the vibrato is one of the most difficult things to learn. For me it just has to sound natural, not like some effect you're applying; like there's a reason for the vibrato to be there. You don't want to get that "nervous Chihuahua" vibrato. You hear a lot of players that make a whole lot out of the "slidiness" of a slide instrument. When you hear somebody like Jerry Byrd or Greg Leisz, for example, it's used in a very economical way. Your pitch has to be very good and your vibrato has to be very good and all the other "slidiness" is sort of after the fact. There's a confidence in your touch that needs to be there before you can really speak a melody.

What does the lap steel allow you to express in your music beyond the colors and textures you get from a standard guitar?

A lot has simply to do with the tone of the instrument. I don't think of tone as something you paint on the music afterwards. A lot of times, the tone is a big part of what you're trying to say. It's not a conveyor of the message, it's part of the message itself. For example, when somebody is speaking to you over the phone you can tell when they're angry or when they're being sarcastic or being funny. It's in the tone. Same thing with the tone of a guitar or a steel guitar. It's part of what you're trying to say.

How did you get into using hollow neck Weissenborn guitars?

Bob Brozman was the first guy who got me hooked on using the Weissenborns. In fact, Bob and I recorded together back in '95. I put out a record called *Counting the Ways*, which is a record of all love songs, and Bob played on *Isa Lei*. Both of us played Weissenborns. It's such a great sound. It's one of the sounds that you hear, then once it grabs you, you're grabbed for life.

There's a guy named Rich Mermer down in Florida who's building them. They're not real traditional Weissenborn instruments, but they really do sound great.

- ¤ Ed Gerhard ¤ -

On your CD *House of Guitars*, you played a number of acoustic and electric steels that many would consider "bargain basement" instruments. You didn't even change strings on some of the instruments yet you somehow achieved the same gorgeous tone as usual.

I thought it might be fun to just get a bunch of cheap old guitars. I really loved the sound of those old field recordings where someone got set up on some old bluesman's front porch with a Nagra tape recorder and recorded them playing maybe a Silvertone or an old Harmony Sovereign. It's just a cheap, stubby, thumpy sounding guitar but the textures that these guys would get out of these guitars you can't get out of a ten thousand dollar instrument. So in my mind, that doesn't make these guitars cheap, it just makes them better suited for the job I had in mind.

I remember as a kid going into guitar shops, you'd see a bunch of guitars hanging on the wall and you didn't know what was a cheap guitar or what was an expensive guitar. They were all *equally* cool. I wanted to try to capture that same sense of discovery about guitars. Some of these were just about impossible to play, but it was kind of fun struggling with the limitations of the instruments to see if I could make some meaningful noise with them.

Your tone on the record is a very personal sound, quite far removed from the brightness and sustain that many players seem to go for.

I tend to favor darker, a little bit more serious kinds of sounds. Part of it is just what I'm trying to convey with some of the music. On *Promised Land*, for example - the first tune – the guitar I'm playing is this little Oahu double-neck. It was strung up to Ab and when I played it, it sounded like it was about ready to explode.

To me, just that *sound* had a lot to say about what the tune was about, a little brighter than usual. I used the same guitar on the next tune, *Poor Wayfaring Stranger*, with the Rare Earth pickup and that got a little bit darker again. I like some roundness in the sound. Treble to me is like salt - once you start getting too much of it, when you get less than that, it seems like it's not enough.

Who do you enjoy listening to on the steel guitar?

Well, I really love Jerry Byrd. Greg Leisz is doing just beautiful work. He's doing such melodic work, not just playing the licks. He has a beautiful sense of melody and construction and I really like what he plays a lot. Of course, you've gotta love David Lindley. He's one of those guys whose pitch is damn near perfect every single note and he's just a really great, expressive player.

Where do you think the non-pedal is going? Is it doomed to a kind of cult status?

Every time I play a Weissenborn in concert, it never fails to make a few people exceedingly crazy. I don't know if it'll ever see the kind of popularity of synthesizers or electric guitars but I think the steel guitar is one of those necessary sounds in music that's always gonna be around. One of the cool things about the steel is that people discover it by accident almost. Once it hooks you, you're compelled to dig a little deeper. I think it brings out some of the best parts of the human spirit, your curiosity, and your search for beauty. That's a good thing.

Can we ever expect to see Ed Gerhard play a pedal steel on stage?

You never know, but I'm not really a mechanically inclined person and the pedal steel to me is like a damn machine. I love the sound of them: Doug Jernigan, Speedy West, and all those guys.

- ¤ Ed Gerhard ¤ -

The pedal steel is just a beautiful sounding instrument. You don't really think of the steel guitar having too many parallels in the world of music. It sounds maybe like a flute because you can change the dynamics after you play the note. In some ways, the steel sounds very similar in it's approach to Indian violin music; the way the notes swell. There's almost a beckoning in the tone. To me the sound of the steel is just so beautiful it's just totally captivated me.

- ¤ -

Pete Grant

Ask Californian Pete Grant to "name drop" some of the people for whom he's lent his talents on pedal and non-pedal steel and you're left with a dizzying list that represents the cream of the crop of the country, folk and rock scene of the last thirty years. The list includes: Jerry Garcia and *The Grateful Dead*, Rodney Crowell, Herb Pedersen, *The Dillards*, Hoyt Axton, Tim Hardin, *The Persuasions*, Paul Kantner, Willie Nelson, Leon Russell, Frank Wakefield, Michael Martin Murphy, Freddy Fender, Peter Rowan, *The New Riders of the Purple Sage*, Stephen Stills, Vassar Clements, John Hartford, Henry Kaiser, and at least fifty more. Pete's steel has also graced the scores of broadcast television programs such as the *Tonight Show, Falcon Crest, Knots Landing, The Dukes of Hazard, The Love Boat, Dynasty* and the *ABC Movie of the Week*.

How did you come to play steel guitar?

It was fairly roundabout, though the first instrument I ever played with lessons *was* the Hawaiian steel. When I was about ten, some guy came to our door with a little acoustic squareneck. I answered the door and he said, "Is your Mom or Dad home?" I said, "I know this is for *me*!" (Laughs). My Mom was home and he said, "I'll give your child a musical aptitude test and if he passes it he qualifies for lessons at Guild Music Studios."

So I "passed" of course, and I took lessons for about a year. It was the kind of thing where you had a half-hour lesson and then went home and tried to figure out what all the notes meant. It was the Oahu method, which was still pretty prevalent – this was 1953. You'd get a new song every week and it was like, "Read that quarter note and don't memorize anything. You're going to play what I give you." I got really discouraged with it and that's totally shaped the way that I've taught ever since.

I was happy playing the few songs that I'd memorized. I played for my parents when they'd have guests over. After a while they bought me a pretty nice steel and an amplifier and I'd get it all out, put the steel on the stand and start playing, and then they'd all start talking, "Oh, isn't that nice. Isn't he a good player?" I'd want to shout, "Shut up and listen!" That was the musical scene that I grew up in (laughs).

Not very inspiring to a young musician?

No. I quit playing music when I was eleven and really didn't pick it up again until about age seventeen or eighteen. rock & roll had no life to it. There was Elvis originally, then all the corporate rock: Frankie Avalon, Pat Boone, and all these things that were just kind of like replacements of something with any kind of soul. Then the Kingston Trio came out and that looked like a real personal kind of thing and they were playing without music in front of them. They were having a good time and it looked to me that they could maybe be popular and maybe get chicks (laughs).

And they got to wear those cool red and white striped shirts.

(Laughs). That's right, all matching shirts. So that intrigued me and I actually took up tenor guitar. Then a friend of mine had a 5-string banjo and I said, "Wow, man, that's really amazing." So I got a 5-string banjo.

When I was about nineteen, I had a fake ID and I'd go to the country bars and they'd let me sit in and play a couple tunes. One band would let me just stand up there on stage and comp and I got to stand right next to the pedal steel – a guy playing a Fender 400. It was a captivating thing. I then took up Dobro because it could do all the things the banjo couldn't do. It could sing and it could also hold its own in a bluegrass band if the banjo player wasn't too overbearing.

The real pivotal thing happened when I was driving up to Berkley to see the *Kentucky Colonels* with Jerry Garcia. He had already shown me some pedal steel licks on the banjo and I was fascinated with all that. It was one of those defining moments. *Together Again* came on the radio and we both listened to that solo and said, "God! We've gotta play pedal steel! We've just gotta."

That was Tom Brumley playing a Fender at that time.

So that took me into pedal steel. When I first started pedal steel I tuned to D^{9th} because with the pedals down that gave me G – which was banjo tuning. So I related it to my banjo fingerboard. Then one day I was noticing that one of my students had much better tone than I had and he had a cheaper guitar. Then I changed to E9th. I don't play C6th well enough that anyone would notice. I don't relate to it as well for some reason. I was always colliding with the 6th sound and frankly, I'm not a big fan of western swing.

Did you play in other non-pedal tunings besides G tuning at that time?

In the '60s, I knew about E tuning and D tuning but I didn't pursue them. I was kind of disenchanted with open G tuning so I sold the Dobro. Then, when I was with Hoyt Axton in '76, I bought a new Dobro because I had a need for it and then a 10-string Dobro because I needed something for practicing on the bus. And when somebody was going to have a jam session, I didn't have to lug 150 lbs. of equipment into some motel room and cart it in between all the people sitting around. I really got into the acoustic side and Weissenborns after hearing Lindley play those. When the song *Look So Good* came out, that was another defining moment of my musical direction. I said, "I've gotta get one of these." I actually tabbed that out for *Frets* magazine a long time ago.

You designed a unique instrument in the history of resonator guitars: the 10-string Zephyr resophonic; a gorgeous instrument.

When I was with Hoyt I bought a brand new 10-string Dobro. It had an 8-string width neck and little outriggers for the other strings. In '77, I went down to Dobro and met Ron Lazar and Don Young and I played my 10-string for them. They'd never heard a 10-string played before. Ron built one for me with a metal body and a nice wide neck. That was better but it didn't have the punch I needed.

The Dobro company changed hands soon after. Their accountants bought the company. They were more open to innovation than the Dopyeras had been. I talked with Don and McGregor Gaines about building one with a solid wood body because I had heard some from other makers that sounded really good and figured that solid wood had something to do with it. Rudy Dopyera had said, "No, it's all in the baffling."

We talked about me designing a prototype and we all had a real respect for the look of the Tricone and the Art Deco style of the design. I submitted a few drawings and that was the one we all liked the best because it paid homage to the Tricone. The first prototype they made for me was a 10-string and all the rest of them were either 8-strings or 6-strings.

I remember a glowing review of the Zephyr in Guitar Player Magazine.

That's right. Rick Turner actually bought the one that he reviewed. He was overcome by guitar lust! (Laughs). Then the Dobro Company changed hands again and they never revived the design.

Do you still play the Zephyr on sessions?

I do. I used it on a record with the *Persuasions*. David Gans and Jim Page stopped by my house on the way to a gig and I played the Zephyr for them. David's a *Grateful Dead* historian and has a radio show on KPFA in the Bay area. Then when he was producing the album called *Might as Well: The Persuasions Sing Grateful Dead* , he called me.

- ¤ Pete Grant ¤ -

The Persuasions are know for their tight harmony acapella sound. What was it like to work with those great voices?

Ah, it was *astounding*! It was the total opposite of what you usually get to do. You know, you're backing up singers and making the singers sound good – and to a certain extent I was doing the same thing. But when it came time for my solo, they were backing *me* up. They laid down the bed of chords and I played on top of it. It was like nothing I've ever done before. It was delightful.

What steel guitars are in your collection these days?

I have a National Model-D, my Zephyr, and a koa wood Stella Hawaiian that was made before the depression when they made the full range of instruments. It has the tree of life fingerboard inlay. I also have a teacher's model Oahu made by Regal. It has a square neck with a deep body with maple back and sides. It's kind of like an overgrown Martin OM with abalone binding and a sprig of life – not quite a tree of life. I bought it at a vintage guitar store and it didn't have any strings or tuning machines on it. I just saw it and went: "Ah, ha! That's an instrument that I need to be playing." I did one session at Jim Messina's studio and the engineer must have come out five times to say, "Wow! That's a great sounding guitar!"

Musicians probably under-appreciate Stella and Oahu guitars.

Exactly. And the Weissenborns are, I think, over-appreciated to some degree – at least by what they're getting for them these days. I also just got a Baby Taylor and put a high nut on it so I can easily fly with that.

What about electric guitars?

I have a black and chrome Rickenbacher, a Recording King made by Gibson that has the Charlie Christian pickup, a National 8-string like Freddie Roulette's that I keep tuned to the Jerry Byrd diatonic tuning, and a Valco with a change-over lever. It's got little cams that allow you to change between three tunings. I also have a '52 Fender double-8 that sounds real good through my tweed deluxe. I've used that on rockabilly gigs with Al Kooper and in the studio with *Rank & File*.

I've got a 10-string Melobar with the soft body that I got from Dave Lindley. I've used it on a lot of sessions because you can get a lot of different tonal characteristics from the two pickups. The neck is slanted at about 45 degrees. I also use it live with a wireless and go out and hang out with the audience. If they're dancing, I'll dance (laughs).

Who are some of your favorite steel players?

On pedal steel: Paul Franklin, J.D. Maness, Hal Rugg, Weldon Myrick, Jimmie Crawford, Curly Chalker and the list goes on. On non-pedal, I really like Jerry Douglas and of course, David Lindley, and I also get a lot of inspiration from players on other instruments: Jerry Garcia, Vassar Clements & Charlie Parker, for example. I just heard [*Sacred Steeler*] Robert Randolph. My God! He sounds like he flat picks.

Many acoustic steel players play in open G tuning but you feel open D tuning offers greater musical possibilities?

- ¤ Pete Grant ¤ -

The basic advantages of the D tuning are that you have a 1-5-1 on the bottom so you can comp chords in much more of a rock & roll or r&b fashion than if you have a 3rd in the chord. You also have an interval of a 4th on the top which is essential for Chuck Berry, Elmore James, Robert Johnson kind of stuff. You have a harmonized scale in 6ths on your 1st string and 3rd string so you can play in your highest range and harmonize it below with a straight bar and slant bar. You can do that in G tuning but you have to use a single slant and a double slant. I find that pretty bothersome.

What other tunings do you use?

My Zephyr is tuned to a D9th – kind of like an E9th pedal steel but with a 1-5-1 on the bottom like a regular D tuning. The top two strings, like the pedal steel tuning, are lower than the next two strings down. I find that really valuable for access to scale notes. In a lot of tunings you have to jump to get the next scale tone. If you're tuned to a major or minor chord, you're either 4 or 3 notes from the next note up so that means you have to jump 1 or 2 frets all the time to get the next scale tone. If you have a tuning that has a 1-2-3, you're never more than one fret away from the next scale tone.

Pete Grant's Tuning (Dobro Zephyr)									
String	1	2	3	4	5	6	7	8	9	10
D9th	E	C#	F#	D	A	F#	E	D	A	D

You've played as a sideman or session player with hundreds of musicians. Who are some of the most memorable?

Jerry Garcia and the *Grateful Dead* for sure; and then Vassar Clements. Vassar is totally awe-inspiring. He inspires you to play better than you ever thought you could. He's the master of phrasing. When I grow up I want to be able to phrase like him.

Hoyt Axton too. When I joined the band he said, "Your job, Grant, is to get the audience off and I don't care what you do. I don't care if you stand on your head or play 100 notes or just 3. If you get the audience off, I'm happy."

I only played with Willie Nelson a couple of times but it was just delightful. I loved playing with Rodney Crowell. Nicky Hopkins is up at the top of the list too. He played with the *Beatles* and the *Stones* and was just a delightful, wonderfully creative keyboard player.

The Dillards was a wonderful band. I grew up listening to the *Dillards* and learned to play banjo like Doug Dillard. So it was a treat to play that music 'cause it was already part of me. When I joined the band I had to learn about 60 songs but I think I knew about 30 of 'em already. I played banjo and pedal steel. I had worked with Rodney and Herb Pederson in a band in LA, so when the *Dillards'* banjo player freaked out and threw his banjo across the stage, Rodney called me to fill in and I stayed on afterwards. I had to quit the road to be a studio guy cause a client would call me up and say, "You're in town? I thought you were on the road. You just missed a big session."

How did you first get into studio work?

My first studio gig was with the *Grateful Dead* playing pedal steel because Garcia hadn't gotten one yet and he wanted to hear pedal steel on *Doin' That Rag*. I also played on one track of *Oxamaxa*. This was back in the drug days. During the first session I think we were all starting cocaine at the time and Garcia called me up a couple days later and said, "Hey, Pete, you've gotta come and re-do your tracks. They're about a half a fret off (laughs)." I stopped taking drugs in June of '69.

Did you play many sessions in LA?

Not all that many considering I was in LA for twelve years. I played for a season on Knots Landing, a season on Falcon Crest, and then every once in a while I'd play odd sessions.

I played sitar on *Taxi*, Dobro on *Alice* and I appeared on stuff like Dukes of Hazard and Dynasty. I did one movie session that they used for library music so I made about $9,000 from that one session.

What do you see as the most difficult aspect of playing steel guitar and was there any particular practice regimen that proved helpful in your career?

Playing in tune is the thing that sometimes haunts me because I get so carried away with playing expressively that I'll just miss some of my notes as far as intonation goes.

I was lucky enough to grow up musically in a really good country band. I left the *Grateful Dead* scene and went through a series of adequate bands then joined the band that Bobby Black had left to go with *Commander Cody*. The band included Bobby's brother Larry and this guy, Hoyt Henry, who's one of my top-ten singers. He was a wonderful musician and a really good singer. At the time, I was just as impressed with Buddy Cage as with Buddy Emmons (laughs). "Okay, I can play a frantic solo here." So they helped tone me a bit and got me to play melody.

As far as blocking, I got a chance to practice five hours a night on the bandstand and then I would go home for a couple hours and practice. Sometimes I'd tape what I did and say: "Okay. What was I *trying* to do?" I knew I was going for something but couldn't pull it off when the moment came so I would try to recreate that moment and go for it then. To the degree that you're thinking, you're practicing and not playing so you really want to do enough practicing so that you're just in the moment playing what should be played. You look at a lot of steel players and they have puzzled expressions on their faces 'cause they're trying to figure it out. "I know that inversion's around here *somewhere*."

What's your music career like today?

I do an occasional session and festival and I play with a couple of local bands. One is a Grateful Dead cover band called the *Deadbeats*. We have a chance to stretch out but we don't stretch out indefinitely. I try to approach the music like Garcia would approach his guitar playing. He was a beautiful person, a gentle, quiet soul who had music everywhere.

I'm also teaching. I think if I won the lottery I'd still teach. I love the process of helping somebody discover how to make music and my students have always done well. Even though I make a lot more money doing the other stuff that I do, I do it because I can and there's not that many good steel guitar teachers around.

- ¤ -

Greg Leisz

The rare ability to play melodically while completely avoiding clichés is one of the reasons that standard and steel guitarist, Greg Leisz, is the first-call sideman for an amazingly diverse group of musicians who span most genres of popular music. Greg's resume' includes gigs and studio sessions for k.d. lang, Joni Mitchell, Sheryl Crow, Me'Shell NdegeOcello, Joe Cocker, Dave Alvin, Mary Black, Lucinda Williams, Tracy Chapman, Bruce Cockburn, Shawn Colvin, and *The Ventures* as well as Beck, *Bad Religion*, *Smashing Pumpkins*, and Brian Wilson.

One would be hard pressed to identify specific stylistic characteristics of Leisz's steel playing because he plays for the song. His taste and melodicism lead him to play exactly what's needed to exquisitely complement the music rather than show off his chops. This open mindedness has led him to continuing collaborations with folk/rock legend Joni Mitchell, as well as with jazz guitarist, Bill Frisell. Leisz's genre-bending steel work and open-hearted approach has led to a rewarding series of albums and live performances with Frisell. The name Greg Leisz on the liner notes is often a reliable indicator of quality music of uncommon sensitivity.

- ¤ Greg Leisz ¤ -

How did you come to play lap steel guitar?

I was a kid playing guitar and I was already enchanted by music in general. I heard the steel and I was intrigued by it so I borrowed a lap steel from a kid who lived in the same town and tried to kind of fiddle around on it. I was drawn to it is the best way to put it.

I probably heard it mostly in the context of the kind of country music that was on TV that I would see occasionally. The records that I listened to were mostly folk music and rock & roll. A lot of the stuff I was hearing was pedal steel and then I took that borrowed lap steel and started trying to copy the stuff I heard from the pedal steel on the lap steel 'cause that's all I had. I had to give the guitar back to the guy – it was his father's – then it was probably another three or four years before I got my hands on another one.

What was your first instrument?

The first lap steel that I bought was the same instrument that I had borrowed, a Fender Champ. I bought one with a matching Champ amp – a '54 – from this elderly lady. They were in great shape but over the years they became completely trashed. I still have that guitar. I actually sold it for a few years and then realized it was my first one so I got it back by trading something that was worth considerably more money for it. After that it grew from there. The second one was a [*Rickenbacher*] Frying Pan; I played that for many years.

Who were your early influences on steel?

The earliest influences I had, because of the records I was listening to at the time, were Sneaky Pete, Buddy Emmons, Red Rhodes, J.D. Maness. Sneaky Pete was very inventive. He had a lot of freedom to play 'cause there wasn't really a genre-specific thing going on. I was trying to develop an extension of my guitar playing on the lap steel. It was a completely different thing but it was more of an approach I adapted to what I was doing. I bought a pedal steel a couple of years later and they kind of branched off in two directions. The lap steel didn't take a back seat, it became this whole other thing in the music I played. A lot of times, the pedal steel was just too big to carry around.

Pedal steel obviously offers more harmonic and pitch-bending capabilities. What do see as the unique qualities of the lap steel and where does it seem to fit best?

As soon as I zeroed in on steel guitar I started hearing everyone from Bob Dunn to Joaquin Murphey to Jerry Byrd, and they all started out with the limitations the lap steel has and all overcame them and created something unique in the context that they were playing. So, the lap steel has limitations and the pedal steel evolved from trying to go beyond those limitations *technically* and to change the tunings while you played. Lap steel evolved to having several necks.

The idea of the pedals was not that you could play a lot of interesting chords but you could change from one tuning to another and not have to have those extra necks. It only became obvious later on that you could bend notes with the pedals while you were playing. So before pedals were invented, people found techniques like bar slanting and getting around on the strings really quickly and the other things that people did, that gave the lap steel its really unique quality. To me, it's the way people were overcoming the technical limitations - and everybody had to do it in a real different way - that made everybody sound different. All the way from the fast single string stuff that people like Sol Hoopii did to the real rich, chord harmonic stuff like Jerry Byrd plays where you can't even tell what string the guy's playing when he changes strings.

Back in the '50s, Byrd used identically gauged Black Diamond strings for his first 3 strings with an unwound 4th string and flat wounds for the rest. That, along with his unmatched technique, contributed to blurring the sound of his string changes.

That totally makes sense because it just sounds like one thing. His playing is amazing. A lap steel is a pickup and a piece of wood or metal, more like a solid body guitar. A pedal steel has got the strings going through a changer mechanism, just a completely different kind of sound. Although the early Bigsbys had a little more of a lap steel sound 'cause he built both. I actually wish the pedal steel would sound more like the lap steel.

As a session musician, I assume you have a lot of instruments. What are some of the electric steels in your collection?

I have a couple of double-neck, 8-string Fender Stringmasters and several Bakelite guitars like Jerry Byrd used to play. I've got two long-scale frying pans that I play a lot. I have a couple of 7-stringers, a Bakelite, a Gibson with the Charlie Christian pickup, as well as a Fender White 6-string, and a National Dynamic. The National Dynamic is the one I use lately probably more than just about anything else. It seems to be very good for recording on pop music and rock & roll.

I have a couple of Asher lap steel guitars – his Ben Harper models. I like 'em for certain things. I've used them mostly with Bill Frisell because they have a lot of bottom. Because of the two pickups, they have an almost cello-like, woody quality that's really nice. I use them mostly with open tunings. The string spacing is wide, like a Weissenborn, and that limits the pickups he can put in them, but that's changing and they'll get even better.

What about acoustics?

Weissenborns, a Sheerhorn, and some old Dobros.

What tunings do you use on non-pedal steel?

On the 8-string double-necks, I mostly use an A6th or a C6th, sometimes changing one or two notes. Usually the other tuning, if I'm playing a double-neck, will be some bizarre tuning that I've made up because of the context of the group I was playing in or sometimes an open E tuning or an extended E7th.

I mostly play 6-string. On those, I bounce around between a straight G tuning, sometimes with a high bass, and other tunings. I've gone through a number of different 6-string tunings. When I first got into lap steel, I used an E chord on top of an A chord. I used that tuning for quite a few years and kind of abandoned it. I found it was really good for horn lines and rock & roll. I liked the fact that I could really get around on the bottom strings and play melodies.

- ¤ Greg Leisz ¤ -

Now, I usually just use an open E or open D. I do the "sus" thing quite a bit – I sus the third and I play in DADGAD tuning a lot. It's a little bizarre playing a slide guitar with no third in it but it causes you to do things that you would ordinarily never do. I also play in a 6-string C6th tuning. I'll take that tuning and sharpen the C's to C# and the G to F# and play it as an A6th. So I kind of interchange those two tunings.

Lately, if I'm in G tuning and I want to do something that's more Hawaiian, I'll just take that middle D string and move it up to E.

Greg Leisz's Tunings								
Strings	1	2	3	4	5	6	7	8
A6th	E	C#	A	F#	E	C#	A	F#
C6th	E	C	A	G	E	C		
E maj. / A maj.	E	B	G#	E	C#	A		
E major	E	B	G#	E	B	E		
D major	D	A	F#	D	A	D		
D sus	D	A	G	D	A	D		
G major	D	B	G	D	B	G		
G6th	D	B	G	E	B	G		

Your playing is notable for its melodiousness and lack of clichés. There doesn't seem to be a "Greg Leisz style" except for your uncanny ability to enhance all the music in which you take part. Was it a conscious decision to avoid clichés?

It's nothing that I ever sat down and thought about. I just don't like to be thinking too much about what I'm doing when I'm doing it. I had some experiences when I was very young, before I even played steel, where I would learn something off a record and think, "I like this song a lot but I don't really like this solo. So I'm going to make up my own solo." So I would compose my own solo and, while I thought at first it would be neat to play my own solo, I discovered in the actual act of executing it that it was very often not successful.

So I discovered very early that, if I worked something out, no matter how much I practiced it, it just sort of left me cold. I started just making the stuff up. Hanging myself out there and making it up right when it happened. I started doing that when I was very young. It became a matter of experimenting constantly.

I'm not consciously trying to stay away from clichés but I think I react - an almost instantaneous reaction - to what I'm hearing. To me, I have a lot of clichés but they're maybe very subtle. I may be playing something in one song that I'll find myself blending into another song. It might be very similar but, in the context of the songs, it seems to work. If anything, the notes that you don't play, the notes you avoid, becomes your style.

- ¤ Greg Leisz ¤ -

You seem to be very focused on making a given song better rather than showing off your chops.

I've always been drawn to songs. From an early age, I was playing with musicians who were singing great songs. I got to work with great songwriters and I've always been drawn to collaborative musical endeavors and finding a place in the song to play. It's served me pretty well in terms of the people I've gotten to work with.

You've had the opportunity to work with a *Who's Who* of contemporary music. Allow me to name some people and get your impressions of playing on their records. Let's start with k.d. lang.

Well, at a certain point in her career, the steel guitar was something she heard as part of her music. She had steel guitar on her records before I worked with her. The first time that I recorded with her was on a record she produced herself: *Absolute Torch and Twang*. She was trying to consciously create her style in the studio using different elements of country music. The fact that she would have a big steel guitar solo in the middle of *Trail of Broken Hearts* on *Absolute Torch & Twang*, was an unusual thing at that time.

On *Ingénue*, the record after that, we were not using any references to country music. She went in a whole different direction. The steel guitar was still part of it 'cause she just likes the instrument. She doesn't feel it has any genre. It no longer represented country music to her or something that was from country music. On *Ingénue*, it was a matter of overdubbing and finding a use for the instrument.

There wasn't really any idea except to use the steel guitar. On *Save Me*, I created a different tuning by using the modality of the song. I can't remember exactly, but if it was in the key of G, the tuning would have F's & C's in it.

Joni Mitchell?

I think she was looking for another color. I was introduced to her through her co-producer at the time and I wound up playing on a couple of her records. It's hard to talk about. It's just sitting down and playing along with the music and trying to come up with something that fits. There was no preconception of what I was doing in that music. I was just there to try something out. She doesn't give direction, so you just play and hope for the best. You don't look at a chord chart. You basically just listen to the music and interact with it. It's like a painting. There are colors that you're providing and when she hears the colors, she uses the ones she wants in her painting. It's *her* painting. I'm just providing colors here and there and she moves 'em around.

Another interesting way she looks at a song is as if it has an architecture. Something like a steel guitar is an arch - long curved lines - where a rhythm guitar would be more like a squared off frame. Somebody playing horn lines would be like filigree – architectural ornamentation. I was able to play live with her too, and ended up playing some lap steel 'cause somebody had to take a solo on some of the songs.

Smashing Pumpkins?

I played a lot of steel guitar but it was just one session. It was for James Iha who had a song he wanted to put steel guitar on. It was just textural stuff for a pop song. It was always on pedal steel with him.

- ¤ Greg Leisz ¤ -

Bill Frisell?

I played on *Good Dog, Happy Man* except for one song that had Bill and Ry Cooder. That was the first time I ever worked with Bill. It was a great experience. I had no preconceptions about what I was going to play on the songs and we just sat down and figured it out on the spot. There are a couple things where just the two of us are playing with no band. I've recorded with him now on four albums over four or five years.

Last spring, we did some shows with just the two of us. He really likes to do that and I really do too. For both of us, it's just one thing we do, but it's definitely one of the highlights of what I get to do. It's challenging in one way, and in another, it's very liberating. I think the space that my head has to be in to play with Bill comes really naturally to me. I have to overcome a little bit of fear of his musical knowledge. I have to integrate what I do and have it work and somehow it does. It's just mind boggling how creative the guy is and how he's evolving his own way of absorbing music from other people. He just integrates what he takes from other people and makes it his own immediately. For me it strikes a resonance with my own way of looking at music.

What's your secret for playing just the right part at the right time on so many people's records?

Well, I listened to a lot of English folk music and modal jazz, like Miles Davis. At one point I was listening to Charlie Christian every day for like two years. You get certain things out in your playing. From Christian, I learned how to play with a swing feel. Before that, I wasn't that great in my rhythmic sense. I played a lot of r&b as a guitar player for a lot years – like Marvin Gaye and Sam & Dave stuff. *That* colors the way you feel music as well. You take all that stuff with you when you're sitting and playing a lap steel part.

A lot of it's just feel. Maybe that's what people hear and they think what you're playing really blends. It's the feel. A lot of times you have to overdub. I don't prefer to overdub, I really like to play live. The whole task of overdubbing is to create the feel that you're not overdubbing. A lot of that is having a pretty refined sense of rhythm and phrasing and space.

How much role does equipment have in getting your sound?

If equipment didn't have a pretty major role everybody wouldn't be so obsessed by it, but you can take four different people and have them play the same instrument and the differences between musicians are going to override the constancy of that instrument.

You have to feel good about the guitar you're playing. When you get a new instrument you think that it's going to make you sound different. Lots of times I like to play an instrument I've never played before because it can make you play differently.

Where do you think the non-pedal steel guitar is headed?

I think people are going to find new ways of playing it in contexts where more people will hear it. Ben Harper uses the instrument in rock & roll in an interesting way. Robert Randolph is doing a whole 'nother thing on the pedal steel.

I went to Hawaii recently and when I think about the whole history of lap style players and how that spread, it seems like there was a golden age that we're way past but there are a lot of people trying to use it in interesting ways in the sounds of today. And that's probably what was going on back then.

- ¤ -

Freddie Roulette

Freddie Roulette's sound on the lap steel is unique in popular music. Nobody else sounds remotely like him. His cascades of notes swirl and sparkle like a handful of pearls thrown on velvet. While often pegged as a blues player, Freddie has command of many other musical idioms including rock, soul, funk, latin and pop, which he fuses together in a melting pot of virtuo licks and runs that create a new hybrid that's his alone.

Born in Evanston, Illinois, Freddie learned the lap steel in grade school. He quickly became good enough to sit in with the best musicians of the '60s Chicago blues scene, eventually playing and touring with blues greats, Earl Hooker and Charlie Musselwhite.

- ¤ Freddie Roulette ¤ -

He relocated to the west coast, and though he remained active on the club scene, released just one recording under his own name until the mid 1990s. Since then, he has enjoyed something of a rediscovery with several new CDs, touring, and collaborations with 60's rock veterans, like Harvey Mandel.

In 1998, Freddie realized a career high point when he appeared as an invited artist at the International Steel Guitar Convention in Saint Louis, Missouri. World-renowned pedal steel players, like country great Jimmy Day, were amazed by Freddie's creativity and astounding technical control of the instrument. These days, he can be found on tour in Europe, Canada, or in the clubs of northern California playing the same fiery licks he's *owned* for more than thirty years.

How did you come to play the lap steel guitar?

I started lap steel back in grade school in Evanston, Illinois; a little 6-string student steel guitar.

Did you start with exercise books?

I used the Nick Manoloff slant bar method. It's an old book that you first start out with. Anybody that plays lap steel knows Nick Manoloff. Since there are no pedals, you had to learn how to get all your chords by slanting the bar. My music teacher used to play with the Sonja Henie band for the Ice Follies. I learned the basics on a 6-string steel then he suggested I get an 8-string steel, which I did. He put a 7th note on it – a natural blues chord.

You used A major tuning?

Yeah, an A7th tuning.

How did you move from a kid in grade school just learning to play to sitting in with blues musicians in Chicago?

I played standards before I ever played blues. I'm kind of an American roots music player because I play more than blues. I played country & western, standards from the '50s – remember the *Hit Parade?* So I learned all the songs from that era; pop music of the '50s. It was a good thing for me to do because it gave me a vast knowledge of chord structure.

Rather than playing a twelve-bar blues, I started out playing compositions *first*. It was a great advantage to me to have done that because I knew chord progressions and melody. Once I started going down to Chicago to play blues, I was able to play blues, r&b or anything else. Everything they could play, I could already play.

Twelve-bar blues was kind of boring to me 'cause I was used to playing compositions. When they started with r&b, I just fell in naturally (laughs).

Do you play other instruments like standard guitar?

I started with a regular guitar. I didn't really like it. It made my fingers hurt (laughs).

I just stuck with the steel. I'm not instrument crazy. I just want to take an instrument and play it well. I liked steel guitar so I just stuck with it. I'm not a harp player. I don't play piano or regular guitar. I just play lap steel. Period.

How did you wind up playing with (*blues harmonica great*) Charlie Musselwhite?

I was with Earl Hooker on the road and got a call from Musselwhite to meet him in Hartford to join him on tour. We wound up all over the east coast and up and down, from Canada to Huntington Beach. After that, I toured with several other people as a sideman until I started making records of my own.

I've been to Germany several times. I have a German album out, as well as *Back in Chicago*, which I did a few years back. I'm finishing another Harvey Mandel album. I've been on a lot of albums with Harvey.

You're in a band with Harvey now called *Nightfire*.

Yeah. We put the band together for recording and mostly studio work. We haven't done any local gigs yet. *Nightfire* plays bluesy originals by Harvey Mandel and me.

What brands of steel guitars do you own?

I've always played a National. I play a single-neck 8-string and I also have a double-neck. One was a gift from David Lindley. I plan on getting a Sierra. The Sierra Company has put out a nice eight-string steel. I've heard a lot about that. It's a beautiful guitar.

What kind of bar do you use? It doesn't look like a standard steel guitar bar.

Those are my prototypes. I had those specially made by an aircraft precision tool manufacturer in Oakland. It's made out of Dacron plastic. They use it out in space where you can't oil your gears. It's tough as steel - one of the toughest plastics on the market. It comes in tubes and he puts it in a cold press, pours hot lead thorough it, cuts it off and I get a pure lead bar covered with Dacron plastic.

I've been using the same bar for over seven years and there's not a nick in it. The reason for using plastic is because it's a silent bar - no noise at all. It takes the high end off and gives you a warm sound. You just kick the high end up on your amp a little bit and that's it. It's a mellow sound. He makes such good bars I haven't seen him in years (laughs).

So as far as bars are concerned, you're covered for life?

I've got about twenty of those bars. I'm covered for life! (Laughs).

What tunings do you use?

I use an A7th and A9th mixture on my double-neck. My main tuning is the A7th – or sometimes [*a variation with*] A-E-G or A-E-A in the bass. I'll make little changes here and there in the studio to get what I want.

I use that double A string 'cause it gives me a bassier sound without overdriving the bass. I use it for little techniques I have when I'm playing rhythm guitar. I'm a good rhythm steel guitar player, by the way. I do rhythms on steel that regular guitarists can't do plus playing all the chord structure at the same time – makes it unique.

Freddie Roulette's Tunings								
Strings	1	2	3	4	5	6	7	8
A7th	E	C#	A	E	C#	A	A	G
A7th #2	E	C#	A	E	C#	A	E	G

Have you ever played in any of the other steel guitar tunings like C6th, C#minor or E7th?

No, because I can get almost all the stuff I need to play progressive chords, and all the alternate chords that go along with them, as part of the color chords, out of my tuning. Sometimes I have to play two movements to get one chord, which gives me an extra measure to play in. If I speed it up, it sounds like one chord. My music is almost always polyrhythmic. Funk especially, fits me so well 'cause I can fit all this stuff in. All you have to do is pay attention to the rhythm pattern that's going on. I can play stuff that regular guitar players can't even get *near*. You develop your own style, which is obviously what I did 'cause I don't sound like any other steel guitar player.

I'm kind of like a synchronous-minded musician. I know my axe frontward and backward, and I know what chord to play if I'm playing with a three-piece group, a four-piece group, or larger. It's more effective to play a few notes rather than a million notes that go in one ear and out the other. You don't need to do that 90% of the time. Like a good harp player or sax player, you play around the chords or inside the chords. I'm having a hard time trying to figure out the theory of playing outside the chords in contemporary music. I get away with it sometimes (laughs).

A few years ago, you played the International Steel Guitar Convention in St. Louis, Missouri. Did you enjoy doing that gig?

That was a great, great experience. I got to play with some of the greatest steel guitar players in the world. These guys are just amazingly great, from Buddy Emmons on down – the kings of the steel guitar. Some of the best country swing I've ever heard (laughs). That's the only thing I cannot play. I *love* country swing but I cannot get the hang of it 'cause I was never oriented toward it or exposed enough to it. It's cool!

You do some volume control effects with the controls on the face of the guitar?

Yeah, the configuration of the volume pot on the National steel is in perfect position where you can grab it. It's not in the middle or way on the outskirts where you can't reach it, so I can play and pick while my hands are on the control. That's one of the main reasons I like Nationals. I don't think it's the best steel guitar out there but it's the best for me to do what I want to do without having to alter the crap out of it. My 8-string has a tone booster in it run by a 9-volt battery. It's completely shielded so it's studio ready - a noiseless guitar.

What about amplification?

One of the things I don't like about it is the highs are not fat enough so I use an old Peavey tube rack top with an Ibanez analog delay – *not* a digital delay because too much digital technology makes my highs thinner. I haven't used reverb in years. The analog delay is just to fatten up the sound and it kind of filters out the compression 'cause I'm driving through a 1000-watt amp.

That gives me a very powerful amplifier. I call it my roadie rig. It'll cut through anything. I like the clean linear sound. If I want to mess with it and make it dirty, I'll use a pedal.

You do a lot of slant bar work.

100% of my playing is slant bar playing. I do very little sliding for a slide guitar player – hardly ever. When I'm doing background and I pick a horn section or keyboard part then I'll slide and do volume and all that stuff.

When you were first starting, did you listen to players like Jerry Byrd, who do a lot of slant-style playing?

Actually, I didn't. I didn't listen to any steel guitar players at all. I listened to Earl Hooker and the way he played single note slide. Earl Hooker used to be a 1940s swing guitar player so he knew more than he was playing. We were playing all this simple blues stuff but he could play much more. I didn't even know he could play all that stuff until he played me some records from the '40s. He was playing at lightning speed. I said, "How come you don't play like that anymore?" I don't know who turned him on to slide guitar.

You don't use finger picks?

I've never used finger picks in my life. I've always been a classical steel guitar player. That's what amazed those people down in St. Louis at the steel guitar convention (laughs). "He doesn't have a volume control, he doesn't have a foot pedal, he doesn't use picks, and he doesn't use a metal bar. He just plugs in and plays (laughs)."

Who has influenced your music and what music do you enjoy listening to?

I don't have one single influence. I like Albert King because of the composition of his songs. I also like his playing, but it's his compositions I like. I like good r&b … Wilson Pickett … I love to play that stuff.

Do you play jazz?

I play contemporary jazz – like [*Miles Davis'*] *All Blues*. I don't like avant garde jazz. I like jazz like the common people who are into jazz like. I'm more of an American roots player. I alter everything I do – even if it's a standard tune. I always have new ideas to put into songs and I like re-arranging and re-orchestrating songs. That's my main deal.

On *Back in Chicago* you play a steel duet with yourself playing the roles of a man and woman having an argument. Your voice was the man and your guitar played the part of the woman. It was both cool and funny because it was so dead on. How did you start to do that?

That's "audio illusion." The steel guitar is a sine wave instrument – same as the human voice. You know we talk in notes - da da, da da. So you have to be conscious of the notes that you're producing when you're talking. People talk in notes and don't even realize it. I did a lot of experimenting with my own voice. I said a word, then I got my guitar and saw that "I'm talking a G …that's a C# … going way up to an A flat and … hey, I'm going to a B flat."

So, I just wrote that down and I talked the notes and then got on the guitar and said, "I'll be damned! It sounds like I just said that." So I call it "audio illusion" – my little scientific name for it. It makes me sound like a really smart cat! (Laughs). I'm kind of like a joker on stage. I should have been a comedian.

- ¤ -

Lee Jeffriess

In his work with *Big Sandy and the Fly-Rite Boys*, Englishman, Lee Jeffriess was a one-man musical encyclopedia of classic rockabilly, early country, and western swing steel guitar. The *Fly-Rite Boys* traveled to gigs in a 1940's bus, played vintage equipment, and dressed the part of an early 1950s band. While Speedy West, Joaquin Murphey and Vance Terry all made their stamp on Lee's style, he combines their influences with his own ideas in fresh, new ways that are informed by a relentless sense of swing. The original songs written by Robert Williams (Big Sandy) for the band served as a showcase for blazing solos by Lee and guitarist Ashley Kingman. Life on the road eventually lost its luster as Lee settled in Northern California to play locally and raise a family.

- ¤ Lee Jeffriess ¤ -

How did you first become interested in learning steel? Were there many resources available in England?

My next door neighbor, when I was about four or five years old, was a Hawaiian player who played a little single-neck 6 or 8-string Fender. I can clearly recall the fella sitting in his living room playing lap steel. He'd play real pretty Hawaiian music and I remember being in the backyard and hearing him and we'd sometimes go to the house and he'd play for us. Then, when I was about fifteen or sixteen, people would play me Merle Travis and Hank Williams records with either Jerry Byrd or Don Helms and I liked those. But it wasn't until I was about eighteen when someone sat me down and played *Two Guitars Country Style* – the Speedy West & Jimmy Bryant album. That really flipped me out! I went, "Oh my God! I want to see one of these things! I want to play it." That was the turning point.

How did you move from desire to playing the instrument?

I got a standard guitar and raised the strings. I didn't really have any idea of the voicings. I just tuned it to a major tuning. Four or five years later I acquired a steel guitar. I was really an upright bass player at the time so I didn't spend that much time with it. I got a double-8 Rickenbacker from Jerry Hogan, who runs the steel guitar convention out in England. Back in the '60s, Jerry was a session steel player who worked with Albert Lee.

I was very into Joaquin Murphey but I was nowhere near figuring that stuff out harmonically. I did have a steel and I tuned it to a tuning that was a kind of Hawaiian E13th. I had an E6th with a 3rd on top – very high-pitched. Now, I wouldn't be able to stand it, just way too high for me. Jerry had sold me the instrument and given me the tunings. I really didn't know what I was askin' for.

I fooled around with that guitar for about a year trying to play along with Bob Wills records and could kind of approximate it, but I pretty much gave up and put the guitar under my bed. I wasn't getting anywhere fast and it was frustrating, so I basically shelved it (laughs). I was working a lot as a bass player so I didn't give it that much attention until I met Big Sandy and those guys over in England. I told 'em I was a steel player. I was lyin' through my teeth! (Laughs). The guitar player at the time, T.K. Smith, said "Move to the states, man. You can come play with us." I was thinking I'd shot my mouth off and shouldn't have said anything.

Four or five months later I was living in the states. I'd moved to work with a guy named Carl Leyland – who later became a Fly-Rite Boy – who was a pianist. I was talking to him on the phone and he had said I'm on my fourth bass player, everyone wants to play electric bass and I can't get anyone to stick with us. I said, "Why don't you buy me an airline ticket and buy me a bass and I'll come over." I was totally joking but he said, "Give me about a month to get it together." And he did.

I was making very good money playing around New Orleans, Austin, and Mobile and then we ended up doing a show with Big Sandy in Austin and they asked me to come to LA to play with them. I didn't want to play bass anymore. I really wanted to play steel. On the way to Austin I had purchased a Bigsby triple-neck from a guy named Dusty Stuart – the guy before Curly Chalker in the Hank Thompson band. We jammed together there and I kind of bluffed it. They said, "Come to LA." So the rest is history.

What was the experience like being with *Big Sandy & the Fly-Rite Boys*?

It was one of those sink or swim kind of things. It was very fun. Early on it was unbelievable - the life of Riley (laughs). I can't think of anything negative about it. I didn't really put in as much effort as I should have done. I could have been a lot more on the ball but I was just twenty-four years old and partying too much (laughs) as you do when you're twenty-four. I'm very fortunate to have met some incredible people, people I would only have dreamed of meeting, getting to play all over the place and having a real good time.

Do you have a favorite among the albums you made with Big Sandy?

No, I like little bits and pieces of all of them and I dislike portions of all of them. From my point of view, I always felt like we got to this point where we were touring constantly and it was like a *Catch 22* thing: you had to tour constantly just to keep yourself afloat. It wasn't like we had been playing the songs for three or four months when we went in and did them. In a lot of instances they were things that were very last minute, like you were winging it. Four months later you're playing a better version of the song.

You and guitarist Ashley Kingman developed phenomenal interplay in the unison and harmony runs that you used as kickoffs and turn-arounds. Did you spend a lot of time working these out?

No, they were head things and we'd sit around while we were waiting to record and make them as tight as possible or we might be working on them a couple weeks before a session. I don't know if there was anything that was, in my opinion, spectacular or outstanding. It was kind of recycled ideas from other things. It was something to get you by. It's easy for me to say now that they could have been better, but of course, they were what they were.

The only good thing about having to do it that way was it forced Robert (Big Sandy) to come up with these really good songs. He couldn't write them four months before. He had to have the pressure of three weeks 'til the project to actually come up with stuff. He was one of those people who really comes up with great things when he's under tremendous pressure. He wrote amazing songs. To me, that's what *Big Sandy and the Fly-Rite Boys* was all about – great songs. I thought these are good songs that are timeless. They could have been written back then but they're kind of contemporary. That's the one thing that stands out about the whole thing. I was in Holland once and this guy came up and said, "You know what? You guys aren't really that good." I said, "I beg your pardon?" He said, "When I look at you all individually, I don't think you're that good. But the whole thing is very, very good." So I guess it was a compliment (laughs).

The swing and drive of your playing never failed to fill the dance floor.

The emphasis was - regardless if you fell on your face or came off looking good - to be as spontaneous as possible. That was the one thing I got from Speedy West. There's no way I could ever play like the fella but I remember talking to him when I first came over to the States. He was my idol at the time. He said, "Dig yourself in a hole and then dig yourself out. Be as spontaneous as possible." That's what he said he and Bryant always strived for. I think if you keep that in mind and just jump out there and try and come up with something, you can surprise yourself or you can fall on your face. But I think that was really good advice.

What guitars have you been playing since leaving the Fly-Rite Boys?

Well, I ran into some financial difficulties a few years back and had to sell my Bigsby. For years I always said, "I don't like those Stringmasters. They sound really twangy to me." But I found out that I just didn't like the way most people set 'em up because they just play 'em on the back pickup all the time, with ear splitting treble. I got this white Stringmaster triple-neck from '63 and started setting it more toward the front pickup and the thing sounded great. I played that for about a year. I loved that guitar! It was definitely on par with the Bigsby. You could get some very pretty tones out of it.

I had that and a few others: a four-neck Wright Custom and a couple of Fender 1000's which I just used as non-pedal instruments. Today, my main guitar is a Bigsby that was constructed from *new-old-stock* parts by Paul Warnick, in Chicago. He and Dave Peterson put them together. It's a triple-8 with five pedals.

Do you use the pedals in your playing?

I use them for chord voicings but very rarely for moving tones. The guys I play with now do some stuff that requires an approximation of Jimmy Day's playing, so I will throw them in there if needed. It's not really my cup of tea. I do like that kind of playing, but I prefer it by Bud Isaacs. He got such a beautiful tone. So I'm coming from a very early pedal steel thing - nothing chromatic or anything like that.

Did you put much time into practicing steel guitar technique – like palm or pick blocking?

Nope. I think I do both but I'm really not that conscious of it. It wasn't until about a year ago when a friend of mine, Bill Dye in Kansas City, who's an unbelievable non-pedal steel player, sent me this stuff by Jeff Newman on palm versus pick blocking. The Newman thing is to really push the pick blocking as he claims it's more efficient. I studied it and it made me really look at what I was doing. I was mainly palm blocking but every now and then I'd use picks.

You *should* think about your technique and practice and, if there's something that's gonna make you do something better, then of course it's a good thing. I think whatever works for you is the way to go. With modern pedal steel, as well as jazz, there's so much emphasis on technique that it kind of kills it for me. You're getting bored pretty fast. You know what you're hearing is hard to do – there's been hours of effort behind it but for what?

I watched Cindy Cashdollar's video and I think it's one of the best things I've seen for new players who don't know much yet about the instrument. I thought it was great; really made a lot of sense.

So, in terms of your technique, if it's not broken don't fix it?

That's right. I'm not a speed picker going a million miles an hour. Joaquin Murphey and Vance Terry both pick blocked pretty much all the time. I've seen them both play and I asked them about it. Vance said, "I pick blocked from the get-go. No one thought about blocking in the '40s & '50s. I always did it that way 'cause I found it kind of uncomfortable to palm block." I watched Murphey and his hand was floating above the strings all the time; I never saw it come down.

Vance Terry never really got the recognition he deserved for his incredible playing.

I've listened to Emmons and Chalker and Murphey and I'd say he's easily as giant as those guys.

What are your main tunings?

Still A6th – I was thinking of going to G6th – I like the lower register better. I'm not really into C6th. Obviously there's no difference in the voicing, but it's a little high for my taste.

- ¤ Lee Jeffriess ¤ -

I use the McAuliffe E13th, but instead of the 7th & 8th string being G# & E, I use B & G#. And I use what I call the Noel Boggs E13th. Vance used that tuning and I just go with what he did. I use Vance's set-up on his Bigsby.

Vance Terry, early 1950s

Lee Jeffriess' Tunings								
Strings	1	2	3	4	5	6	7	8
A6th	E	C#	A	F#	E	C#	A	F#
E13th #1	E	C#	B	G#	F#	D	B	G#
E13th #2	E	C#	G#	F#	D	B	G#	E

Who are some of your favorite players? Do you listen to pedal steel players at all?

You've listened to *Steel Guitar Jazz*, right? Buddy Emmons with Sonny Rollins' band? Apparently, he gets freaked out if that record's even mentioned. I've heard he says he was depressed for months after makin' that. He thought it was the worst ever made. And when I listen to it, my God! It's unbelievable. I think he's just a phenomenal swing player that can touch on bop and all that.

Initially, I was into Speedy West and Herb Remington. Then, not much later, I got into Joaquin Murphey. I get more of a buzz out of Joaquin or Curly Chalker before they went to pedals. Are you aware of those cuts that have been reissued of Curly with Hank Thompson?

On the radio transcriptions of Joaquin with Tex Williams you can literally hear the audience as well as the band hold their collective breath when Murphey was about to come out of the gate.

The floor drops away, doesn't it? I got to meet Joaquin on several occasions. The first time, I sat in [*producer*] Mike Johnstone's livingroom and watched him play for about three hours straight. It doesn't get any better than that (laughs). He didn't once repeat himself. He had hundreds of tunes stored in his head; a huge repertoire.

I've heard he was kind of depressed about the E9th pedal sound becoming the dominant sound while his 6th chord-based style fell somewhat out of favor when everyone went to pedals in the '50s.

Yeah. I asked him about that and he said, "No, I didn't like it; I didn't like what it did and I thought it was a gimmick." To him, the E9th was a novelty tuning. Guys like Jerry Compton, who was a buddy of Joaquin's and a phenomenal steel player in his own right, used to say, "C'mon, Murphey, you could play that E9th thing and be makin' a lot of money. I know you don't dig it, but why not try it? You could have a second career out of this." But Murphey was adamant that he didn't want to do it. He held out 'til about 1968 or '69 before he tried pedals.

Did you listen to any of the Hawaiian players?

Not really. I liked the west coast guys. A friend sent me some stuff by the Japanese steel player, Lion Kobayoshi. That guy plays very good jazz and Hawaiian. He's a great musician. I've listened to Jerry Byrd, Joaquin, Speedy and Herb Remington play pretty Hawaiian stuff. They're putting a 1940's pop angle on it. Now, from a purist standpoint you might say, "That's not *really* Hawaiian." I don't know what makes it faux or real, but I'm just not as "gung ho" about it as a lot of people.

What are you doing these days and what are your musical plans for the future?

I'm playing around the San Francisco Bay area and trying to keep my hand in. I've been doing some recording with a couple of different people like Johnny Dilks. I did bits and pieces with a guitar player who's a Merle Travis-style player. I'm not looking to go out on the road. The last couple of years when I was touring, I was constantly thinking about my wife and daughter. I felt guilty about it and decided to get a regular job. I'd had my fill. I don't regret any moment of it but how long can you do that for? So I'm doing French polishing and furniture restoration and, if I can get to play at least once a week, I'm happy. I'm also hoping to get an instrumental album out soon.

- ¤ -

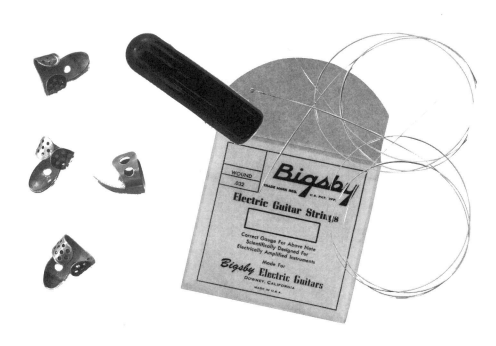

Jody Carver

Jody Carver's career in music took many unusual twists and turns. The son of vaudevillian Zeb Carver, Jody was an active professional musician in the 1950s appearing on TV with Arthur Godfrey, recording, doing studio work in New York, and playing clubs. He was a featured Fender endorser along with Leon McAuliffe and Noel Boggs. He enjoyed a long and close association with Leo Fender as a traveling sales representative for the company and later, for *CBS* and *Music Man.*

In 1958, Coral Records released the record *Hot Club of America in Hi-Fi.* Along with guitarist Johnny Cucci, Jody's steel work was astoundingly fluid and exciting. They sounded like Speedy West & Jimmy Bryant, but with a definite New York, ethnic edge on tunes such as *Miserlou, The Third Man Theme,* and *Brazil.* Jody's "pick click" percussion and volume pedal effects were quite innovative. Today, the original *Hot Club* recording is a much sought-after collectible. As of this book's publication, Jody plans a CD reissue and is writing his autobiography.

SACRED MUSIC

WALTER JOHNSON
STEEL GUITAR ARTIST

at CALVARY BAP. CHURCH
Rev. HEDGEMAN   ARDMORE, PA.
on
THUR. MAY 9,1940-8:30 P.M.

assisted by the Following Quartettes

FAMOUS MORNING STAR   ISRAEL LIGHT
EOLEUM GOSPEL SINGER   KING OF KINGS
CONNIE WILLIAMS - BLIND GUITAR ARTIST
SELECT SOLOIST
ADMISSION 25c

Gospel music, especially that of the African-American church, has had a long and profound influence on American popular music. Performers from Sam Cooke and Aretha Franklin, to the hard boppers, soul jazzers, country acapella harmony groups, and even turntable-scrubbing rappers have all drunk deeply from the well of black church music.

Nevertheless, for 60 years, a unique genre of steel guitar music remained known only to the members of two related sects of Pentecostal Church communities: The House of God, Keith Dominion and the Church of the Living God, Jewel Dominion.

Troman Eason, who had studied with a native Hawaiian player in Philadelphia during the 1930s, introduced the steel guitar into House of God worship services. In the early 1990s, Florida folklorist, Robert Stone discovered that the Hawaiian steel guitar had become essential to religious services throughout the 26 states where these sects had congregations. This musical "hothouse" nurtured a culture that was largely untouched by outside influences. Stone dubbed their music "Sacred Steel" and produced a cassette release of the music in 1995 for the Florida Folklife Program. The recording created an immediate critical stir that led to a series of CDs by Arhoolie Records, videos, concerts, tours, and international visibility for the musicians.

Steel guitar pioneers Willie Eason (Troman's brother), Calvin Cooke, Ted Beard, and Henry Nelson - like Clapton and Hendrix in secular music – were revered in their church communities for their abilities to stir a congregation. The next generation of Sacred Steelers includes lap steel virtuoso, Aubrey Ghent, the Campbell Brothers (Chuck on pedal steel, Phil on guitar, and Darick on lap steel), as well as Sonny Treadway, and the late Glenn Lee.

Perhaps the most visible proponent of the style is pedal steeler, Robert Randolph, whose meteoric rise in popularity earned him a Warner Brothers' recording contract and press coverage befitting a rock star. The success of the Sacred Steel movement in reaching the broader public continues with new recordings, festival appearances and club gigs, books, and a traveling photographic exhibition in the works.

Darick Campbell

Darick Campbell's father is State Bishop and Pastor at the House of God Church in Rush, New York. When not on the road with his father, Darick can be found on the bandstand contributing powerful steel guitar solos and ensemble parts to the music of the *Campbell Brothers Band*. Influenced by Henry Nelson and the Jewell Dominion's Bishop Lorenzo Harrison, Darick uses a wah pedal as a tone control to produce an edgy, boxy sound that goes right to the gut of listeners. Years together have helped the brothers develop the ability to turn on a musical dime based on the response of their listeners. While the enraptured faithful have been known to shout spontaneously or break out in impromptu dance moves, secular audiences have often been surprised to find themselves utterly swept away by the incessant groove of this music.

- ¤ Darick Campbell ¤ -

Darick, who plays for his audience first, wouldn't have it any other way.

How did you come to play steel guitar and what was your first instrument?

I started off on drums with my brothers and made it to the highest point in the church organization, playing in Nashville at the national congregation, which is called the General Assembly. I would play with all our top players: Ted Beard, Calvin Cooke, Henry Nelson, and my brother, Chuck Campbell. Playin' with them guys, the way I played the drums, I always liked to accent things that they were doing on the steel and try to play with them. Instead of being a flashy drummer, I just kept the main timing, if you will. Just listening to what guys were doin' on steel, it was just amazing to me how they would make their instruments sound.

And locally, Chuck worked at night and when we'd have services on Wednesday and Friday nights, he wouldn't be there and the service didn't seem the same without the steel guitar. So I decided that I would try to learn the steel guitar 'cause I have another brother, Phil, and he was usually playin' the bass at that time. In 1980, I picked up the steel guitar and that's when I tried to apply myself and learn it.

What does the sound of the steel guitar bring to the church congregation that's different from the sound of the organ, the instrument most people probably associate with church music?

The difference the steel guitar brings is almost like another human voice because the steel guitar actually mimics the human voice. The different moans, the different leading lines that the vocalist is singing, the steel guitar will actually pick up and carry the song.

The sound seems to really excite the congregation. Excite is probably the wrong word.

No, that's a good word. It really evokes the spirit in people. The organ has the same effect by the way, but the organ is more about chord progressions than lead lines where the steel is about one or two-string lines that really resonate about the church. If you're good enough, you can close your eyes and it sounds like someone is singing.

Were there any steel players in the secular world who influenced you besides the players you heard in the church?

Not until lately. Chuck was more influenced by the country western guys such as Jimmy Day. I listened to him by way of Chuck. Growing up in the church, we weren't allowed to listen to outside music. Listening to it and being influenced by it and trying to bring it to the church and play it, we weren't allowed to do that (laughs). At the same time, I'm not naive. Some of the top guys have listened to 'em [*players outside the church*] and been influenced by 'em. That's my personal belief.

- ¤ Darick Campbell ¤ -

It sounds corny, but I got everything I learned from the church. I don't mean any disrespect because I respect all different types of music and recognize that everybody has some talent and gifts. I don't have any problem giving credit to the players who came before.

You and your brothers are certainly going on to influence a whole lot of people. Nobody can listen to your music and not move.

Oh, wow. Thank you. If I may add, now that I'm able to hear different players…the Allman Brothers, Freddie Roulette, Buddy Emmons and all these other people that are out there, when I hear them, man, it's amazing what they do with the instrument! Now mind you, we had opportunities to hear the guys on the *Hee Haw* show but they didn't have big spots on there. Most of the stuff they were doing was like chord progressions and every once in a while they'd get a solo but it wouldn't be that long.

What's been the reaction when you and your brothers play festival dates from audiences who are hearing your style of steel playing for the first time?

People come up with amazement. They say they can't believe the steel guitar sounds like that. Some people come up and ask, "What is this instrument?" (Laughs). They want the instrument defined so we explain it. People are thoroughly impressed by the music that we play for them.

What's your main guitar these days?

My main guitar is a Fender Stringmaster 8-string [*Fender Deluxe-8*] . Now I'm also playing a Sierra 8-string. I love it, man! The Fender-8 was the steel of choice in the '60s & '70s from Ted Beard, Calvin Cooke and Henry Nelson who is Aubrey Ghent's father. Calvin Cooke and Ted Beard moved on to the pedal steel but Henry Nelson stayed with the [*Fender*] 8-string. When I heard the man play, and the way he played, the sound he got from the instrument was just phenomenal - I just had to have one. They were hard to come by. When I finally landed one, I had to get work done to it. I just loved the instrument to the tune that I bought three of them and gave one to my nephew who's learning how to play. The sound that the instrument brought was just awesome to me. Now that I have the Sierra, it's a different sound from the Fender but the Sierra's amazing as well.

How would you describe the differences between the Sierra and the Fenders?

The Sierra sounds cleaner. I believe it has more sustain as opposed to the Fender. The strings go through the body on the Sierra and that helps resonate through the wood and it's got a metal plate through there that gives you that unbelievable sustain. Tony Williams at Sierra has been really gracious in working with us. I like it, I really do, but to be honest, Fender is the top-notch guitar for me. It just fits. I'm looking for a Dobro now. It's a beautiful sound, man.

What tunings do you use?

The tuning I use is an E major with a C# on top. I think they call it a 6th, but I'm not good with the theory part of it. I use a Shubb bar and a Stevens bar.

- ¤ Darick Campbell ¤ -

Darick Campbell's Tuning								
Strings	1	2	3	4	5	6	7	8
E6th	E	C#	B	G#	E	B	E	B

You get an amazing sound with a wah pedal – almost like the sound of an amplified harmonica.

(Laughs) Yeah. I'm using a Morley wah pedal. That was influenced by the Jewel Dominion of the Church of the Living God - a guy named Ronnie Mosey, under Bishop Lorenzo Harrison. I was greatly influenced by them. They are phenomenal players. I'm influenced by Aubrey [*Ghent*] too. It sounds like a woman singing with Aubrey.

Do you do volume effects with your hands?

Up top, that's right. I got that, again, from Henry Nelson. Man! He was just amazing. Aubrey Ghent is blessed with it as well. He can almost make it sound like he's whistling. When the guy used to do that - wow! It's so emotional that some people will cry or get excited. That's what I try to get to in my playing - where I can touch people.

Your brother Chuck is an incredible pedal steel player. Do you play pedal steel as well as lap steel?

I have a 12-string GFI but because of the group's format, Chuck plays the pedals and I play the lap. The lap is my favorite to be honest with you.

What do you think is the hardest thing about learning to play the steel guitar?

You've got 6, 8, 10 and 12-string guitars. The hardest thing to me is understanding the changes - the I, III, V, VII. There are different ways of doing it, but I go by frets. You go to the A, back to E, then to the B, and some times you go three frets back for the minor. Understanding the basis of that in the way we play, that's the hardest part to grasp. Learning licks or scales, I think that's the easiest part.

Do you think it comes out in your steel playing if you're nervous?

Yeah. The way we were taught to play, you're not supposed to wiggle the bar so much. You only wiggle the bar for sustain, not when you first start out. We have this phrase that we coined, "You got to have a solid hand." If you don't have that solid hand your playing won't sound as good as the experienced guys. Time plays a factor. It comes with experience, so the more you practice, the better your hand will be. Being nervous plays a role because you've got to have the right timing, the right cadence to actually get the notes you want to achieve and how you want them to ring out.

My method is to always think of my guitar as a voice – somebody singing. You don't want to crack notes or slide into notes. You want to hit them as pure as you possibly can.

What kind of gigs have you been playing with the *Campbell Brothers Band*?

We've been doing mainly festivals. We just did a couple of pubs with Ropeadope Records. Mainly we're doing stuff with the arts.

- ¤ Darick Campbell ¤ -

What's it like playing with your brothers? Do you think being family helps you communicate as musicians?

(Laughs). It's a great experience, man, to the extent that we have a set formula, if you will, that we use but so often we're able to let loose and go for it and I know the guys will be there. We've been playing together at least twenty years or more. Now that we're playing together with two steels, it's awesome 'cause normally, there's only one steel player.

Do you have to be careful to stay out of one another's way?

Well, yes. The formula is Chuck is first and I'm second. He leads out and what I try to do is find little gaps in between and just get in there and stick it out. I guess we look at it like the jazz guys - like a horn section - that's the best way to look at it. Now we're working on harmony parts to play together.

I'm a very emotional guy when I'm playing (laughs). At any given time, I'm subject to letting loose and the guys, they understand that and they allow me to.

Ten years ago, the world outside the Keith and the Jewell Dominions really didn't know much about steel guitars being played in the church. Now there are videos, CDs, and you're playing to audiences outside the church. Do you think all this has been a good thing? Has there been any kind of backlash in the church?

In the beginning, yes, because the church had a strict issue about playing *outside* the church as well as *for* the church. They felt you'd be greatly influenced by it. You can't serve two masters, if you will. For a while, I was in that frame of mind as well. But thanks to Bob Stone for coming and discovering us and hooking us up with Arhoolie Records, I actually feel now that we're doing what our church teaches. That's to go out and spread good news and glad tidings to the people.

A lot of people won't come to the church because of the preaching so we're actually taking the music to them. That's the new wave going through the church now.

I understand Jim Campilongo the country/jazz guitar player from San Francisco was so moved by your performances he found himself a church to attend where he now plays at services.

Oh, man! Yeah! A beautiful guy, too. He does some steel stuff on the lead guitar that blows me away. He's beautiful, man. That's the type of experience we're running into. Different guys come to the show and say, "Wow, this is nice!" So we say, "You can also come by the church and if you're a player, bring your instrument." We had a guy this past Sunday – he's from Italy. He brought his guitar and started playing with us. That's where our playing has evolved. I give a lot of credit back to Bob and Arhoolie for getting the word out there.

When I play, it's mainly for other people. I don't play for *my* pleasure. But I am enjoying myself, if that makes sense.

Are there kids coming up in the church who are taking up the steel?

All the time. This is a farming ground that will always be. My nephew, Carl Campbell is learning to play. I've got a cousin, Jason Haygood – he's learning to play. Down south, a guy named Kashia

Hunter is learning too. There are some even younger who have the interest in playing. I try to explain to them as much as I can that you have to be a student of it and you must love it. If you don't, it's gonna be hard to accomplish what the great guys have been able to do.

- ¤ -

Aubrey Ghent

Aubrey Ghent's congregation is likely to refer to him as "doubly blessed." An Elder in Nashville's Keith Dominion Holiness Pentecostal Church, Ghent is as widely recognized in the church community for his rafter-rocking preaching abilities, as his fiery lap steel improvisations.

A Florida native, Elder Ghent is the nephew of Sacred Steel pioneer, Willie Eason, and the son of Henry Nelson whose playing was extremely influential within the church. The astonishing fluidity of Ghent's steel playing - often on a 6-string Fender Studio Deluxe - puts him on a short list of masters of the instrument. Within the sacred steel community, his peers recognize him as a virtuoso of the genre.

- ¤ Aubrey Ghent ¤ -

Secular listeners have described his approach to this traditional Hawaiian instrument as sounding like Aretha Franklin. Like the best improvisations of jazz guitar great, Wes Montgomery, there can be an almost palpable sense of having "survived" one of Aubrey's musical tornados of "praise music." He is quietly proud of his abilities and grateful for the opportunity to share his message with a wider, secular audience.

How did the steel guitar become part of the Keith Dominion Holiness Pentecostal Church?

Steel guitar in the church, at least the Gospel style the way we usually play it, originated with my uncle, Willie Eason. Willie was from Augusta, Georgia and later moved to Philadelphia. He connected with one of the church's bishops, J.R. Lockley, and started traveling with Bishop Lockley, whose diocese was on the west coast of Florida. That's where Willie did a lot of his playing in the infancy of the House of God Church. Willie would play on the street corners and in tent revivals and that's how the steel began to develop and migrate throughout the coast. Willie's brother actually learned to play from a Hawaiian.

What's the role of the steel guitar in the church's music?

The role of the steel is to take the lead part in the band for the church services. When the congregation finishes the song, the steel guitar picks it up and rolls with it. Therefore, you have to have a pretty attentive, skilled, steel guitarist who really knows how to follow as well as take the lead. They have to know the song and have a good ear.

What do you think the sound of the steel guitar brings to the congregation? It's a much different sound from that of the organ, which many people associate with Gospel music.

In the House of God Church, the people have gotten used to the steel guitar carrying a sound that imitates the human voice. They seem to become excited over that sound - the different voice-like qualities of the strings and how they sound in relationship to the human voice. It's like folks who go to festivals, or go to hear bands in the secular world. They've come to expect that sound over the last seventy or so years through the generations and they look for that special sound of the steel. The most exciting and popular players in the House of God are the steel players.

How did you come to play the steel guitar?

Well, my first instrument was a regular Spanish guitar. I had heard Willie Eason and the other players in the church. I elevated the strings and used a different type of string to give me the steel effect. I did that at the age of nine. Later on, at about age eleven, I acquired a Hawaiian steel that my grandfather bought for me.

Did you spend any time with secular music?

I did have a chance to play in my high school's jazz band. That was basically as secular as I've ever played.

- ¤ Aubrey Ghent ¤ -

What type of steel do you play today and what tunings do you use?

I would love to get my hands on another Fender, but right now I'm playing a Sho-Bud. I use Dobro tuning – what the old-time musicians used to call a Vestapol tuning. It's a tonic tuning. Some of the other players adopted E9th tuning, C7th tuning and so on, but I've been using this tuning for years. I pitch it to A or G usually. I've used a regular old Stevens bar since I was 11 years old.

Aubrey Ghent's Tuning						
Strings	1	2	3	4	5	6
G major	D	B	G	D	B	G

Have you ever played pedal steel?

I played pedal steel about 20 years ago, but my main interest has remained the regular lap steel because a lot of our younger people were getting pedal steels and I wanted to remain with the old school because I knew I could develop it so much. I felt if I could master that and display it that it would impress (laughs).

You have so much emotion and energy in your playing, as well as an amazing ability to improvise on the instrument. Did it all come easily or did you have to work very hard at it?

I had to work at it. It's really just like anything else, like a craftsman has to work at the skill they're trying to perfect. It's the same way for steel playing. You listen to other players and you try to work at getting it as perfected as you can and it doesn't come overnight. It takes a few years to get it to where there are less mistakes (laughs).

Did you listen to any secular music for inspiration or were all of your influences from the church?

Actually, most, if not all, of my influences came from the church. As I got older, I started paying attention as far as style and perfection to a lot of players, including secular players, but I learned and developed the church style.

There are few players who can play an exciting, hot solo then turn around and play a hymn that moves people the way you do.

Gee, thank you. I participated a week ago in church services with a group of folks who were hearing me for the first time. They were so amazed that they were almost speechless at the tone as well as the sound you can develop from a bar on strings.

What are you thinking about when you improvise?

Well, you formulate from the chords. If you play independently of others, you're gonna have to chord as well as solo – with each string doing different things in the solo. Some players use more chording than single strings but we're coming to the point that a lot of players who're coming after us have begun to do a whole lot of single string playing. I'm one of the younger pioneers, but I've been playing over thirty years.

- ¤   Aubrey Ghent   ¤ -

The liner notes to your Arhoolie CD quote you as saying you wanted your steel to sound like a female opera singer. Do you listen to singers for inspiration?

That was about the best way I could describe it at the time. I listen frequently to Mahalia Jackson. From the time I was a youngster, I've attended symphonies where opera singers were involved and, of course, I've tried imitating those sounds. But basically, the sound of Gospel singers like Mahalia and the singers from the Caravan - I don't know if you remember the old *Caravan Gospel Singers* – influenced me the most. Aretha Franklin too - I especially liked her rendition of Amazing Grace.

You're as well known for your preaching as your steel playing. Has the steel guitar had to take something of a back seat as you've gained more responsibility in the church?

There was a time when I thought it would take a back seat to my ministry but, for the last few years, I've been playing as much as I preach – probably equally.

Prior to 1992, the world outside the Keith and Jewel Dominions really knew nothing about your use of steel guitar in the church. Now, there have been festival appearances, CDs, and even a documentary video. Has all this public attention been a good thing?

Well, I think it brought a good thing to light. There are some in the church who disagree. They feel that it's indeed a sacred thing and that it belongs solely in the church and should not be taken outside. I think it's been hidden long enough and the bursting open of a new style of playing steel guitar should be spread.

It's certainly enriched the lives of many people including those whom you haven't met and may never meet.

That's why I'm here.

Is there anything you'd like to do with the steel guitar that you haven't yet accomplished?

I would actually like to take the style to the *Grand Old Opry* here in Nashville. That's where I would like to introduce the style of playing. I think it would reach a wider audience and inspire them that there's another style of steel playing besides the bluegrass or country style. So that's my goal and I think I'm close.

- ¤ -

172

CAJUN MUSIC

Cajun music has a long and complex heritage rooted in medieval France. The exiled Acadians in Louisiana intermarried with other ethnic groups, evolving into a new ethnic group called the Cajuns. During the 1920s and 1930s, Cajuns experienced a period of increased americanization, prompted largely by the discovery of oil in Louisiana, as well as the construction of new highways.

In addition to its French heritage, Cajun music was also influenced by the music of the Creoles of African descent. While the accordion was the primary instrument of Cajun music, Cajun bands added the steel guitar, bass, drums, and even banjos and mandolins to their lineup. By the late 1940s, however, the accordion again dominated Cajun music.

Though it's unclear who first introduced lap-style guitar playing into Cajun music, the Hackberry Ramblers, led by brothers Lonnie and Floyd Rainwater, are among the first Cajun bands to record with the instrument. The group formed in 1930 and began recording in 1935.

While today, it has been largely supplanted by the pedal steel, throughout the 1940s and 1950s the lap steel guitar was a familiar sight on Louisiana bandstands. Ann Allen Savoy's excellent book, *Cajun Music: A Reflection of a People,* features many archival photographs showing non-pedal steel players who include: Jack Brock, Lonnie Rainwater, Dusty Rhodes, Atlas Fruge', R.C. Vanicour, Rodney Miller, Claude Sonnier, and Dick Richard.

Papa Cairo

Among the best known Cajun steelers was Julius Angelle Lamparez – better known as Papa Cairo. Unlike many Cajun musicans, Cairo took music lessons as a child, learning to read and write formal music notation. He turned professional at age fourteen as part of the trio, the *Daylight Creepers, and* later joined the *Louisiana Rounders,* among other bands.

Cairo was ubiquitous on the Cajun scene of the late 1940s & 1950s, contributing to Chuck Guillory's 1949 hit single *Big Texas* as well as records by Rufus Thibodeaux, Harry Choates, Ernest Tubb, and Doug Kershaw, one of the most commercially successful Cajun performers. His style was the most swing-influenced of the pre-pedal era of Cajun steel guitarists.

- ¤ -

Shirley Bergeron

Shirley Bergeron

Singer and steel guitarist Shirley Bergeron recorded largely with his father, accordionist Alphee Bergeron, and their backup band, the *Veteran Playboys*. Shirley made his recording debut in 1957 with two songs at a radio session and then spent most of the 1960s doing singles for the small Lanor label. His 1962 single, *French Rocking Boogie,* fused the traditional Cajun sound with rock & roll. Shirley Bergeron died in 1996.

- ¤ -

Clarence "Junior" Martin

Clarence "Junior" Martin

Junior Martin is recognized by his peers as a master of the pedal and non-pedal steel guitar in traditional Cajun music. His use of bar bouncing coupled with pick blocking technique works well for the fast pace and note flurries characteristic of the Cajun style. He has been a sideman to many leaders over the years, most notably accordionist Jo-El Sonier. A master craftsman, Junior is as well known in Cajun music circles for his superbly crafted, custom Cajun accordions as his steel guitar prowess.

- ¤ Clarence "Junior" Martin ¤ -

How did you come to play steel guitar?

Well, when I was a child growing up, my family were all accordion players and that's what I wanted to be – an accordion player. So I picked $25 of cotton during one week and I told my uncle at the end of the week that I wanted to go see about buying me an accordion. He said okay but when we got on the way goin' we were listening to country music and he said, "Listen to that - the steel guitar is so popular that five years from now there won't be one accordion left. You need to learn how to play steel." So, it sounded pretty what I was hearin' and I changed my mind. We started lookin' at accordions and they were $27.50 and the steel guitar was $25. I came back home with a 6-string lap steel guitar. No legs, nothing. You just put it on your lap. It was a Harmony guitar.

I played on that for about six months and then kind of improved to a little better guitar called a Fender. It cost $33. I played on that one for a long time playing dance jobs. It was much better. I wish I still had the first one but I got rid of it, not knowing at that age it would have been nice to keep the original steel that I learned on.

Fenders are versatile guitars.

Even when I bought a new one – a double neck 8-string with no pedals - it was still a Fender. It had the small humbucking pickups. I played on Fender for a long time. I played that for probably three or four years before I went to the pedal steel. It didn't have the rods, it had cables and it didn't work too good. I finally went to Emmons and Sho-Bud and the pedals worked much better on those.

How did you move from a kid learning the instrument to starting to play professionally?

I listened to records and this guy played that I could hear every Saturday. This guy would tune my steel and I'd watch him all night long and listen to the records learning one song at a time. If I have any good advice to give anybody that's learning how to play, not only steel guitar but *any* instrument, it's learn one song as good as you can so you really sound professional on that *one* song. Once you do that, the rest of it is really easy. A lot of songs relate to others. If you try to learn a bunch of songs at one time – a little piece of one song, a little piece of another song – you'll only slow your learning.

Who were your early influences on the steel guitar?

The one that inspired me the most was Rodney Miller. He's still playing. Dick Richard was the one that I watched a lot. Dick was a real good player at that time. Dick is in an old folks home now and he's paralyzed on his right side. Rodney Miller was much younger, a little older than me. He played the steel, fiddle and guitar. He kind of set the pace for steel guitar players. The style he had, everybody wanted to learn.

What was unique about the way Rodney played?

His open string work. He played more open strings than the other steel players. Dick Richard didn't play open strings much. It was just a different style.

Did you listen to Papa Cairo, probably the most famous Cajun steeler of the '40s and '50s?

I did, and I liked a lot of what he did but it wasn't my style 'cause it was a 6th tuning, either C6th or A6th. It's kind of swing stuff he played. I can play a little bit of that style but it's not what I like to play.

- ¤ Clarence "Junior" Martin ¤ -

What tunings did you use then and what non-pedal tunings do you use today?

It was a G tuning which is still what I use. At that time, the C accordion was more popular which made you play with a G open tuning. It's still the most popular tuning today.

The standard Dobro tuning?

Dobro tuning is D, B, G, D ,B, D. The steel guitar tuning we play for Cajun music is G ,D, B, G ,D, B all the way up. On a 6-string, it was G, D, B, G, D, G. But now, on the 10-string steel guitars, it's G, D, B all the way up - all major.

Clarence Junior Martin's Tunings										
Strings	1	2	3	4	5	6	7	8	9	10
G major	G	D	B	G	D	G				
G major	G	D	B	G	D	B	G	D	B	G

Beyond the tuning, what makes Cajun-style steel guitar different from other styles?

Bouncing the bar and a type of a picking called a pick blocking technique. You start off by picking a string and going up. You start with your fingers on the string all the time the way I pick. When you go back down the strings, the pick is what mutes the string not the palm of the hand like a lot of players. They mute with the palm of the hand. Not me, I'm using the picks.

Is pick blocking something that came naturally to you or did you put a lot of practice time into it?

No, it was something that came natural to me. I knew I picked different than other people but I didn't know what it was called 'til I went to school in Nashville to learn how to play country music. I learned speed picking and that's when Paul Franklin told me, "Did you know that you pick block?" He said that even as a kid nobody could understand his picking technique. He said, "You're playing Cajun music by pick blocking so all you have to do is bring that over to country music." It was much easier once I understood what he was talking about.

What kind of bar do you use?

It's a BJS bar. They made me a special bar about 15 to 20 years ago. I bought one of their regular bars for E9th, for country and I had a bar that was made by my son-in-law that was stainless steel but it didn't have the best sound. When they saw what I was playing they said, "Why don't you let us make you a bar? We'll call it the *Junior Martin Cajun Bar*. It's going to cost $85 but since we enjoy your playing so much we're gonna give you this bar." They made it to my specifications. They drilled out the back to take some weight out of it because we bounce the bar around so much that you don't want it too heavy. It's tapered on the right and left and it has special chrome. That's what I've used all these years. It's a great bar. I *love* it.

- ¤ Clarence "Junior" Martin ¤ -

What do you think is the hardest aspect of learning to play steel guitar?

Probably the left hand is the hardest thing to master. You can pick with the right hand and do decently but that left hand is so critical. Any good player doesn't watch the right hand; they watch the left hand all the time. The tone comes from the left hand. Of course, the pick blocking is important to keep it clean. If you can't mute it clean, you're gonna be muddy and sound terrible. Some people are good muting with the palm of their hand. I wasn't fast enough so I had to find another way.

What's the role of the steel in a Cajun band? Do you have to try to stay out of the accordion's register?

It's different than country. You play pretty much *with* the accordion. In country music, you stay out of the way of the singer or the other instruments that are playing lead. Not Cajun music. It's like all five members on the bandstand are playing at the same time. You play all the time in a Cajun band, you don't hold back.

Are you doubling the melody with the accordion?

Sometimes it's melody, sometimes it's just improvising – kind of like a riff you're playing behind him.

Is most of your playing today on a pedal steel?

When I play Cajun music with a Cajun band, I don't play the pedals that much. If you play with an accordion player that has a Bb or Ab or F# accordion – weird keys – we play the pedals on that because we have to. We can't find a place for the capo. If I'm playing with a band I'm not familiar with, I find out what key he's going to play in and I tune my open strings to that. On my double-neck it's tuned for Cajun music and I use a capo – whatever it takes to make it sound Cajun.

You're refering to your pedal steel guitar?

Yeah. This is a pedal steel guitar that I made the body for myself. I make steel guitar bodies for a company called Pedalmaster, owned by Roy Thomas. This particular steel guitar that I made is a beautiful thing. It's all gold-plated. I made the body out of birdseye maple mixed with zebrawood.

Do you still play gigs on lap steel?

Oh yes. I have a lap steel that I made. I bought the pickups and hardware from EMCI Steel Guitar Company and I made the body myself. It has ten strings. It can be used as a Dobro or as a lap steel. It's based on this guy who invented an electric Dobro that's made with a cat food can - a 35-cent cat food can used for a resonator. His name was Mars. About fifteen years ago, he came out with this resonator electric guitar. It has the same sound as a Dobro. We took one apart to see how it was made. It's amazing.

Ironically, considering how your uncle steered you away from accordion to steel guitar, you make most of your living as a master accordion builder.

Yes, that's my main job. I get to play 'em a little bit now. I'm not a great player. Because I work on 'em so much I know 'em by heart; every note in every key, backwards and forwards. It's a lot of fun.

- ¤ Clarence "Junior" Martin ¤ -

It's fun to work on a steel guitar too. I used to buy a new steel probably every two years. Since I got this new one, my wife doesn't want me to get rid of it being it's gold-plated. She says you can get another one but you're not getting' rid of this one (laughs).

Tell me about some of the musicians you've played with.

My first band that I played with was Adams Hebert. It was popular and made a lot of good songs. I played with him for a couple of years and my uncle, he was also with Adams Hebert, and we started a band of our own for a couple of years.

From there, I moved to the big bands. I was getting pretty good. I played with probably the best big band, Laurence Walker. Rodney Miller, the guy that I liked so much was playing with him before and he moved on to play with Aldus Roger. I played with Walter Mouton and Aldus Roger.

I played with Jo-El Sonier every night for seven years. Jo-El is about five years younger than me. As a kid he was so advanced. When he moved to Nashville, we stayed in touch. He has about twelve of my accordions.

I played a lot of country music with Joe Douglas for twenty years. Toward the end, it was more Cajun than anything. I've played a lot of the steel guitar conventions.

I play with a band called *Fatras*. After they pay the musicians, they donate all the money they make to needy organizations. They're not great players but they're great people. They're having fun out there.

Music has been important. I didn't depend on it for a living, but Cajun music has been part of me for all these years.

You've developed a special friendship with Lucky Oceans, who was the first steel player for *Asleep at the Wheel*.

Lucky and I have become good friends. He came down to my shop about ten years ago wanting to learn how to play Cajun music on steel guitar. I gave him about a 3-hour lesson and I didn't see him again for about 6 years. He moved to Australia and then came back down here a couple of years later and he had gotten to be so good at Cajun music it's unbelievable. Now he's got a band in Australia that plays zydeco and Cajun music. When he comes, he stays with me. He gives me lessons on country and I give him some on Cajun music. He's got a little lap steel and he plays with all those bands around here.

Steve Riley of the *Mamou Playboys* went to Australia and I asked him if he knew Lucky. He said, "He sat in with us every night." Steve had Roddie Romero playing lead guitar and after Lucky played one ride on the steel, Roddie wouldn't play again (laughs).

The last time he came to my shop we had every steel guitar player in South Louisiana and Texas – 135 people came and we had a big black pot of jambalaya and we cooked for all those people. It lasted from 6 at night to 1 a.m. We had about twenty-five good steel guitar players, playing country and Cajun music. We're lookin' to do this again.

- ¤ -

ROCK & ROLL

The musician sitting at the crossroads, playing all manner of spine-tingling moans, tremolos, and shivers from a guitar played bottleneck-style is an American cliché. Nevertheless, the contributions of early blues musicians like Robert Johnson, and lap-style guitar, Black Ace remain indelible and form the palimpsest on which much of rock & roll was written.

A postwar Chicago blues scene without the magnificent contributions of Muddy Waters is absolutely unimaginable. From the late 1940s on, he eloquently defined the city's aggressive, swaggering, Delta-rooted sound with his declamatory vocals and piercing slide-guitar attack. In the world of country music, Hank Williams and the western swing of Bob Wills, along with thousands of other better or lesser known combos, melded country music with the blues to help kick-start the revolution known as rock & roll.

Bill Haley's first band, *The Saddlemen,* ultimately became the very first wildly popular rock & roll band in history - *The Comets.* With Al Rex on bass, Billy Williamson on steel guitar, and Johnny Grande playing piano and accordion, Haley fronted the group wearing a ten-gallon Stetson covering his trademark curl, a hair style he developed to take attention away from his blind eye.

The Starlight Wranglers, Scotty Moore's band before Elvis, featured non-pedal steel player, Millard Yow. Yet despite this early visibility, by the late 50s, the lap steel was largely passé in most rock music. Its last gasp likely was Santo & Johnny's landmark recording of *Sleepwalk.*

David Lindley is the musician most responsible for re-introducing lap-style guitar into rock music in the 1970s. His playing on Jackson Browne's early recordings introduced a generation of lap steelers to the magic of the instrument. The re-popularization of non-pedal steel has slowly grown over the years. Today, steel guitar can be heard in rockabilly bands, country rock bands, surf bands, and many other roots-oriented rock sub-genres.

Santo & Johnny

Santo & Johnny

As composers and performers of *Sleepwalk*, likely the best known steel guitar instrumental of all time, Santo and Johnny Farina hold a special place in steel guitar history. Born in Brooklyn, New York, Santo on steel and Johnny on standard guitar, played together from childhood. By 1955, they were local favorites at clubs, variety shows, and teen dances. *Sleepwalk,* co-written with their sister, Ann, was recorded in 1959 and became a number one hit. The song has enjoyed a second career in hundreds of movies and commercials. The brothers had several other chart hits into 1964. Over the course of their career, Santo & Johnny recorded over 40 albums. Santo's treble-dominated Fender Stringmaster tone and simple, melodic style connected with listeners and years later, seems to evoke a more innocent era. Johnny Farina continues today as an active musician on both guitar and steel.

- ¤ -

David Lindley

Musician's musician is a term often bandied about, but, in the case of multi-instrumentalist David Lindley, it's an understatement. World music pioneer, first-call sideman to the cream of the crop of rock & folk performers, bandleader, lap steel stylist and master of multiple ethinic instruments, composer, performer on film and television scores – Lindley's done it all.

A native of Southern California, David's skill on banjo and fiddle, while still a teenager, enabled him to win the *Topanga Canyon Banjo and Fiddle Competition* five times. After his work in folk-influenced bands like the *Dry City Scat Band* and the visionary group, *Kaleidoscope* in the 1960s, Lindley turned to rock music as the guiding force behind Jackson Browne's recordings and concert performances for most of the 1970s. From 1981 to 1990, he practically re-defined the word eclectic in three albums with *El Rayo-X* , his innovative band that covered rock, ska, reggae, Tex-Mex, surf, New Orleans first line, and everything in between. His lap steel playing with *El Rayo-X*, using vintage Rickenbacher

- ¤ David Lindley ¤ -

or National lap steels, was hugely influential, as was his re-discovery of the koa wood Weissenborn Hawaiian guitars of the 1920s.

His instantly identifiable, melodic playing on myriad string instruments has graced albums by Bob Dylan, Dolly Parton, Rod Stewart, Linda Ronstadt, Rory Block, Ry Cooder, Warren Zevon, James Taylor, the Pahinui Brothers, Emmylou Harris, David Crosby, and Graham Nash, to name just a few out of hundreds.

The 1990s saw Lindley collaborating with avante-garde guitarist Henry Kaiser on recordings in Madagascar and Norway, as well as touring as a duo with percussionists Hani Naser and Wally Ingram. He also dropped his major label affiliation and began to self-produce and distribute his recordings. Lindley continues to play selected sessions and film scores, tour with Wally Ingram, and showcase the lap steel guitar in his live performances and recordings.

What are your earliest memories of listening to music?

The *Griller String Quartet* used to rehearse at my grandmother's house. My uncle used to accompany them. I would sit under the piano and, sometimes, I would put my skull against the soundboard which was wonderful when my uncle was playing. It would totally scramble my brain.

I was probably three or four and I can remember looking at the strings and the tailpieces and they were gigantic, and of course, the cello was huge. I remember looking inside the piano and seeing all the strings. I just loved the way they looked. That got me interested. "Can kids do this? Oh, yeah, of course."

Who were some of the other musicians who first inspired you?

I had access to my dad's record collection and he had records by Andre's Segovia, Carlos Montoya, and later on, I remember him getting a Sabicas album. Of course I liked rock & roll – especially the guitar player that played with Rick Nelson, who was James Burton. I just loved the sound of that guitar and said "Oh, boy is this good! Why does he sound different?" The slinky strings and all that stuff - I had no idea about string gauges or anything. I also liked Duane Eddy and players like that.

My dad had Udai Shankar 78's so I heard the Sitar and the Vina and he had Greek records too. He had reams of stuff and he would always be buying them and he played them all the time so I would hear them. My brother started studying piano when he was six. I would hear Wanda Landowska on the Harpsichord all the time – *the Well Tempered Clavier*. Too much harpsichord can get to you after a while, even Wanda, as good as she was. It was the cage of flies. All through the walls I could hear it. I used to know the *Brandenburg Concertos* just about note-for-note in my head.

What was your first instrument?

I started on a baritone Ukulele. My dad had a little ukulele and I used to mess around with that. I borrowed an old Lyon & Healey guitar from a friend of mine. It had bad strings and was hard to play. My dad saw I was interested so he and my uncle went down to Bernardo's Guitar Shop in east LA and bought a Mexican guitar.

- ¤ David Lindley ¤ -

I'd go to this music store in Pasadena where Jim Keltner was the drum teacher and I would play every guitar on the shelf if I could. It just kind of accelerated from that. There was a club in Arcadia called the *Cat's Pajamas* and there was this guy named Mike McClellan who knew all kinds of stuff and I took some lessons from him. He gave me two or three lessons and, from then on, I learned how to steal stuff by watching.

How did you first investigate lap style playing?

I was in a bluegrass band and we had a Dobro player. At first, it was Pete Madlum who was a really fine Dobro player and he would play different styles. There's a group called the *Six and Seven-Eighths String Band of New Orleans* and they played string Dixieland. The slide was like the trombone and the clarinet was taken by the mandolin. Doc Souchon was the guitar player; FDR's favorite band. So, we would listen to these records and Pete learned to play like that and it was different than a lot of the Dobro players that I had seen in bluegrass bands, like Leroy McNeece and Uncle Josh.

I liked that approach and there were also some other players around at the time. Being a 5-string banjo and fiddle player, I would be able to watch all this stuff. As I'd step back from the microphone they'd step up and then I would *watch.* I learned a lot that way - by that ability to steal stuff by watching someone play. I could figure it out by watching them and retain it.

Who was the first person you heard playing an overdriven electric lap steel sound?

I heard Freddie Roulette one night at the Albion Ballroom. I was upstairs in the dressing room and I heard this guy crank up and I said, "Holy shit! What's that?" I ran downstairs and saw what he was playing and said, "Yeah, I know what one of *those* is." That was it – the beginning of the end.

You play a lot of different instruments. What do lap-style guitars allow you to bring to the music?

Lap steel or Weissenborn' you have to play 'em differently because the electric's sustain will pile up if you play 'em in a certain way – at least the tone that I use. The electric approach was more or less a vocal approach. That's how I went at it. The acoustic approach is something else – more of a piano or a harpsichord that slides.

You get a tremendous dynamic range out of your acoustic Weissenborn-style instruments.

Oh, it's just amazing how a hardwood or semi-hardwood top as opposed to a spruce top made it possible to do all kinds of things - the rhythmic stuff that you can do with that. I used to hear all different ways of playing that instrument and then I figured out that you can play claw hammer guitar stuff on a Weissenborn. Why not? It's limited, there are only certain things you can do, but it's limited in the same way that an oud is limited. It opens up other things.

How many different instruments do you play?

Oh, God … seven or eight.

Is there anything with strings on it that foxed you - that you just walked away from or said, forget it?

I had to stop playing pedal steel because that's *all* I would do and I wouldn't play any of the other instruments that I really liked. I wouldn't play any fiddle and then I got rusty on it so I kinda had to stop. Every once in a while I think about going back and learning it. I'm in the middle of the Oud right now and I think that's what I'm going to stick with for a while. The techniques are *so* difficult. It has a really short neck and no frets. You have to play it like an ant. You have to be aware that instead of 13 tones to the octave you now have 42. It's a completely different musical system.

Did you ever practice formal steel guitar technique like palm and pick blocking?

Yeah, I did. In fact, the first time I ever saw behind-the-bar [*bending*] stuff was Mayne Smith who played Dobro in a band that I was in with Richard Greene. A great Dobro player.

Do you use a bullet bar?

No, I don't. I use a Stevens with a thumb pick and three finger picks. I use a bullet bar when I play pedal steel. I'm making my own bar now. I found a gunsmith who has all of these old ends of barrels. The guy has got all kinds of machines and this fabulous, really heavy stainless steel and different degrees of it. It's just the best steel ever so, if you get a bar out of that stuff, it'll sustain forever.

With all the instruments you play, string gauges must be a pretty big deal.

Yes! [*I carry*] Not only an assortment of strings for all the instruments, but also in the cases themselves. Some of these things – like a saz – you have to pre-make the strings or use extra long banjo strings. Same with the bouzouki. I have a string deal with D'Addario who seem to make the best strings for everything. The quality of the winding on the guitar strings - especially on the Weissenborn - where you're gonna play with a steel, lasts a long time.

Many of the players I've interviewed name you as a key influence. They often mention how incredible your intonation is. Is this something you had to work at?

I kind of played until it sounded right. I can remember listening to myself – like on the Jackson Browne video – I'm playing consistently sharp during one period. Every note was sharp. It was some kind of Doppler from where the microphone was or something. I always tried to play it in tune. I would do it as a combination of looking at it and listening at the same time.

You managed to do it on high-energy, up-tempo music as well as the slower stuff. That's the challenge.

Now my ears are shot. We played *really* loud. My ears have been worn a little bit more than I would like. Ear protection is a big thing – especially for an instrument that has no frets or that you play with a slide. Also when you sing and you play a slide instrument, it's gotta be there. I think every musician my age and a lot of the guys from the grunge era who played super, super, super loud got nerve damage. There's a difference between the kind of hearing problems that are just from loud music than when you get into hissing and ringing and all that. It's a different thing. You can learn to ignore it even though it's always there. I know it's ringing now but I don't hear it if I'm not listening for it.

Do you try to avoid wearing headphones on sessions?

I wear headphones like I always did. I just don't listen to it as loud as I used to.

- ¤ David Lindley ¤ -

Your sound, both on acoustic as well as electric, is pretty much instantly recognizable. How hard do you think it is to cultivate an individual sound?

It's one of those things that you get if you play all the time; you play a certain way. Also people have been hearing my stuff for a long time. I started playing in the 1970s so there's thirty years of Lindley, in tune, out of tune, what have you.

That whole thing with the overdriven amplifier with the lap steel, I can remember I was sitting in the dressing room of the Avalon with Duane Allman when I was with *Kaleidoscope*. Us, the *Allman Brothers*, and I think, Charlie Musselwhite all shared the bill. A guy came in with a lap steel and Duane got up and went for it at the same time I got up and went for it. It was one of those things like a baseball bat, you know? You put one hand over the other. We did that and he put his hand on the top of the peg head and won. So he checked it out. It was a little Fender; a nice one. He was playing in the dressing room then he handed it to me and the same thing dawned at the same time - you can play this thing with a bottleneck *and* you can put it into an amp and turn it up really high. I can remember that moment and man! The first time I plugged a National into an amp it was just like the Ampeg reverb-a-rocket and I went "Oh, boy, is this good!"

The Bakelite Rickenbachers were pretty much passé by the late 1960s except for a hard-core group of Hawaiian players who had always appreciated them.

That's right, but there were country players too. There were people that would still play that style along with the Hawaiian players - the Jerry Byrd 7-string Bakelite thing. And there were a couple of guys in Texas who played 7-strings and did all the pedal effects behind the bar. One guy in particular - Blackie Taylor told me about this guy - he said, "This guy is the best you'll ever hear and he uses really light strings so he can bend 'em behind the bar and he bends two strings at once and does all this stuff." It was really an eye-opener. The trick to doing that is you have to work out your fingertips like a Kung Fu master if you bend 'em behind the bar and then slide the thing up 'cause it's like a razor blade. You gotta be tough!

Jerry Byrd used to use the same gauge for the first three strings to get that super smooth sound.

(Laughs). Of course! That's so good. With as many unwound strings as possible he'd get that beautiful thing going where you don't get any sizzle. The dynamics of the Rickenbacher and the Nationals, Supros – things like that – it's another world entirely.

Have you retired the Rick sound from your musical arsenal?

No, I've been playing them. When I play with the *Blind Boys of Alabama* I use that sound. I play a Supro. It's kind of a similar set-up where the strings go through a [*magnetic*] field. The Supros have a plate that goes over the top of the strings.

How did you get into pedal steel?

Blackie Taylor had a double-neck and on one neck he had a guitar neck with frets. The bottom one was just regular pedal steel. You played the first two pedals and instead of going up to the four chord it would go down into the five chord. He did it just the reverse. I said, "You can do *that*?" "Oh, Yeah, you can tune these things to whatever you want." Oh, boy!" Then that started this whole thing off with the pedal steel.

- ¤ David Lindley ¤ -

You were one of the musicians who caught on early to the recording properties of inexpensive instruments like those with microphonic pickups.

The main one was the Danelectro. That was a particularly unique sound. First of all, to get a Reggae guitar scratch sound, it's real important that you have something that will do the real super high end because for a lot of the rhythm stuff, you don't press the string down on the frets, you just kind of approximate it. There's no dampening thing. You just kind of press it down then you go to the next chord and kind of press it down. Meanwhile you're scratching with the pick. And for a lot of that sound, since I played banjo, I was familiar with how banjos react and a Danelectro was closer to a banjo than a guitar, that's why I liked 'em.

Your 1980's band, El Rayo-X covered reggae, ska, Tex-Mex, rock & roll, and just about everything else. How did that band come about?

El Rayo-X – the first one – was like studio musicians except for Baboo and Ian Wallace. I didn't have a bass player then. I did a lot of that myself. It's fun to do that too. It's me times three sometimes – hey! There's three of me now! I always liked the early reggae stuff like the *Pioneers*, the *Greyhounds*, the *Rudy's, Desmond Decker and the Aces,* and the early *Toots and the Maytals* – all that stuff.

I was living in England at the time when the *Skatalites* were playing. In '69, '70 and '71 I was in England and the whole skinhead thing was going on. I loved reggae music and ska and I thought, "Boy! This is just good stuff!" [*Imitates English accent*] "Wait – Lindley, you're not supposed to go in that place there. They won't like it." Fuck that! I'd go into this Jamaican bar across from the recording studios and play the jukebox. I remember going there with Jackson [*Browne*]. "You gotta hear this stuff! Check out Desmond Decker and these are the *Israelites*." We'd go nuts. And since we were fans and we weren't British, they left us alone (laughs). We could have easily *died* and they wouldn't have found us for a week.

I heard Cajun music at the same time for the first time and said "You can put this Cajun fiddle over top of a ska tune easily." It worked great, and in fact, it's probably what people were listening to on the radio down there in Jamaica and Haiti and the Dominican Republic. They'd hear all these radio stations from New Orleans. That whole area has big radio stations that blast. You have something about the Gulf of Mexico from the tip of Florida all the way around to the Yucatan and with everything that's in there, something happens and it's all *good*. You hear Vera Cruz harp music, you hear real Cajun stuff and you hear all the Tex-Mex and it's just all wonderful stuff and it's all similar. And when it comes down to it, it's all just music and the only thing that makes it a little different is texture and interpretation and that's about it.

How much of your "go for broke" lap steel solos – like on Brother John with El Rayo-X - are improvised? Did you work that stuff out or just turn up the amp and go?

After we learned it, we could take it wherever we wanted and then there were certain passages and lines that would signal that we were gonna go do something and I always liked that approach: "Okay, guys, listen for this riff – here it is – after we do this then we go into this next thing."

I tried to keep it different every night, as different as possible. One reason is to entertain myself and the other reason is so it wouldn't sound all the same.

You've been almost single-handedly responsible for renewed interest in the hollow-necked Weissenborn Hawaiian guitars of the 1920s. How did you first hear these instruments?

- ¤ David Lindley ¤ -

I had first seen them when I was teaching at the music store in Pasadena when I was about nineteen years old. Across the hall in one of the studios was a [*solid neck*] Kona. I'd been used to hearing Dobros and stuff so I checked this thing out and it was great. Ooh, boy! Lockmiller and Connor - these two guys that played at the Ice House - well, Jim Connor had a [*Martin*] 000-45 that he had set up like a Hawaiian guitar and he played the *shit* out of it. It had a huge sound and bass which a Dobro didn't have. Some little voice inside said, "Remember this. Make a note of this."

The second time I saw somebody do that it was James Burton. He played a Harmony. He'd put a Hawaiian nut on it and played Dobro stuff and it was beautiful. He has a wonderful style with beautiful tone and approach to it. Then that same little voice said, "Remember this too."

I first got hold of a Weissenborn and I said, "This is even *better* because it's got a hollow neck and it sounds louder than anything I've ever heard." So I started playin' that, got hold of a Sunrise pickup, put it in the soundhole and that was that.

What tunings do you use - are they all enharmonic variations on Open E tuning?

Yeah, a lot of it, especially when I was playing with Jackson, was in open E. Essentially, just a [*Spanish guitar*] first position E chord. I'd tune it to E to F to G and to A sometimes on a Rickenbacher. You'd have to change the first string every night 'cause it'd break. With the E tuning I used to raise the 3rd and use the 2nd fret as a base position. You'd get this minor 7th, a beautiful sound, and then you could play all kinds of different things on there. Then I got into a C tuning which was the tuning that Leo Kottke used on his 12-string, with a *3rd* on the top and the tonic on the bottom. I use that a lot. Starting at the bottom, it's C-G-C-G-C-E. And then of course, there are other variations of that and standard Dobro tuning.

Do you feel that your steel guitar playing suffers from your spending time playing other instruments?

Not really. They kind of compliment each other. You play the saz [*Turkish string instrument; forerunner to the Greek bouzouki*] and then you go and play the baritone Weissenborn. You get this huge sound out of it and it's nice to be able to switch and you just readjust your amp or your box slightly. It keeps your brain flexible. The hardest thing that I had to learn to do on stage was to play the 12-string guitar and then play the saz because the saz has very, very light strings in three groups of two. And a 12-string guitar, you have to manhandle the thing. It's a weird kind of thing. To play it in tune you have to press hard but not too hard. If you're doing bar chords and things like that, you have to go to the Shaolin Temple for a couple of years to learn to play both of 'em in the same set. With the other stuff it's not hard.

You did two exceptional records with Henry Kaiser: *A World Out of Time* in Madagascar, and *The Sweet Sunny North* in Norway. What were those experiences like?

Those were so fun. I'm so glad I did those, especially Madagascar (laughs). At the beginning of when we were going to record, there was a witch doctor/medicine man type of guy there and he was blessing the project. The city of Antananarivo hadn't had any rain for a long time. They had a drought going on there. So we started to play and all the lights went out in the studio. So there were all the musicians and a lot of other people all sitting around in this room drinking rum. Suddenly there was thunder, lightning, and rain and the medicine man goes "These guys are cool (laughs)." It was one of those times where you go, "What the hell is happening?! This is too weird!" Henry and I just looked at each other and all the hair on my arms stood up and he said, "This is a good sign."

- ¤ David Lindley ¤ -

Here we were all these white guys in Antananarivo. The engineer and producer were from Germany. We would go back to our hotel and we'd come out in the morning and there'd be all these people there wanting to check out these crazy Americans. They were having a revolution at that time. People walking around in fatigues with semi-autos and stuff. The American embassy said, "Don't go. There's a travel alert for Americans." We said, "Ah, fuck," and went down anyway. I felt the change too. The gearshift. This Greek chorus said, "Boy, you gotta get out more. There's a whole lot of stuff around. Check it out." That was Henry's idea to go down there.

How did your duos with percussionists Hani Nassar and Wally Ingram come about?

Hani was over at my house one day and I'd always wanted to play with two people because I had seen Ali Farke Toure and said, "This is a good way to do stuff." So I decided to put that together with Hani. I'd seen an oud player with a dumbek player or a guitar player with a conga player. Lightning Hopkins used to play with just a drummer; his electrified acoustic, and then a drummer and it was always good. Then Hani went to do some other stuff and went on to do stuff with Wally. The thing with Wally is more like the original idea I had.

I understand you and Wally try to engage the audience about political and social issues that are important to you.

Yeah. I don't like to preach anything but I have on occasion gone off on genetic engineering and letting people know that one of the reasons they may have stomach problems is because of the genetically engineered corn and soybeans and what it does to the digestive system. I'll throw things out, but you know, that can get to be a little too much sometimes.

A lot of times people just want to come to a show and forget about that shit. You serve a better function in helping people forget about that stuff rather than constantly reminding them of it so life becomes an ongoing horror show for folks. They don't like that so I don't do that as much as I used to.

Lets talk about your work on sessions and film scores. You've done probably thousands of sessions. Do you have to be something of a musical chameleon?

Yeah, unless they're hiring you for what you do. I've started taking only projects that I like. I'm going to do a Ziggy Marley thing next week and then I'm working on Warren Zevon's newest album and then I did a thing with Ry [*Cooder*] for a kind of Walter Hill HBO movie.

Who are some of the most fun people to work with in sessions?

Ry definitely is really, really fun to work with.

Have you played lap steel while he's playing bottleneck at the same time?

We've done that. It's fun to do. Sometimes one will play more percussively than the other. We've done a lot of bottleneck and lap steel stuff. There's a bootleg out of us live in Osaka.

You're both very aware in your approach to the instrument of the Blind Willie Johnson style - milking the beauty out of just a note or two.

Blind Willie Johnson was *the guy*. He and Robert Johnson had that approach that was so wonderful.

- ¤ David Lindley ¤ -

And then there's also Ry's approach. On all his records there's a certain kind of approach that's a *textural* approach. He'll play a certain way: "Bonka chank bonk chank bonka chank."

I remember when we went out on the road with my daughter and me and Ry and Joaquim [*Cooder*] and we did this series of concerts in Europe and Japan. I tried to figure it out. "Okay, if Ry's going to play a lot of bottleneck guitar I've got to play something lower than that that's not going to eat him up." I said, "Baja sexto is a good idea, but that's hard to play, so regular old 12-string's the next best thing. Let's put this together and tune it way down like a baritone guitar and you don't want octaves 'cause that will eat everything up so let's just put on two sets of D'Addarrio light gauge bronze and tune it down." I played that on the tour a lot – just a Danelectro 12-string with two sets of bronze strings on it.

I've read comments from you in the past that people like Linda Ronstadt and Dolly Parton are really easy to work with in the studio because they can clearly articulate what they want to hear.

Yeah, it's so easy – especially Dolly. Dolly said, [*imitates cranky old guy voice*] "Lindley, play like an old man." I said, "Well that's the only way I *can* play." "Well that's why you're here." (Laughs). It's real fun to work with people like that rather than someone who's afraid to say something or they don't know what they want and they're waiting for you to save the tune. A lot of times I used to have to come into a situation where it was like, "Okay. Make something out of *this*. Make it *way* better than it was when you first came in." I'd have to do that and it would take a lot out of me. You'd have to second-guess them sometimes and, a lot of times, I would take it in a direction that they wouldn't like.

Do you watch the movie while you're recording a film score?

Sometimes I do that and other times it's a chart and you have a tempo and you don't look at anything. Or you have one person - like Ry - who would look at the chart and he would lead everything. You watch him like you watch a conductor and you play along with him or else it's just dry, no TV screen at all. You just play *this* and they're gonna cut to this later so we have to play it like it's walking speed. I've done stuff with James Horner where he knows the exact tempo because he has a computer program that printed it out for him.

Have you played on film scores with a full orchestra reading notation while youre role is to improvise your part?

That's exactly it. When I played with Ry on the thing that we did for Geronimo, I had an actual part written out in the score for the mandolin and bouzouki and stuff so I've done that too. That's really frightening. You get all these musicians there. Really seriously good players and you're right behind the string section. There you are with your little mandolin. "Excuse the hat. Don't mean to be a bother. I'm just gonna mess this up a little bit."

- ¤ David Lindley ¤ -

You get intimidated, you know? Everything is just wonderfully played and it's interpreted and it's not stiff and it's good and then they come down to you and your part begins to fuck it up! What you don't want to have happen is for people to turn around in their chairs and look at you. That's a little bit too scary for me so I kinda stopped doing that kind of thing. "I'll come in later and overdub it. Okay?" (Laughs).

It's quite a stressful way to earn a paycheck.

Scoring stuff and doing soundtracks – it'll kill ya. The pressure will put you in the hospital. I watched Ry a couple of times, and in his own words, he would slowly deflate like a balloon under the chair in the living room and he'd turn this grey color 'cause the project was eating him up. It was really awful and he said, "Don't ever do this. Don't you ever do this kind of thing - you'll end up *dead*." [*shudders audibly*]. I've done soundtracks and it's always: "We need it tomorrow or day after tomorrow." [*director*] Penelope Spheeris calls me up and says, "Can you do a banjo tune by then?" I said, "Sure", went in the studio and did it and that was the only time that kind of thing was okay. People drop like flies from doing this stuff unless they're really prepared or they have some generic stuff on disc they can plug in.

Your original score for the children's recording of Laura Dern reading the *Song of Sacajewea* was an exceptionally beautiful score.

It turned out really well. I'm really sorry that the company itself [*Rabbit Ears Productions*] didn't get further than it did. They got bought out by BMG and BMG has been waiting to reproduce things. It was a lot of fun and I also did another one with Garrison Keillor that was based on parables from the New Testament. I did some of that stuff with the really strange instruments – the psalteries and the Middle Eastern tambours. It was really fun and it turned out great too. They show up on eBay from time to time.

Has the proliferation of inexpensive home recording equipment made your life easier?

It's really fun now especially 'cause there's now a lot of this really high quality recording equipment that you can put in your living room. A 24-track digital machine is pretty small.

You don't have the pressure of the meter running in a big commercial studio.

No. You don't have *any*. You can get up four in the morning, turn it on, play something - "Hey, that's *good*" - and then go back to sleep. The really important steps are when you mix it and then when you master it. Especially with digital stuff, it's best to mix it onto an analog format. That's what we did. We went into Jackson Browne's studio and got all the levels right then put it onto an Ampex ATR two-track.

So you keep all the warmth of the analog process?

Yeah. You take the 1/2 inch two track and master from that as opposed to having it *all* digital. Anything that's in the power train that's tube or analog adds to it a lot. Also when you make the CDs themselves. I learned so much working with [*mastering engineer*] Joe Gastwirt. He's got all this custom stuff he's built and he runs things through this and run things through that and I say, "Wow! How did you tighten that up?" He says, [*imitates nerdy engineer voice*] "Well, it's a box (laughs) and it's not the original box either. I changed some components (laughs)."

- ¤ David Lindley ¤ -

I've also been collecting tube microphones for a long time. When I see one that I've always wanted to use or I remember one that sounded good on some recording session I'd buy it if I could afford it. It's hard to find a lot of these things but, then again, there are some really good new ones out there. People are making good tube microphones and wonderful pre-amps now.

One final question, how did you first get the notion to don your trademark polyester wardrobe?

Lightning Hopkins - he wore polyester with orange shoes and kind of ochre pants - *so* good. He was one of my heroes so I filed that away. The *African Brother's Dance Band* wore plaids, stripes, and polka dots. It's so good! Your clothes move on stage for you! After the gig you wash 'em in the hotel sink with those little bottles of shampoo, in the morning it's dry, you throw it in your suitcase and go. I've got over 200 polyester shirts.

- ¤ -

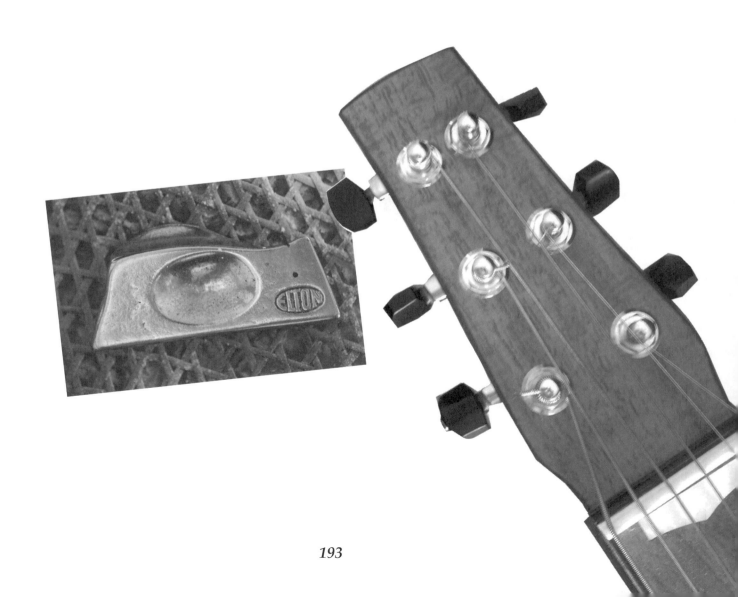

Gary Brandin

Gary Brandin may well be the most heard steel guitar player in the history of the instrument. His steel guitar work on *SpongeBob SquarePants* - tone of he highest rated children's programs on TV – is heard by more than sixty million viewers per month. In addition to lending his talents to many classic episodes of the animated series, Gary has a regular gig with the Los Angeles-based "surf-noir" band *The Blue Hawaiians*. After many years as a pedal steel player in country music, Gary rediscovered the tonal possibilities of the non-pedal instrument. His steel guitar adds considerably to the lush textures of the *Blue Hawaiians'* music. *The Vanduras,* his band with his guitarist son, Geoffry Brandin, takes the steel guitar on a genre-melding excursion into the worlds of surf and cinematic musical soundscapes.

- ¤ Gary Brandin ¤ -

How did you come to play the steel guitar and what was your first instrument?

I didn't start playing music until I was about twenty-five years old. My wife and I moved into this house in South Pasadena, outside of LA, and all of our neighbors were musicians - all bluegrass musicians. They got me interested and I ended up playing guitar and mandolin in a couple of bluegrass bands.

They used to take me over to the *Palomino* on Tuesday nights to listen to the house band that had J.D. Maness playin' steel and I was sort of interested in the instrument, but wasn't initially grabbed by it. Just by chance, I acquired a pedal steel and I ended up bein' the only guy in the neighborhood who had a pedal steel even though I couldn't play it. Since I had one, everybody kept coming over to jam with me to play country music and I ended up, within four months of acquiring that single ten guitar, working five nights a week in country bars.

What was your first lap steel?

A Bakelite Rickenbacher that I still have. I bought it for $200 bucks in the late '80s. I tuned it up, played it a few times, then put it under my bed and forgot about it. It's still under my bed (laughs). At one point in the early '90s, I put an open G tuning on it and played it through my Supro Thunderbolt amp, which is a 30-watt, class-A amp made back in the '60s. I'd run the lap steel and turn the amp up all the way for a pretty good David Lindley sound. That's how I started playing around with lap steel. I'd always been a pedal steel guy and never thought much about playing a non-pedal guitar because I didn't think I was good at it and I thought it was too limited. I just hadn't developed an approach to it or a real interest in it.

Today you're playing a lot of non-pedal steel on a regular basis. What changed your mind?

When I had a few years off, I started listening to other music and completely forgot about country. I wasn't thinking about getting into music again, then I ran into the *Blue Hawaiians* who called me to audition for the band. They weren't interested in pedal steel so I borrowed a Stringmaster from one of my students and went to the audition. I could play C6th without pedals so I got the gig.

They're a surf rock band so I had to change my *whole* approach and the way I looked at my playing as well as my equipment. You couldn't play a gig with the *Hawaiians* through a solid-state amp. I went to a smaller tube amp – my Rickenbacker 30-watt amp that I used all the time, even on country gigs – and went out and bought a Magnatone double-8 from the early to mid-fifties. It's kind of like a Stringmaster with the long scale and two pick-ups and a blend knob. It's really a beautiful guitar but it didn't quite have the sound that I was looking for. It had virtually no sustain. I'm not really an expert on guitars, I just know what I like.

I had a friend who had a whole bunch of steel guitars and he had this wooden double-8 Rickenbacker that sat on three legs. I borrowed that for a few gigs and it had the *sound* - a big, fat Rickenbacher sound along with all kinds of sustain. It would just sustain all day. So I bought one of those and it's my main guitar for non-pedal; just a great sounding, very stable guitar.

What's the role of the steel in the *Blue Hawaiians'* music?

That's what sort of lit a fire under me because it was left up to *me*. They just wanted someone who could play it and play it in tune (laughs). My son would come to some of the gigs and tell me I was sounding too country or muting notes too much. There's also a [*Hammond*] B-3 in the band so I had to develop my own space in the sound of the band where I'm not competing with the keyboard or the guitar player. There were some songs where they gave me parts to play but, other than that, they just left developing a role for the steel in the band up to me.

I developed a style where I try to put it somewhere where it's not a keyboard and not a guitar. It sort of finds it's own space. Everybody's really encouraging as far as using the steel and it's the first band I've been in where I'm being asked to please play *more*.

Your solo on the song *Swinging Hula Girl* from the *Blue Hawaiians* CD *Sway* really caught my ear. It swings while still staying in the Island bag.

That's funny because I had just gotten my Magnatone at that time and I didn't have a clue. I had just joined the band and hadn't played any live gigs with them. The playing on *Swinging Hula Girl* is actually my country approach but, you know, I think that it was what that song called for. If we played that song now I'd probably play it the same way. Same thing with the Sponge Bob stuff. It's more accessible from where I'm coming from.

You did a wonderful "surf noir" project with your son Geoff called *The Vanduras*. The surf noir genre, in general, seems to draw from a lot of influences: surf music, spaghetti western scores, 1960's spy movies, the *Shadows*, and more. Some bands, like the *Aqua Velvets*, have moved increasingly to tunes where many songs seem based out of diminished or augmented chords. The *Vanduras'* sound strikes me as more listener friendly. Was this a conscious decision?

It *was* a conscious decision. Pascal records approached me to do a steel guitar CD. I cringe when I think of a steel guitar CD. My son and I sat down and listened to some steel guitar CDs and I pointed out how great the playing was – these guys are just amazing players – but with the exception of a very few, none of them have any original ideas. They keep just playin' the same stuff. They all think they're gonna do the better version of *Sleepwalk*. They just don't get it. I've got the first Santo & Johnny album and you can hear how lacking his playing was in terms of technique but his ideas were fresh. You listen to a lot of younger players and they have fresh ideas. So we decided not to not make a pickin' CD where you're out there trying to outplay the next guy and say nothing musically or making the steel sound like an accordion album. I didn't even want to put *Rope and Pineapples* or *Lost Beach* on the CD but my son insisted on putting them in.

He wanted to show that dad could pull off the technique stuff when he needs to?

(Laughs). That's the kind of stuff I wanted to stay away from and get into the more cinematic stuff. In any musical form, I feel it's the song that's most important and it's the song that people remember. I don't think anybody can sing a Van Halen or Eric Clapton solo but they can remember the songs. I want to put the steel guitar in music where it becomes the song rather than using the song to show some musical acrobatics that are meaningless except maybe to other pickers.

Here's an example. I've got this old 45 of Jerry Byrd doing *Memories of Maria*. You listen to that and it's the *song*. The song is beautiful and Jerry Byrd just uses the steel to play the *song*. It's a good example of the steel just staying within the context of the song. I don't buy steel guitar instrumental albums other than somebody like [*ambient pedal steel guitarists*] B.J. Cole or Bruce Kaphan. Whether you like that sort of thing or not, at least they're trying to go somewhere with the instrument. More players need to sit down and try to come up with new directions and different ideas.

- ¤ Gary Brandin ¤ -

As a regular on Nickelodeon's *SpongeBob Squarepants* animated cartoon, you're very likely the most heard steel player in America. According to USA Today, *SpongeBob* pulls in 56.1 million monthly viewers, with over 18 million of those in the 18-to-49 category. This is unprecedented exposure for a steel player. How do you and the *Blue Hawaiians* go about cutting tracks for the show?

When we first started doing *SpongeBob*, we had no idea it was going to be popular. We just thought it was some little off-the-wall thing. We recorded most of that stuff back in 1999 and it's just gone crazy since then. I get fan mail from people that just love the music. They don't even know it's a steel guitar, they just like the music.

Do you actually look at the on-screen footage while you're playing?

I did on two episodes. The one I like the best is called *The Reef Blower.* That one I played along with from the beginning to the end. They'd say, "Do songs that sound like these but aren't these songs." I just made up the melody to fit the cartoon. The first half is kind of mellow and calm. Then in the second half, he straps the leaf blower on and goes berserk. That's our version of *Hawaiian War Chant* done in reverse. I'm doing these whoop slides and I threw a cha-cha-cha in there on a stop because I thought that was funny (laughs). For other episodes, we just give them songs that they want done differently so they don't have to pay royalties and they just buy us out for the song. We don't spend a lot of time on them. The rhythm section can pretty much copy what's on the original recordings and then it's up to me and the bass player to come up with a different melody. We've given them so much music they chop up what we give them and use it as cues [*brief musical interludes*].

I hope that's good exposure for the steel guitar. I don't think it's really representative of the instrument but at least it does put it in the consciousness of young people to a certain degree. So maybe it will be more of a standard sound in the future. It's hard to say.

How much effect does equipment have on a player's sound and how much is in a player's hands?

I'm real particular. It might be different for somebody else, but for me I've gotta play through a tube amp. I can't go back to playing through a solid-state amp. I played through solid-state amps in the 70's. In the early 80's, I switched back to a tube amp. I can't even play through a high-powered tube amp; it's too unforgiving. I play through an old 1956 Rickenbacher M-15 that is about 30 watts with a JBL D-130 in it. It's a cathode bias so it has a nice compressed, saturated sound even at low volume. It just gets that *sound*. I go back to the Jerry Byrd records and early steel guitar stuff from the 50's and

60's. Those guys were all playing through tube amps and not necessarily big tube amps. There's just a sound that they got that you don't hear any more with guys that are playing through big solid-state amps.

True. Jerry Byrd got that saturated, rich sound with lush harmonics on his early recordings. You don't have that harshness that happens with solid-state gear.

Exactly. For a long time I couldn't put my finger on what it was I was hearing on those old steel tracks. Then when I finally started experimenting with amps, there it was – the sound. It has its limitations, but to me, it has far more advantages than limitations. With the gigs I do nowadays, I mike my amp and I'm fine. Same thing with pedal steel. The last tour out on the road with Heather Miles we were touring with Merle Haggard and I couldn't use my amp and had to use Norm Hamlet's Session 500. It didn't sound horrible but there was something missing.

So I'm a *big* tube amp guy. I've kind of gone crazy with 'em. I own thirteen tube amps and they're all different. On the *Vanduras* CD I mostly use a 6 or 8-watt Magnatone Lelani amp – one of the mother-of-toilet-seat models. For pedal steel, I played through my M-15. For *Rope & Pineapples*, I used my 1953 Silvertone with a single-12 speaker because it's a brighter amp.

Once you find out how to play through tubes and how to set them to their sweet spot you can't go back to anything else. It just becomes part of the instrument.

Where do you see the non-pedal steel guitar going? Is it on its way out or here to stay?

Well, non-pedal is like anything else. Fender was almost ready to discontinue the Strat back in the mid-60s until Jimmy Hendrix came along and resurrected it. They weren't getting sales compared to the Jaguar, the Jazzmaster, and the Tele. So it depends if somebody comes along that does something with the steel that catches the attention of the general public. It would have to be introduced into pop music or at least the popular consciousness. I don't know if *SpongeBob* is gonna do it because it's still pretty one-dimensional. You have to show the public a little more than having them think, "What's that wacky instrument?"

Maybe it's better that it's sort of a cult instrument 'cause then it doesn't wear out its welcome. There's a lot to be said for that. Maybe it's better if it just sits off to the side and does cool things and kind of interjects itself sometimes then backs off. It helps the instrument stay unique. As long as I'm playing it and having a good time and there are young people out there who are learning to play it, I don't think it's really important that it ever becomes a mainstream instrument. I've seen too many trends come and go. As soon as something becomes a new trend it's going to become an old trend sooner or later. Steel guitar hasn't really ever worn out its welcome. It keeps that mystique happening and mystique is a good thing.

- ¤ -

Steve Howe

S teve Howe is a legend in rock music. In his work with the classic 1970s supergroup *Yes*, Steve brought influences from jazz, ragtime, country, and classical music into the world of arena rock. His versatility on standard guitars extends to his use of non-pedal and pedal steel guitars, which he often plays in unconventional ways. While best known for his trademark Gibson ES-175 hollow-body standard guitar, Steve's use of steel guitar in his music forms a consistent thread throughout his career as a professional musician.

- ¤   Steve Howe   ¤ -

How did you first come to play the guitar and who were your early influences?

I was about ten and I wanted to get a guitar. It took me about two years to convince my parents that I needed a guitar *badly*. At that time, I had just started to look across to America - this was about 1955 or '56 - and in my parents' collection there was a surprising amount of good music. In there were two kinds of music which both involved guitar. Les Paul and Mary Ford - those old 78s of theirs - and Tennessee Ernie Ford, who I discovered had Jimmy Bryant and Speedy West playing guitars. I don't think I was buying records quite then but I soon started.

Bill Haley was sort of central to the way I was doing my young boy, pre-teen revolt by jumping on the rock & roll thing. Still to this day, Franny Beecher and Scotty Moore played excellent guitar. It was great to meet Scotty Moore a couple of years ago. He was really, really charming. I felt that those two guys, at that stage, were the leaders of the pack.

So hearing this music was kind of the fall back music in my life, in addition to whatever I could hear on the radio. Hearing those musicians – Les Paul, Jimmy Bryant and Speedy West – was a great inspiration to me. It wasn't the focus of my attention, but my first influences were definitely those three people.

What was your first lap steel guitar?

It was a Gibson BR-9 student model. I added gaffer tape, believe it or not, to where the fingerboard ended so I could get some crucial notes, like a top E. I dearly loved that guitar. It was my first steel experience and my first inspiration. I didn't appreciate, at the time, that most of the guitars that I was listening to, from *Santo & Johnny* and many other steel guitar players, were Fenders. The Gibson didn't actually give me the sound that I was seeking, although I did still use that guitar for a long time.

Your extensive collection of guitars was documented in your book with Tony Bacon *The Steve Howe Guitar Collection.* What acoustic and electric steels do you currently own?

I've streamlined my steel collection a bit since the days of the book. I haven't got any BR-9s right now. I've got an EH-150 [*Gibson*] double-neck that I like very much. The necks aren't joined - they're separated. It's a marvelous guitar but I'm a little disappointed that it's an 8-string 'cause most of my steel guitars are 6-string, if I can get them. I used that guitar on my album called *Portraits of Bob Dylan* on a song called *I Don't Believe You* because it has a kind of searing sound that's quite different from a Fender. I've also got an Ultratone that I love. It's in perfect condition – lots of Bakelite, lots of pseudo Art Nouveau stuff on it - and that's quite a nice sound as well.

I've got my infamous Fender dual professional steel which is, I think, a 1956 double-neck. That twin neck has become my main instrument. I've got two ShoBuds – a 1976 maple single neck. That's the one that's been recorded the most. I have used other ones onstage but the one I have now is a red, Professional II model. I experimented and customized - you might say, bastardized - that guitar and took the D9th tuning off in favor of a Hawaiian style 6th tuning and I even put a Fender pickup in it. I took off all the pedals from the C neck.

I like to experiment occasionally with guitars but I don't do it much myself anymore because I tend to mess 'em up (laughs).

Then I've got my Dobro which I recently had renovated and that has an interestingly embossed sort of look. It's got a weird kind of finish, a kind of raised look about it. That's a wonderful guitar. And then I also have a really marvelous guitar that I used on *Natural Timbre*. It's a Martin 00-40H. That guitar is miles away from a Dobro because it's just such a pure, natural, clean sound. It doesn't have the affected sound you get with a Dobro – which I love – but it's nice to have that balance. I think of that Martin as my sort of mellow sound and my Dobro more as my hard sound.

What tunings are you using on your 6-string steels?

If I'm not going to be thinking about anything special, then I'm going to use an E major tuning which doesn't go down, it goes up again on the bottom. It's [*hi to low*] E-B-G#-E-B-E but the bottom string is an octave above what it should be for a regular guitar so you get a kind of doubling effect. I like a root on the bottom. I use other tunings as well. In the old days, I used to have a minor tuning so I could go from major to minor. Then I decided that if I really wanted to improvise like I was doing on *Going for the One* [Relayer album with *Yes*], the other neck was actually in regular guitar tuning – normal, everyday tuning: E-B-G-D-A-E. That meant I could go on there and play without actually thinking about normal steel positioning like I do when I'm in a chordal tuning. Then I discovered that a lot of steel players are playing in A and I felt a bit alien because I could never quite see things from an A perspective. I'm more comfortable in E.

With *Yes*, Jon [*Anderson*] decided to sing *Going for the One* in D, so I had one neck in E and the other neck in D. One night I started in E and then the band came in in D (laughs). That was a very memorable moment for me.

Do you find that you have to be especially careful with your blocking when playing in standard guitar tuning?

Oh yeah.

You never really studied conventional steel guitar technique. Do you play with finger picks?

No I don't. I was very pleased to learn in about 1966 that I play a bit like Albert Lee in the way I hold my plectrum with my first finger and thumb and pick with my third finger and a bit with my 2nd finger. Doing that on a steel guitar came very naturally 'cause I can get lots of the effects that guitarists get with fingerpicks. I don't get all the sounds that are possible but I get my own distinctive sound – a bit like I do on Spanish guitar 'cause I've never really had nails. Even there, I'm playing a sound that's quite unorthodox because most classical players are used to that nice, sharp sound you get with nails. For good or bad, I've gotta go like I know.

I found a very unusual steel bar. It looks like Bakelite but it's much harder. It looks kind of like tortoise shell – a very unusual small, round bar. It's unlike the kind I usually use, where it comes up a bit so you've got a gripping surface. I use a bullet bar on the pedal steel. I can't play with it on a 6- string though.

Do you have to be extra careful in switching from standard guitar with its fixed intonation to steel guitar which is intonated by placement of the tone bar?

- ¤ Steve Howe   ¤ -

I think pitch is a very fascinating thing. I put myself through occasional checks and I discovered that my basic instinct is to always be in perfect pitch. I'd be flying around on stage doing things and usually my final note is a fade-in to a chord with the vocalist coming in singing. It's pretty concerning for everybody if I'm not spot on. What I do is I play the note just where I want it - where I believe it is - and I've got a tuner strategically placed where I can see it. When I go right up high in the very top octave, and I go for a note say, three octaves above open E on the first string, it's nice to know what the hell you're doing.

Did you immediately see a role for the steel guitar in the progressive rock music *Yes* was doing?

Yes, I did. When we came to *Close to the Edge* that was when I introduced steel into *Yes*. It was on two tracks. By the time we did *Tales from the Topographic Oceans*, I used it on side three as my main instrument for quite a long section which was kind of daring 'cause we were playing like space cowboys then, weird time changes and even not playing at the same speed. *Gates of Delirium* had a great tune to play on the steel guitar, and *To Be Over* had pedal steel, so I was bringing steel into *Yes* all the way, really.

When did you begin playing steel on stage?

I first started playing a pedal steel in 1975 and by the time I was recording *Relayer*, I was really trying to find out what I could do on it. In the tune *To Be Over*, there's a place where the whole band stops and I double-tracked the part I play. To play that on stage was an absolute thrill. I'd gotten used to playing a bit of steel and in *Going for the One*, I also played standing up. I still use the ShoBud.

I keep my Dobro playing a lot more simplistic because of the human, physical possibilities, but I find that with my Stringmaster, the sky's the limit. I moved to that guitar because I believed I could make those sounds on a standard guitar but I couldn't make them as well. I didn't actually want to start making wild crazy noises on my guitar, though I do open up and play quite wildly on it quite often. They were sounds I could have made on the guitar but I found when I could go to another instrument, I was so *relieved.* I could go beyond what I'd imagined I could do.

In the studio particularly, I know I've had a lot of fun with the steel. I did a record with Billy Currie called *The Transportation*. On one track, he said, "Why don't you put some steel guitar on there?" and I said, "Oh yeah -I've got an idea." I did a little trick I used on a few solo tracks where the steel guitar goes down to the chord and I have another steel guitar [*in the track*] below and it goes up to the chord. If you kinda do that in harmony you get this marvelous *nrrhhhhhh* (laughs) and nobody knows what the hell is going on! (Laughs) Because just in the mid-point, they cross over. So I love the kind of effects sometimes that you can get, though it's a bit hard to reproduce it on stage without a pedal steel.

Who are the players who have most influenced you on the instrument?

I am completely over the moon about somebody. About five years ago, I was in America and I turned on the television and there was this girl singing then she played a bit of violin. I listened to that voice and she was so good! The camera pulled back and there were a bunch of guys all playing acoustic instruments. The song ended and I didn't know who any of them were and the guy said, "Thank you *Allison Kraus and Union Station,*" and that was it.

Over the next couple of weeks I hunted out some recordings and found some of the things they did and kind of followed their career a bit, just enjoying them. I noticed that Jerry Douglas was on a lot of these records and I started hearing his playing - so smooth and just great. Each new album they did together, he started being not more predominant, but worthy of being predominant. He gained so much weight in his colorful sound. Then on the new album, *New Favorites*, he just excels totally and utterly, as he does just about everywhere he shows up.

What he's done for me is that my hopes for the Dobro guitar are not only being fantastically advanced by him but it's made me think, yeah, I can get more from this instrument too. I love it dearly, particularly because, at times, I've even considered stopping the guitar and just concentrating on steel for a while -though that wouldn't mean exclusively Dobro by any means. So I was pleased to see that Jerry had an electric lap guitar on the album.

In thirty years or more of making music from progressive rock, heavy rock to ambient and acoustic music, two threads seem to weave through your music: a consistent melodicism and an awareness of musical texture. Is that something you're consciously striving for or just a natural by-product of your influences?

In my first five years of playing I guess I was somewhere or the other with playing the guitar. I made leaps and jumps and when psychedelic playing came along, I'd only been playing about seven or eight years yet it's amazing what I played at that time. I've never actually thought about it like this before. I started playing in '59 and by '67, I was onstage hurling about on that 175 [*Steve's trademark Gibson ES-175*]. Most probably I did make an early leap from playing like Hank Marvin and the *Ventures* to trying to copy Django. I was slowing down records and trying to find out how to make those changes and runs. My mind started to become full of chord changes and it still can if I allow it to.

There was a great day in my life when I bought a Fender Tremolux amp. I was sure it was the amp I wanted. I got home and I put it in quite a small room and I plugged in my precious 175 which I'd only recently gotten. So the two things came together and I was almost frozen at how good it sounded. "Ahhhh! Wow! That sounds so good!" Why it sounded so good was to me, it sounded just like Kenny Burrell (laughs). To me, Kenny Burrell, besides Wes Montgomery, had the ultimate jazz guitar tone. It always sounded well produced. Even his very early records, I'm sure, he was the kind of guy– and I'd love to hear it if I'm wrong – who said, "Can we get the mic position a bit better?" or "Can we just put a bit of compression on this here?" Somebody intervened and I think it's *him* 'cause it's so consistent.

I spent a little time with Tal Farlow some years before he died and I've got some photos I treasure. In certain registers, his sound was very cagey, but usually when he had Eddie Costa on piano and Vinnie Burke on bass - when those three were playing together - there was a great deal of sound compensation there because the piano compensated tremendously for the dryness of Tal's sound. When Tal got up in the higher register, he would fly like no other guitarist except maybe Hank Garland, but Tal really did fly around in the upper register and that's where the sound really developed well.

You and Martin Taylor had the unique experience of recording a CD using the vintage instruments from the late Scott Chinery's collection, as well as serving as the producer of *Masterpiece Guitars*. Did you play any steel on that record?

I played a Bigsby on a tune called *Tailpiece*, which I was very excited to play given this was one of the earliest pedal steel guitars around. I found that a wonderful guitar to play and on the same track, I played a Bigsby standard guitar as well. That record is available on 20th Century Guitar's website [*www.tcguitar.com*]. I played a Dobro on one track that we didn't end up using.

That was a beautiful experience because for two weeks we had full access to these instruments. We had great, great fun exploring all the guitars and we also had the pleasure of having somebody there to set up any little details because we weren't just looking at them, we were playing them. So if they needed restringing, a bit more preparation, or had a fret buzz, we had a professional guy there. It was a fantastic experience.

Is there any kind of music that you haven't tackled that you've always secretly wanted to do?

In a way, I've never reached deeply into the pocket of either classical or jazz. I've never done an album that's all classical or all jazz. But I've kind of spiced my music up along the way with both of those elements. I certainly don't think it's over (laughs). Country music hasn't had a big focus for me though things like *Natural Timbre* allowed me to do a few country pieces but not exclusively because I wanted to explore the acoustic domain in every style.

I should mention my fascination and enjoyment of country swing. I like Leon McAuliffe. I have one of his guitars. I have his four-neck Fender. When I opened up the case, it had a green piece of lined paper with Leon's tunings. It's a wonderful piece.

Where do you think the steel guitar is going?

My hope would be that both of them [*pedal & non-pedal*] will go on and have an equal importance. It's deceptive sometimes, which one somebody's playing, until you go to the unique qualities that each one of them has. Certainly, the chordal movements that pedal steel has are very hard to achieve on a non-pedal guitar. You can do quite a lot of things as so many people have shown. The value of both is equal. I don't think I can open up as much on the pedal steel because I'm more used to lap steel. In one respect, pedal steel tries to disassociate itself with country music and there's no reason why that's the only music it should be in. There are a lot more openings and I hope that more people take those openings. I'm going to possibly dedicate a whole period to playing steel because I know I can get a lot of sounds out of there. I have a lot more to learn about both of them, to be honest.

- ¤ -

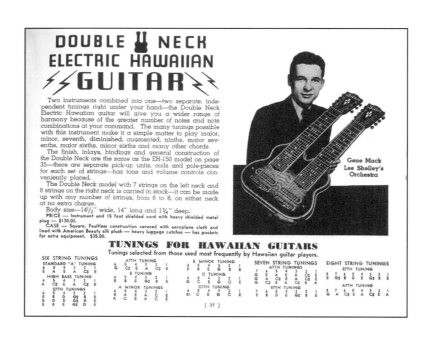

World Music

The steel guitar music of Hawaii was one of the first non-western styles of music to be documented at the dawn of recorded sound. By the mid 20th century, the sliding sound of a bar on metal had become popular and could be heard in music from Mexico, Germany, Japan, Tahiti, India, and many more places around the globe.

As today's musicians freely cross-pollinate their music with pan-cultural elements, the sound of lap-style instruments can be heard in diverse and exciting new settings.

HarryManx

Harry Manx brings the sounds of India to the blues. Combining bluesy lap-style guitar played on lap guitar or the mohan vina (a 20-string member of the guitar family created and named by Indian musical guru Vishwa Mohan Bhatt) with his distinctive vocals, Harry creates a new musical experience. Born on the Isle of Man, Manx immigrated to Canada as a child. In the mid-70s, he traveled to Europe and spent the next ten years performing in cafe's and bars, honing the musical skills that would provide the foundation for his later musical experimentation.

By the mid-80s, Manx was touring regularly in Japan and living in India. During Manx's stay in Japan he came across a recording of the legendary Indian slide guitarist Vishwa Mohan Bhatt. Manx was so moved by the musician's work that he contacted Bhatt and made arrangements to join him in India. There, he became a student of Bhatt's, studying with him for five years.

- ¤ Harry Manx ¤ -

The two traveled together in India, performing in front of large audiences with Manx playing the tambura, a four-stringed instrument used to provide a drone. Bhatt would not allow him to play the mohan vina live at the time, as he was still a student. Years later, having successfully mastered this complex instrument, Manx now incorporates the mohan vina into his own shows. He has been called an "essential link" between the music of east and west, creating musical short stories that fuse the essence of the blues with the Indian raga tradition.

How did you come to play lap steel guitar?

I was in Europe and I was playing regular guitar and then one day I saw one in a shop - an old Gibson electric. I bought it, took it home, and I had a book of Hawaiian music in open E7th tuning. I went plowing along with it for about half a year and got a few notes out of it. I remember clearly one occasion in Switzerland, the dog next door started howling every time I'd play that lap steel! (Laughs). When I was learning to play, there was nobody to learn from until a certain point when I connected with Vishwa Mohan Bhatt. 'Til then, I just sort of plowed along on my own trying to figure out the tuning and where to play the chords and notes. It takes a while to figure it out if you don't have a system already made up.

I went from there to getting a regular kind of a Dobro. I stuck to the bluegrass tuning [*Hi to low*: *D-B-G-D-B-G*] and learned a few songs but it wasn't really my style. I sat down and started thinking about this whole thing and I just took a regular guitar and jacked up the strings and put it in open D tuning. From there, I started to really figure out how to play music with the slide. That was really the start for me and I'm still playing that tuning.

What guitars are you playing today?

These days I have three instruments on the stage: a 6-string banjo which I play in open D, a 6-string Martin D-35 which I bought from Randy Bachman who claims that it was the guitar on which he recorded his big hit, *Takin' Care of Business,* and my mohan vina - a 20-string Indian slide guitar. Those are the main instruments in my arsenal right now.

How did you meet Vishwa Mohan Bhatt and learn the mohan vina?

I pretty much moved to India in 1986, and two or three times a year I'd go to Japan to make some money, and then come back to India. I started studying Indian music but there was this big gap between my instrument of choice – which was my slide guitar at that moment in time – and what I was trying to do. On one of my trips to Japan I heard a record of Vishwa Mohan Bhatt playing Indian classical music on the slide guitar. As soon as I heard it, it sort of clicked for me, "Yeah, that's the thing. I can keep playing slide and learn Indian music."

When I went back to India in the early '90s, I looked up a friend who gave me someone else's number and finally, I got to Vishwa Mohan Bhatt. He was living up in Rajasthan. I called him up and said, "I'm from Canada and I play the slide guitar and it would be nice to drop in and meet you some time." He said, "Yeah, come on up. I'm here now." So I went there – it was a couple of days on the bus and the train.

- ¤ Harry Manx ¤ -

I went there and I had this 6-string guitar I bought in Japan – a Yamaha or something. It was real cheap – and he asked me to play a song. He had never seen somebody playing the slide like that on a six-string Western guitar. He really liked it and he said, "I'm going to show you *my* instrument." He played about three notes and I just stopped in my tracks. After hearing that, everything else I was doing in my life sort of lost meaning in that split second. So I thought, "I'm gonna hang with this guy and see if I can catch some of that magic he has." Him playing a few notes just blew me over. I ended up stayin' with him for five years.

I hung with him, and every morning, I went there and studied with his two sons and we did exercises and started slowly. They got me into ragas and then we would tour around and I always played tamboura which is an accompanying instrument to soloists in Indian music. I learned to play that thing and after five years Vishwa said, "Go to the West and see what you can do." He said, "You're playin' pretty good now; much better than that other guy I made the record with, Ry Cooder (Laughs). I said, "Well, I don't know, he's pretty *good!*" (Laughs).

So I left India and went to Brazil for a year because my wife's from there. I couldn't get her emigrated into Canada so we stayed there and I ended up playing with a lot of Brazilian musicians in club gigs. From there, I came up to Canada and released my first record *Dog My Cat* which got the Independent Music Award for *Blues Album of the Year.* I put out another one recently, *Wise and Otherwise*, which is also doin' pretty good.

Wise and Otherwise is a beautiful album.

Thanks. I'm real happy. From my perspective in India, I couldn't see what it was like to play in the West anymore. I hadn't been living in Canada for twenty-five years. It was really a mystery. I'm glad they've really taken to the music. I was kind of afraid they'd sort of laugh it off as kind of a new age joke – me playin' blues on the mohan vina. But it seems to have taken hold and I'm very grateful about that.

How do the three influences of the blues, Indian music, and the lap steel guitar tradition all inform your songwriting?

One of the things when you play a lap steel guitar, you're sort of limited with the chords that you can actually produce. That's the reason, I guess, that they have pedal steel guitars that have all sorts of other options for getting a lot of notes so you can make complex chords. But on a six-string, in open D, you're limited to major chords and one or two minors. You have to work with that limitation on the chords. You can't play every kind of song on the instrument unless you figure out a particular tuning to do that. I play only one or two different tunings. I play D major, D minor and D major *7th* and then I capo to change my keys.

What are the notes of your major seventh tuning?

From the bass, D-A-D-F#-A-C#. I just drop that high D note down to C#. That's how I play the song *Coat of Mail* [on *Wise and Otherwise*]. Another variation I'm working with now is dropping the A's in D-A-D-F-A-D tuning down to G, giving you D-G-D-F-G-D which gives you a very interesting tuning. I've recorded a new album with Kevin Breit who plays on the new Nora Jones record and with Cassandra Wilson. I used that tuning for at least one of the songs and we got some great tones out of that.

- ¤ Harry Manx ¤ -

I found the Dobro tuning, D-B-G-D-B-G, a little limiting for a self-accompanying singer songwriter. The D-A-D-F-A-D works for me mainly because I can do a rotating bass between the two Ds and there are a lot of nice rolls – similar to banjo rolls – that you can play in that tuning. It's very rich tuning.

Kevin Breit showed me a very cool thing. He plays a National, bottleneck style. He had an open D tuning and he took the lowest D string and dropped it down to a G – a lowdown, nasty, way-too-low G. It rattled against the neck and it sounds wonderful. He's on the last three or four Cassandra Wilson records and you can hear him do that. It's a great idea.

What style bar do you use?

I have been using a Tim Sheerhorn bar but lately I've used a Dunlop *Lap Dawg*, it's like a Sheerhorn copy but shorter. I find that little extra weight nice. I never play with a slanted bar. I learned that a little in the early days, but I didn't do anything with it so I always play pretty much in a straight line.

Vishwa Mohan Bhatt uses the axle from a Honda scooter as a slide bar. He holds it like a pen in a raised position. He never touches more than one string at a time. He gave me one of those and I used it for a few years.

Can you describe the mohan vina?

On the top there are eight strings. Of those eight, I only used the slide bar on three strings. There's also one short one – like a banjo string – which is also tuned to the root. Then there are five other strings which I simply strum with my thumb as a kind of chord or a reference. If you're playing a raga for instance, you'd want those notes on top to be tuned to the essential notes of the raga. Underneath those strings and running parallel to them, are twelve sympathetic strings. Their tuning heads run all down the neck and they're tuned to the particular raga you're going to play.

If I'm playing a song, I'll tune them to major or minor. It's essentially an F-hole guitar that's been modified to handle all these extra strings. The original one was a copy of a Craftsman – a German guitar – that Vishwa had. Mine were made in Calcutta by the same guy who makes Vishwa's and Debashish Bhattacharya's guitars. I've got a bunch of them in case I lose one.

Who else do you enjoy listening to in the world of lap steel guitar?

I like Kelly Joe Phelps' music a lot. I knew him before he was known and we became friends. I'm a big fan of David Lindley, and Ry Cooder and Johnny Winter. I find all these guys great players. Muddy Waters played some killer, sweet, little licks. And I listen to a lot of Indian players: Brji Bhushan Kabra, Vishwa Mohan Bhatt, and Debashish Bhattacharya.

Debashish is an astounding technician and a profound musician.

He and I played together this summer at the *Calgary Folk Festival* and it was really wonderful meeting him. We did some good damage there! (Laughs). These Indian guys, when they're good, they're really, <u>really</u> good. They just kick ass. They practice forever - way beyond what most us in the west really get into.

One of the more obvious differences in the way many Indian players approach playing melodies, as opposed to Western players, is to play many notes with a great deal of bar movement and a single strike of the string.

That's exactly it. Brij Bhushan Kabra, the great Indian slide player, is famous for taking one strike from the right hand to play four notes; a very lovely style. The other thing they do with the left hand is to play in circles. If you can imagine playing from A to B back to A [*it sounds like*]Ah-Ah-Ah- without stopping when you reach the next note, but heading immediately back. This circular motion is what gives them the imitation of the human voice with the slide. There are note steps there.

In Indian music, it's called the *meend* - how you approach a note. That's something that you study very intensely. Do you approach a note from below it, above it, or can you approach it directly from another note or do you have to go through several notes? This kind of thing they've studied a lot and they know a certain approach will give a certain effect: some may sound exciting, some extremely beautiful. They pay a lot of attention to the *meend.*

Tell me about your relationship with blues music. Who influenced you and do you consider yourself a world music musician? A blues player?

I think both of those categories suit me pretty well and I tend to get billed in both those roles. I left my home at fifteen and went to live with a blues band. By seventeen, I was working with a lot of bands as a sound technician in Toronto. I worked at a club called the El Macombo club, a famous blues club in the '70s & '80s. I got the house gig and got to mix sound for Willie Dixon, Muddy Waters, John Hammond – a lot of great bands and players. I can remember running home after the gig 'cause I had the groove in my head that Willie Dixon had played and I just had to grab my guitar and see if I could still remember it (laughs).

That was very inspiring and made a deep imprint on me. When I was nineteen, I moved to Europe and started busking and I worked a long time there - ten years – playing mostly blues. Along the way as a street artist I played all kinds of popular music and that was good training too.

You also learned how to capture an audience; an audience that could leave!

Yeah, the street's like that. If you learn to hold them you really do well and if you don't you can die of starvation out there. I had some fat years on the street in Japan in the '80s. It wasn't unusual to make a thousand bucks on a good day. It was a gold mine before their bubble burst in the early '90s.

How did you come to cover songs like *The Thrill is Gone*, on banjo, and Hendrix's *Foxy Lady, on lap style guitar?*

I come from that generation of music. I've always played *The Thrill Is Gone* but only recently on the banjo. I did Hendrix stuff when I was working in Brazil, more or less tongue in cheek. It's about the most unlikely thing you'd want to play on the vina but then people started to enjoy it. Some people have noted that it's quite risky to do songs that have already been done really well by great artists. The risk is always that you'll be compared. But I kind of threw caution away because I noticed the live crowds really like those pieces so why not throw them on the record too?

Your career right now is mostly as a solo artist. Do you miss the interaction of playing with other people?

I play with other people sometimes and I played as a session musician in Japan but I find there's so much to learn playing solo, so much to be explored.

- ¤   Harry Manx   ¤ -

It's so challenging to see how much you can accomplish with just your two hands and I'm still very fascinated by that journey.

- ¤ -

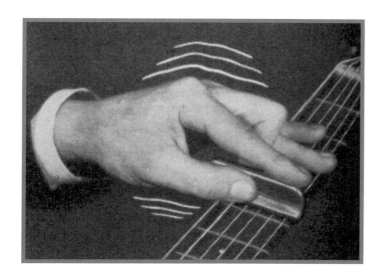

*Better living through science, from Nick Manoloff's
Hawaiian Guitar Method, 1936*

Bob Brozman

Bob Brozman's music redefines musical diversity. As a performer, his energy and virtuoso abilities on lap-style, bottleneck, and fingerstyle standard guitar have made him popular with concert audiences around the world. He has been a pioneer in playing lap-style instruments in diverse world music settings that blend rhythms and timbres from Hawaiian, Indian, African, Japanese, Okinawan, Caribbean, Greek, and Gypsy music with blues and even Hip-Hop.

Born in New York in 1954, Bob discovered National metal-bodied guitars at age thirteen, eventually becoming a world-renowned expert on their history and an authority on historical Hawaiian music. He amassed a large collection of 78 rpm records from which he has produced and contributed liner notes for five CD collections on the Rounder and Folklyric labels. In 1988, Bob recorded *Remembering the Songs of Our Youth* with the Tau Moe Family, an album that re-created the family's Hawaiian music from the late 1920s.

Bob's continued passion for National guitars led him to write *The History and Artistry of National Resonator Instruments* - the definitive book on the subject - in 1993.

- ¤ Bob Brozman ¤ -

His earliest records focused on traditional blues, early jazz, and calypso. His catalog now includes more than twenty CDs with his most recent projects involving collaboration with over four dozen artists from more than thirteen different countries. In addition to producing educational videos for *Homespun Tapes*, Bob is an Adjunct Professor at Macquarie University in Sydney, Australia where he lectures on ethnomusicology. He is also working toward creating a foundation to help third-world musicians obtain playable instruments, strings, and basic recording equipment.

How did you come to play lap-style guitar?

I started playing guitar when I was five years old. When I was about eight or nine, I started hearing blues music and being attracted to it. Then, when I was about thirteen, I had my first exposure to a National resonator guitar and it just sent me over the moon. I liked everything about it. My first guitar was a [National] Style-O and then, soon after, I got a [National] Tricone. I got them in pawnshops in New York City. So, throughout my teenage years, I played a lot of blues and only just a little bit on my lap.

During that time, I would purchase any LP that had a picture of a National on it. I found this copy of *Old Timey Steel Guitar Classics* put out by Arhoolie that had a Tricone leaning on a chair on a front porch somewhere. So I bought it for the *photograph* and on there was one track by Sol Hoopii. That really turned my head around and I resolved at that point to start collecting 78s and to start playing lap-style.

Now, I've been playing guitar almost forty-three years and lap style almost thirty years. Having said that, any musical instrument is sort of an infinite path of learning and improving.

Do you consider yourself equally proficient on both standard guitar and lap steel?

I can play all kinds of very fancy non-lap guitar – high speed picking and all this fancy harmony and read a foreign newspaper and translate it for you at the same time. But the lap guitar demands all your attention. For one thing, it's literally less than a millimeter between heaven and hell in terms of intonation. Nothing sounds worse than a beautiful song played with slightly off intonation.

The other thing I've realized over decades is that the process of playing a musical instrument literally is: "How do you feel emotionally, and what are you doing about it in practical terms with your muscles?" Intellect almost doesn't even come into it. It's expressing emotion with muscle movement.

So, taking that idea a little further, you imagine that your feelings as a musician are a curved line and your muscle movements are stair-stepped, straight-line movements – like calculus – trying to describe a curve with straight lines. You have to make the stair steps as tiny as possible. The slide guitar forces you to become aware of those gradations and my goal as a musician is to make my stepwise muscle movements so fine that they resemble, most closely, the curve of my feelings. Debashish Bhattacharya is a musician who has gotten closer to that than anybody. His stair steps are invisible.

How are you doing in meeting your goal?

My stair steps are invisible at times, but what sounds really smooth and professional to my fans might sound really jerky and awkward to me. The path of growth in music never stops.

You mentioned Sol Hoopii. You listened very carefully to the early acoustic Hawaiian guitarists like Sam Ku West and Sol. Can you talk a bit about their styles and what set them apart?

Absolutely. First of all, there's a law that applies in any discipline: 90% of everything is crap. The 10% that's not crap goes all the way from good to mind-bendingly transcendental. So, in every generation of musicians, there's really only a few that are in that higher 10%.

First, I'd like to go a little earlier than Sol. Tau Moe, who I'd have to say is one of my main gurus, was actually a similar age to Sol and recording in a similar era. Stylistically, however, because he was from the country and not the city, his steel guitar sound, even though it was recorded in 1929, really sounds like 1915 - the generation before Sol, musically speaking. It's very folky, it's very ethnic. There's no jazz involved and barely any ragtime involved. Sol was the guy who really took it to the next generation by going to LA in the mid-'20s and hanging out with black jazz musicians and trying to imitate horn lines. He really took it to a new place, both with his technique and with his ideas.

Of that late 20's period, Sol is absolutely my favorite followed closely by Sam Ku West, who was a beautiful player but less adventurous than Sol.

Even today, his combination of relaxation and incredible technique really stands out. The ascending glissandi you do up the first string while playing a forward roll sounds like Sol. What aspects of his style did you adapt for your own?

It's actually a *backward* roll. The guy who invented that was Frank Fererra but he never used it to roll upward. It's basically a triplet and you can break it up in the same sense that Django Reinhardt's rhythm section is broken up by going: one-and a-TWO-three-four…one-and a-TWO-three-four. So, Fererra perfected that thing of going: duttle-a dut …duttle-a-dut … dum-dum. Duttle-a-dut … duttle-a-dut … dum-dum … to get those triplets to start phrases. Then Sol just took that a little bit further. That's something I've been doing for many, many years.

Hawaiian guitar playing has really informed my other guitar playing with techniques that don't belong on normal guitar. With fingerstyle guitar, somebody seems to have set down a rule that you're only allowed to touch one string per pick and I just think that's absurd. So I do all those triplet movements over one string, over three strings,or as a strumming movement over all six strings.

So, Sol is a musician that teaches us the value of pure mechanical practice. Debashish is an extreme example of that. He gave a workshop at my house where the first hour was simply spent on the major scale and the 65,336 combinations of practice exercises that you can do with that (laughs). Debashish's nuance of note is just unbelievable. We all already know as slide guitar players that any note can be articulated 500 different ways. With Debashish, it's more like 5,000 different ways.

- ¤ Bob Brozman ¤ -

To western ears, the salient feature of Indian guitar playing is to play many notes with a single pick attack.

That's one of the stylistic flags and that act alone really makes you a better Western steel player too, believe me. You start with two notes, then three, then four notes with one stroke. It really improves your bar work.

Let's talk about steel guitar tunings. You use a wide variety of tunings. Can you give a primer on the tunings you use and the kind of music to which they lend themselves?

I started in low bass open G as my first open tuning. I think there's a fascinating story behind that tuning. Basically, the guitar came with colonialism all over the world. In my work, I'm collaborating with cultures that are victims of colonialism 'cause that's where all the interesting music happens. The western view is that its music is considered the legitimate music and everything else is "world music" or "folk music." In point of fact, if you make Europe's musical culture of equal size to any other musical culture, you will quickly find that the bizarre culture on the planet is the European one. They have a really strange way of looking at music.

For one thing, the temperament system of tuning is so unnatural. The Greeks figured out the modes by taking a string and dividing. You divide a string in half and get an octave higher, you divide in 3^{rds}, you get the 5th, you divide in 4^{ths}, and you get the octave again, and so forth. All of these divisions of the string generated notes in what we call the modes. A seven-note major scale, for example, is a mode.

All of those seven notes, whether major or minor, Arabic mode or whatever, are all comprised of simple whole number ratios, like 4 over 3 or 2 over 1. None of these numbers are higher than 10. Now that system works beautifully if you're in the modal key. It was the construction of the keyboard that revealed the problems with the system. So, the Europeans came up with this twelve tones to the octave tuning compromise in order to make things sound kind of in tune in all keys.

As we all know, things in nature that are beautiful are nearly always mathematically simple. So therefore, these beautiful, simple whole number ratios got detuned with a bunch of decimal mathematical noise added to them. To me, one of the ugliest sounds in the world is the equally tempered major third on a piano. It sounds like a car horn. This is why guitarists struggle with their B string. If you're in standard tuning, your B string should read 7 cents flat on a tuner in order to sound natural. So, basically, the whole European tuning system is unnatural.

The hierarchal way of looking at things is the whole problem with western civilization. It's an experiment that happened and the world only got one chance. Western civilization got hold of everything with its method of objectifying people and animals. Instead of being part of something, you're above it and therefore have the right to control it, exploit it, or destroy it.

So why have I said all this? When native people were confronted with the European-tuned guitar and strummed it in standard tuning, it didn't sound pretty. So the least number of turns of the pegs to get to a pleasing sound gets you low bass G tuning. So, open G tuning shows up in Mississippi, Mexico, Hawaii, Africa, Cuba, the Philippines, and India.

I began with low bass G as a blues player and moved into it for Hawaiian as well. In all my guitar playing, I play the following families of tunings: standard, open G major, G minor, G add 2nd, and G suspended – G with a 4th.

- ¤ **Bob Brozman** ¤ -

The same applies to D tuning. I play D major, D minor, DADGAD, and a set of C tunings where the major or minor 3rd is on the top string.

Bob Brozman's Tunings						
Strings	1	2	3	4	5	6
D major	D	A	F#	D	A	D
D minor	D	A	F	D	A	D
D sus	D	A	G	D	A	D
G major	D	B	G	D	G	D
G minor	D	Bb	G	D	G	D
G add 9	D	A	G	D	G	D
C major	E	C	G	C	G	C
C add 9	D	C	G	C	G	C
Double C	C	C	G	C	G	C

Everything you know in G tuning, move it one string closer to your face and it works in D major. Everything you know in D tuning, move it one string away from your face and it works in G tuning. In G tuning, move it one string away from your face and it works in C major tuning. I tune the E to Eb for minor and I tune it to D for an add 2. I even sometimes tune it to C – so that the first two strings are both C's for the ultimate open tuning which is neither masculine or feminine.

In the past, you've been known to comment that the more complex the tuning, the less hand work required. Do you still feel that tunings like C6th, which offer close voiced harmony, are inherently less desirable?

It's really a matter of personal choice. I really like having to do all the work with the bar. Because that bar is an extension of my heart in terms of expression. I play a little bit in C# minor to get that western swing sound, but you start relying on the tuning as a gimmick and it just has a characteristic sound. If I play in open G, I can play Mexican music, Arabic music, Hawaiian music, blues, anything. If I use a C6th, it's gonna sound like western swing or '30s & '40s Hawaiian so it's very restrictive, stylistically. It has a kind of clichéd sound to it. In open G, I'll drop the middle G to F# and raise the middle G to A. That gives you a D6th or a Bm7, which was Sol's invention. He was really the father of the thing.

His effect on western swing has rarely been acknowledged.

Absolutely. If you listen to early western swing it sounds like Sol's later recordings.

You were practically a one-man revival for National metal body guitars but recently, you've been using wooden body guitars on stage and in recordings. Did your ears need a change?

No, not at all. I still continue to use the Nationals. I love the wooden Hawaiian guitars 'cause they're just another voice. On my current solo touring rig I bring a standard Tricone, a baritone Tricone, and a Kona Bear Creek and sometimes, a massive baritone 7-string Bear Creek. My little Kona is a 23" scale so it's meant to be tuned to A. I tune it up to C so it just sings like a bird. The 7-string is meant to be tuned down to F but I tend to tune it up to A. Again, to get this high tension sort of singing treble.

What do you think about the hollow-neck Weissenborn design versus the solid neck Kona design?

Apples and oranges. It's hard to compare. For old instruments, I prefer the Weissenborns. For new instruments, they're just two different animals. The only square-neck Bear Creek I have is the 7-string, which is a hollow-neck Weissenborn Instrument. But, the dimensions are quite different. I gotta be honest with you, I've really come to prefer the Bear Creek to the old Weissenborns for most applications.

There are two kinds of woods used in the [*vintage*] Weissenborns and David Lindley and I have very different tastes regarding that because of the way we play. We're friends and we play together beautifully. He likes the more open, straight-grained guitars and I like the curly stuff – and it's not for the look.

I'm very interested in material science around guitar making and what physical attributes result in what kind of sonic results. With the open grain wood, when you strike the note, it's actually louder than the curly ones – maybe 10%, even 15% louder. But, with less dense straight wood, the energy of the note dissipates more quickly. A lot of Hawaiian guitar playing is on the first couple of strings above the 12th fret. What I'm looking for is a guitar that gets louder and louder above the 12th fret.

If you take a Martin guitar, or an open-grain Weissenborn, or a lot of the Weissenborn copies that are being made, as you get above the 12th fret the ratio of the pick sound…the puh-puh-puh-puh… begins to have more power than the ringing note. With the curlier Weissenborns, because I play on stage with a microphone, I'm willing to give up 10% of the initial volume in order to have 80% more sustain. The Bear Creek I play has even more sustain and, man, that thing just sings. You can go have breakfast and come back and the note's still ringing.

You and Led Kapaana have developed a near-telepathic ability to complement one another's playing. How did this come about?

If you see Ledward and me play live and you close your eyes you'd think that there's four people sitting there. Two are playing and two are just giggling like schoolboys. Even on slow beautiful stuff we'll sometimes giggle and chortle 'cause we're just knocking each other out. Ledward is a guy whose joy of music is just about more than anyone's. He's just a natural musician.

I made two albums with him. I had met him eight years before and jammed in an all-Hawaiian club. Then 8 years later, I was invited to come in the studio and do *Kika Kila* with him. No rehearsal; we just sat down, "Okay, how about *Mai Kai No Kauai*? Okay, 1, 2, 3, 4 – let's roll."
That whole record is basically like that - a jam session.

At that time, all I knew about was 1920s and '30s Hawaiian playing. Those players always had a rhythm guitar and never had to play rhythm for anyone. I'm trading choruses with Ledward so I had to develop some technical language of rhythm playing on steel. I figured out a couple very cool techniques for accompaniment.

Then, after touring for 60 or 70 shows since then and recording the 2nd album, the telepathy is really there. Now, my language of rhythm playing on steel guitar is much more developed. With the telepathy we have now on stage, either guy can change to a different song and within a 16th note the other guy'll be there. That's one level. The other level is the sound of things dampening and opening up very gradually. If Ledward starts doing a damping phrase….bup-bup-bup-bup-bup…it sends me a message that doesn't even get into my brain. It goes directly to my arm muscles and I'm with him.

How did you come to adopt hip-hop and Reunion Island rhythms to the acoustic steel?

You understand you're talking to a highly opinionated person, right? I make it my business to only spout opinions on things that I know about. My opinion is this: the 4/4 pop rhythm of American music is infecting the entire world and destroying musical cultures right and left everywhere. That beat is the most boring, lifeless beat ever invented by human beings. For musicians, it's very important that they know that the rhythm of pop, musicologically speaking, is no different than military marching music or Polka music. *Now*, how hip is that?

In the 20th century, the rhythm of popular music changed about every ten years until the rock beat came in and then things kind of froze for about 40 years. The first new interesting beat in popular music came from Hip-Hop. Why?

Rhythmically, the world is divided into two cultures: the colonized and the colonizers. The colonizers are interested in the beat. They see the beat as something you follow and something you march to. The colonized, who are marched upon, see the beat as something to react to. The interesting thing in music is the "and." In blues music, most guitar phrases either start on the *and* before one or the *and* after one. In African music, the one is even less important. In Reunion music, the *and* is the quick *and* of a triplet – the opposite of a shuffle. A shuffle is: 1-2-THREE-1-2-THREE. In Reunion music it's: 1-2-3-4-1-TWO-THREE-1-2-THREE. I encourage musicians and audiences to support their own local culture instead of buying into this Americanization.

If I'm stuck in a rental car somewhere I'll usually try to find a Hip-Hop station. I don't really care about the lyrics or the samples or the lifestyle. I just like the beats, as a musician. The difference with hip-hop is that the bass drum is put in surprising *ands* and it swings. When you hear Hip-Hop, there's a mental hi-hat in your head going: 1-2-3, 1-2-3, 1-2-3. It's a swinging quality.

You've played in all these different musical genres: blues, Hawaiian, West African, and Okinawan. How has it changed your music and how has it changed you as a person?

I would be the first person to point a finger at a dilettante, someone who's just dabbling in different musical styles. I'm fully committed to the styles that I attempt to play. I'm also fully prepared to be told by anybody I collaborate with that I'm doin' it wrong. My attitude is very different than some more famous collaborators.

I've never been a rock musician. I don't show up with a big entourage. That means the party I'm working with is not afraid of me and not looking at me as a meal ticket. We sleep on the same floor, eat the same food, and split the money 50-50. My attitude is something like an anthropologist. When I work with someone, I'm practicing four levels of anthropology.

One, the physical: I'm literally looking at their pupil diameter, their respiration, and the subtle muscle movements in their arm to see how each individual musician breathes his own music.

Level two: the musicological - what makes Okinawan music sound Okinawan? Level three: social and historical - I make it my business to know the history of the place. The fourth level would be a kind of social, behavioral level. What's the best way to ensure the comfort of the person I'm working with?

So, I don't meet these guys half way. My primary goal is their comfort and their happiness and that just makes good music and great friendship. I would do anything for any of them and they would do anything for me. There's a free flowing exchange that doesn't feel like pushing or pulling. So I don't feel I lose anything at all, I gain massively.

What specifically, have you gained?

From Djeli Mousa [*Djeli Mousa Diawara plays the kora, an African harp-lute*] I gained the ability to sit in front of another musician and be forced to play a piece of music that I've never heard before , with no rehearsal. In Djeli's music there is no overall structure but it's full of microstructure. So I learned to sit on the edge of my seat and pay attention.

What I learned from Takashi [*Takashi Hirayasu plays the Okinawan snakeskin banjo*] is there's no music that's too simple for you. You can always bring the beauty to the music.

What I learned from Rene' [*René Lacaille is a master musician from Reunion Island in the southwestern Indian Ocean*] is kind of a rhythm liberty. Now I feel almost to the point where I can put a beat anywhere I want to at any time.

From Debashish [*Debashish Bhattacharya, is a master of the Hindustani slide guitar*] I've learned some of the biggest lessons of all. When you're confronted with such a wonderful musician, it's kind of like a mirror for your own flaws and shortcomings. So, I went through quite a process of discovering the many flaws I have and then learning to accept them and go forward from there.

The things I'm learning about music are becoming more basic, more general and fundamental. If someone forced me to boil down the act of playing music to one verb – you get one verb to describe what it is – then that verb is to *be*. As corny as that may sound, the slide guitar leads you more efficiently toward that goal than normal guitar does because you cannot let down your attention for a minute when you're playing slide.

Working on this record with Debashish these last few weeks has really confirmed what I knew to be true. Playing music teaches you how to be a person.

- ¤ -

Debashish Bhattacharya

Debashish Bhattacharya is but one droplet in the two thousand year old musical stream that is Indian classical music. He performs this music, however, on lap-style guitar - an instrument used in Indian music for less than sixty years.

Debashish and his siblings began to learn Indian music from their parents before learning the alphabet. In childhood, he mastered many Indian classical instrumental styles and vocal music from different musical teachers in Calcutta. He became a disciple and student of Brij Bhushan Kabra, the father of Indian classical guitar, and trained under Pundit Ajoy Chakrabarty, the eminent Indian vocalist, as well as sarod master Ustad Ali Akbar Khan.

Debashish gave his first guitar recital at the age of four on *All India Radio.* In his twenties, he evolved a unique style of playing guitar, synthesizing selected features of various other traditional Indian instruments such as the Vina, Sitar, Sarod and Kannur. In 1984, at age twenty-one, he received the *President of India Award.*

- ¤ Debashish Bhattacharya ¤ -

He developed his own acoustic steel guitar after years of research and experience. Like many Indian string instruments, it has sympathetic strings that vibrate in consort with the guitar's primary strings. His latest venture is a manufacturing effort to make his designs available to other players around the world.

What are your earliest memories of music?

Many. I remember attending many performances of our great legends of Indian classical music when I was a kid. My father used to take me to listen at music festivals where there were all-night concerts; from 10pm to 8am or sometimes, 7pm to 6am. These were big concerts with maestros who are the equivalent to God to Indian music lovers. Specifically, by name, they were Usted Ali Akbar Khan on Saroud, Pandit Ravi Shankar on Sitar, and vocalists Ustad Bade Ghulam Ali Khan and Amir Khan.

I understand that vocal music is very important to the study of Indian instrumental music.

Yes. My father and mother were very deep in vocal music going back beyond six or seven generations in that same profession. So we are basically *genetically* vocalists. The custom in our family is to give the lesson when the human brain forms - from two to five years. My brother Subashish Bhattacharya is a prominent tabla player and we all got the same training from the age of three.

Was there any kind of steel guitar tradition in India when you were growing up?

Since the arrival of Europeans to our country in the 14th century with the British East India company, Calcutta has received very many slide guitarists, as well as Spanish-style guitarists. Tau Moe, the Hawaiian slide guitarist who stayed from 1941 to '47 in Calcutta, has been a great influence to Bengali music lovers and guitar players of a new generation. They took the instrument but tried to play our own music on the lap steel guitars - all sorts of contemporary songs.

In 1951 or '52, black and white movies started in our country. At that time, the songs were so popular that people wanted to play those film songs on the lap steel guitar. So steel guitar playing got much more popular. That period - from 1952 to about 1970 - was a prime era of contemporary songs all over the world; a golden era of music. That love of film music still exists in Calcutta.

Brij Bhushan Kabra started another trend in 1958. He started playing classical Indian music in the societies where the maharajas and the royal families used to listen to him. He moved from a 6-string to a 7-string guitar but instead of six, he used three main strings. If he were in the key of E, he tuned them to EAE or DGD, in the key of D. The other four strings were towards the body and were drone or supporting strings called chikari.

These drone strings were like those on the sitar. He became very popular through collaboration with two other musicians, Hariprasad Chaurasia, the legendary bamboo flute player, and Shivkumar Sharma, who played santoor. [*The santoor is similar to a hammered dulcimer and is played using mallets to strike the strings*].

Their album, *Call of the Valley*, is timeless. It's still in print and available on CD.

Ah, yes. Their first record was an all-time great. Still, it is a best seller in our country. So, all these three were coming up with their own style of performance that was unique and became legendary.

- ¤ Debashish Bhattacharya ¤ -

Without any doubt, Brij Bhushan Kabra, in our classical raga music, is the pioneer of Indian classical steel guitar.

How did you come to play the guitar?

My father was a government servant, apart from his musical personality. One day, my father came back from his office with a small round hole six-string guitar. My father said, "I have a colleague who needed some money. So I gave him the money but he's honorable, so he gave me his guitar in exchange for repayment."

My mother sat with me one day when I was three to engage with that guitar and me. She found that by putting a steel bar over the frets she could play the Sa, Re, Ga, Ma, Ba, Dha, Ni, Sa …that's Do, Re, Me, Fa, So, La, Ti, Do in Indian form. She taught it to me and told me to play and I remember, I was sitting the whole day and in the evening, when my father came back from the office, I was almost playing the national anthem on guitar.

Seeing that quick transformation in me, my parents thought that guitar would be a venture for my future. I left everything and kept on playing and within a few days, I was playing all the songs I knew from my father and mother - like Indian classical compositions called khyal.

So, from the age of four, I was a child prodigy and *All-India Radio Calcutta* invited me to perform on a children's program. I studied in various parts of the ocean of music: learning classical vocals, learning sitar, sarod, and tablas. I have learned from *so* many teachers in different times of my life. This has given me awareness, from my childhood, of many directions in music and that has been a blessing in my life.

There seems to be an enormous range of emotion in your music and you seem to have the technique to execute anything that you can think of. How did you build your technique on the instrument?

Well, I don't know how to speak about technique because the technique always came to me as a blessing either by practicing or even in my sleep. I dreamt some techniques in my sleep and woke up and started playing. It was so electrifying, those memories of getting that information from someone whom I have never met in my lifetime. Talking about those blessings, those memories of power that somebody has given me from somewhere I tell you, the fingerstyle I am playing today was almost explored through an invisible power in myself.

I also practiced western lap-style guitar with Rajat Mandi, who was a great lap steel teacher in Calcutta. He's still alive. I studied only two years – age five and six. I played tunes like *Sleepy Eyes* and *April in Portugal.* Those tunes were very rhythmic and tuneful but didn't have any emotion – the emotion I carry from my generations – at that point in my life. I regularly meet my teacher Rajat Mandi now who told me, "If you hadn't learned that music it would be a great loss to Indian slide guitar because you chose a very big ocean to swim in and crossed the barrier of all cultures." I used to play a small song, *Bonanza* [*the American TV Western theme*], and I remember I was playing that piece in my home as a kid and I discovered that the double pick with thumb and first finger is much easier for me than picking with the thumb and middle finger. That was a joy.

That memory was a blessing in my classical performance of Indian music on lap steel guitar. Every week I was sitting with my sitar teacher and whatever he was playing on sitar I was doing on my guitar – that double picking with thumb and first finger. This gave me, later, the power of doing any staccatos on slide guitar more powerfully than anyone can do with the first finger and middle finger. The thumb is the strongest finger in all five fingers.

Tell me about the Hindustani slide guitar. You were the first to move the chikari - or drone strings - to the audience side of the instrument.

Since childhood, I played all the classical instrumental styles and ragas on the 6-string guitar. At the age of twenty-one, I got the *President of India Award*. I stood first in the *All-India Radio Competition* which is a very prestigious competition for young up-and-coming musicians of our country. I was the first Indian guitar player who stood first. I competed with sitar and Sarod and all Indian instruments. But, inside of me, was a pain developing for two or three years.

If only my guitar could get a resonance like sitar or sarod, which we call *gunj*, which is the Hindi word meaning resonance of the body. So I was thinking every night what to do to get some more activity in my guitar. At that time, I was seeing some guitars in shops with *back* chikari on the body side. I was also seeing some of my future guru's followers who were playing slide guitar in that way – in the back with the thumb. But to engage the Chikari with my thumb was not my idea because if you engage the thumb in the chikari, you are playing all the other strings with your weaker first and middle finger. More than 60% of Indian classical guitar players in our country still play with those weaker fingers.

I went to a company called Gibtone in 1984 and asked them to make a guitar with a wood appendage parallel to the fretboard and put the chikari *facing* the audience. They also put the resonating strings in the back at my direction. That was the first form of the Hindustani slide guitar. It was a round hole guitar.

1984 was also the year I saw my guru, Brij Bhushan Khabra. I met him one night with my father after a show in Calcutta. He interviewed me for six hours. He wanted to know why I played this

Brij Bhushan Kabra & Debashish Bhattacharya

way, because my technique and my instrument was completely different than his. It was like a police interrogation (laughs). After that interrogation, I played for him with my brother Subashish. We played raga *Shree* and *Yaman* and he encouraged me to play more. Then he told my father, "This boy has unique blessings. If you'll permit me, I would like to be his second father and take him with me and see what I can do for him. I want to give him my music, but what he has discovered is unique in its own way and I don't want to change that so he will feel his own arch of emotion. I want to keep that and put it in a more educated way with his own explorations."

So, I went with him all the way to Amadabad, leaving my family for ten years. So I stayed there for ten years in a musical concentration camp. He made it possible for me to come from a boy of many innovations to a master musician.

Do you change tunings to match the mood and mode of a given Raga?

In India, there are thousands of ragas but I play mostly 150 to 200 ragas in which I feel comfortable to perform professionally, but I know many more than that. My innovation was to get a group of ragas in a particular tuning. In a given tuning I practiced many, many ragas. In another tuning, I play another group of ragas that have the commonality of the scale. Suppose I'm in E major tuning, the first open strings are: E, B, A, G# - an E major scale. If I have a raga in which B and G# are dominant - there may be other notes major or minor, it doesn't matter - my preference will be E major for that raga. But if the B and G notes are dominant – not G# - then my preference will be E minor. If E, A, and C# are the prominent notes, than I use A major. If A and C are prominent, then it will be A minor. This gives me enormous opportunity to play any Indian form of music and allows you to take more advantage of your open strings.

How many string are on your guitar?

Twenty-four strings. My guitar has six "strum strings." I never changed my guitar from six to three strings because I feel if you take a single string from a 6-string slide guitar you lose many harmonics in your whole guitar's resonance. You have three octaves of E, two of A, and the 3rd string G# which is the 2nd harmony of E. Some musicians in India play 4-string or 5-string guitar. I don't believe in that. If you take a leg off the human body it is unbalanced so I never believed in taking strings off the guitar. To me the guitar is like the human body and should be balanced.

Do you play only single notes with the tip of your bullet bar or do you ever play chords?

I play double stops but not very often in Indian music. Indian music is like a flowing river of melody. Indian melodies are formed by the passage between the notes with particular melodic nuances. So, for that melodic movement you're not allowed to use double stops. In other forms of popular or semi-classical music or my own compositions I play all the techniques of Western culture.

You've designed what you call a *trinity* of new instruments for lap-style playing. Please tell me about them.

I was never happy with the tone of the instruments we used in my country for Indian music. In India, we always got the voice of American, or German, or South American guitars. We never had our *own* culture in our guitar. It was always like we were importing foreign stuff into our music. I wanted to get a better Indian character in my instruments – closer to sitar, santour and sarod. The instrument's identity, I believe, is not in its look but in its character or identity. So I wanted to give a new voice to my instruments - my own cultural voice.

This 24–string guitar which I play is the sound of four Indian traditional instrument's voices blended in one voice. The 6-string guitar sounds like the lower octave of the vina. The 4th string area of the next lower octave gets the sound of saroud. The other string areas in the other octave give a blend of sitar, santour and violin. Why violin? Because slide guitar really lives in between bowing and plucking instruments. It relates to the piano and violin – the most known classical instruments in the west.

Because it includes all the instruments in one, I named it in a Sanskrit name, chaturangui, which means a guitar with additional blend of four tones. The *gui* is added because this is a guitar, it is not a vina. All over the world the guitar has its own voice, which is why it is so popular.

The second one is a double-string guitar like a 12-string. This is the first form of 12-string guitar in which we hear a cry with more emotion and better sustain in sliding form. When we glide a bullet bar on double strings it sustains better. This is called the gandharva - a sound that belongs to the cosmic world. The sound portrays the beauty of the goddess of the Gandharva.

The third of the trinity is called anandi, which sounds like a ukulele but again, in a slide form.

Will people be able to purchase these instruments?

These guitars will soon be coming to North America under the name *Debashish Guitar & Company*. I didn't want to have a company but I have seen that without control of your production you cannot satisfy yourself. These are not regular guitars. These are my own dream and my own "babies" so I wanted to have more care and control of the process, at least in the beginning. I don't want to have these like a selfish, egotistic musician. I want to share these with my fellow musicians. I have also written the first-ever book on Indian classical slide guitar. It will be coming out very soon.

I have recorded these three new instruments in studios and sent a sample to my great gurus, Ustad Zakir Hussein and Bri Bhushan Kabra, who sent me a very nice letter. He said that when he heard this trinity of slide guitars he was so emotionally moved that he wrote with tears in his eyes. Being with a guru as a son is always a blessing that cannot be bought.

How has interacting with western musicians, like Bob Brozman, affected your music?

Bob is one of my most beloved brothers in the western field of music. In 1996, we first worked together in Stephan Grossman's idea of East meets West called the *World of Slide Guitar* tour. We traveled throughout the West Coast with Martin Simpson and Subashish Bhattchaterya on tabla.

Bob is a very educated guitarist. His approach toward music is multidirectional. He doesn't like to do a thing over and over. He likes to take the challenge of playing music from many other cultures in his own way. That was very inspirational to me. I was all the time doing the same thing in India without any other inspiration. Bob has taken away some of my loneliness because Bob is doing the same thing that I was doing in my country alone.

We have just completed our first duet recording. For this I came to California from Calcutta. We have not yet decided the name of the album. One song on the album is a lullaby I wrote. Basically, I am a gypsy with my guitars. I barely get a chance to see my family in India. So when I'm in India, I sing every night a lullaby to make my baby sleep. So one night when my baby had gone to sleep I lit the bed lamp and wrote down those notes. When we were in the studio I told Bob, "You are allowed to do anything but always think of the sound of whispering a lullaby in a baby's ear. Don't make any sound that makes her wake up." He did beautiful harmonies.

I am also working with *Remember Shakti* and I have blessings from the great maestro of guitar, John McLaughlin, since I got the chance to work with him. *Remember Shakti* did so well they won four Grammys.

- ¤ Debashish Bhattacharya ¤ -

John is taking a year and a half break from touring and working with a bunch of musicians in his home. We speak often by phone. We are looking forward to working together again on the road.

So, boats from two oceans came together with a bond of love and started floating together. The music we make together will be a new music.

- ¤ -

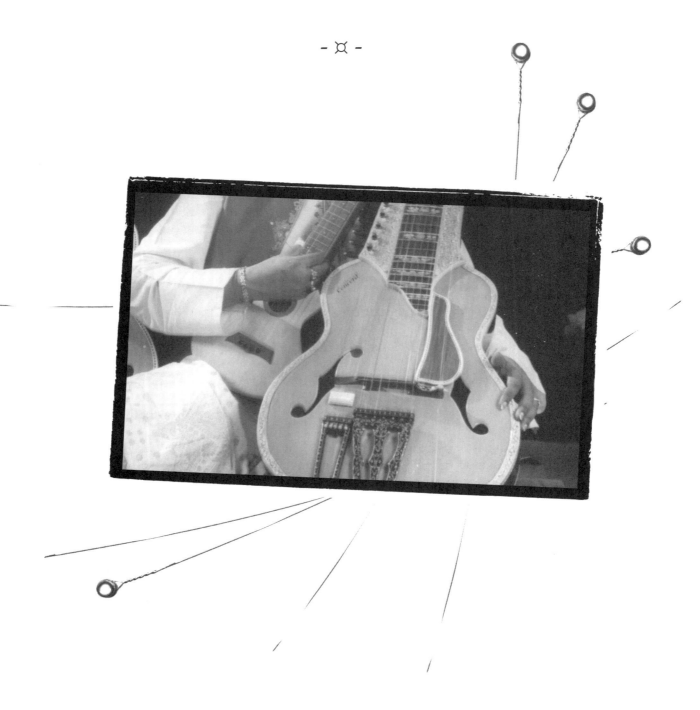

THE
INSTRUMENTS

VINTAGE STEEL GUITARS

Guitars created specifically for lap-style playing have been around for over one hundred years. The popularity of these instruments once outstripped that of Spanish guitars. As the steel guitar slowly slipped off the musical pedestal of the world's imagination, the instruments remained. Though largely relegated to closets, under the bed, music store walls and pawn shop shelves, they were still played by a smaller, but fanatically loyal constituency. Despite the fact that steel guitar became something of an underground instrument over the last forty years or so, there are still many fine vintage instruments to be found, and often, at prices far below those of vintage standard guitars.

The field of guitar design, in general, has long been an area of fertile inventiveness. There have been some instruments that were beautiful from a design standpoint yet proved to offer poor utility for players. Other guitars, while possibly lacking in aesthetics, offered outstanding tonal qualities.

There is a well-known quote by Jerry Byrd to the effect: "If you can play, it doesn't matter what guitar you've got. If you can't play, it doesn't matter what guitar you've got." While there is a lot of truth in that comment, there are certain instruments that seem to have consistently inspired steel guitarists over many, many years.

There are a number of fine books in print oriented to collectors. This is not one of them. Rather than attempt to discuss the plethora of steel guitar makers of the past and all the minutia of various models, this chapter focuses on a select group of classic instruments. Though no longer in production, they're still highly desired by players. Nevertheless, evaluating the merits or detriments of various guitars is very subjective and a personal decision for every steel guitarist. One's "holy grail" is another's "piece of junk." While this listing is incomplete, it offers a look at a number of acoustic and electric instruments that have stood the test of time as successive generations of musicians have appreciated, owned and played them, and then passed them on to the next generation.

Right
1929 Martin
price list

MARTIN *Hawaiian* GUITARS

Especially constructed and adjusted for Hawaiian Steel playing

Style No.	2-17 H	Mahogany Amateur Size	$ 30.00 Retail
Style No.	0-18 K	Koa Concert Size	$ 45.00 Retail
Style No.	0-28 K	Koa Concert Size	$ 75.00 Retail
Style No.	00-40 H	Rosewood Grand Concert Size	$100.00 Retail

Detailed Descriptions and Illustrations on Request.

Made and Fully Guaranteed by

C. F. MARTIN & CO., INC.
Established 1833

Acoustic Steel Guitars

Martin

The instruments of the C.F. Martin Company of Nazareth, Pennsylvania are among the most desired, played, and collectible acoustic guitars of all time. The Martin aesthetic favors simple, understated design elements, the finest tone woods and a clear, ringing tone that musicans have found adaptable to a wide range of popular music. Martin's Hawaiian guitars were some of the earliest and best instruments created for lap-style playing and were used by many of the pioneering professional Hawaiian guitarists, such as Sol Hoopii and Frank Fererra.

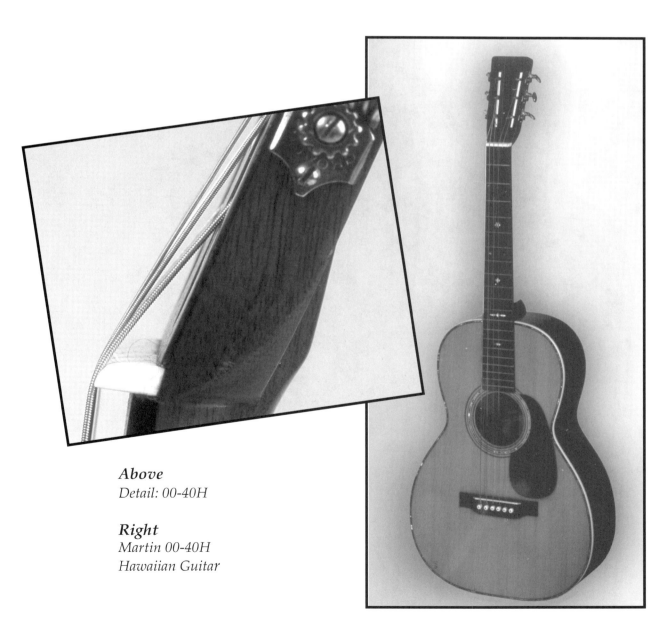

Above
Detail: 00-40H

Right
Martin 00-40H
Hawaiian Guitar

MARTIN GUITAR
0-18 KOA
HAWAIIAN STYLE

KOAWOOD BODY, MAHOGANY NECK,
EBONY FINGERBOARD AND BRIDGE, PLAIN
INLAY AND POSITION DOTS.
THE UNSURPASSED MARTIN GUITAR
EQUIPPED FOR HAWAIIAN STYLE PLAYING
PRICE $40.00
OTHER STYLES MADE TO ORDER

February 1921.

Above
Martin 00-28H Hawaiian

Right:
1921 advertisement

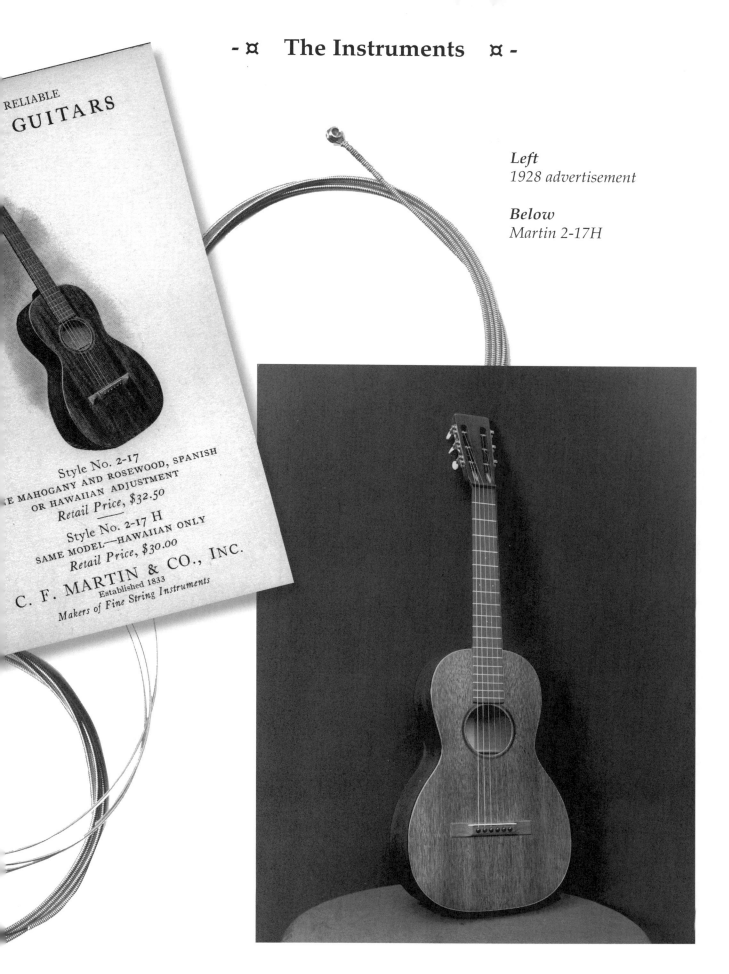

RELIABLE
GUITARS

Style No. 2-17
E MAHOGANY AND ROSEWOOD, SPANISH
OR HAWAIIAN ADJUSTMENT
Retail Price, $32.50

Style No. 2-17 H
SAME MODEL—HAWAIIAN ONLY
Retail Price, $30.00

C. F. MARTIN & CO., INC.
Established 1833
Makers of Fine String Instruments

Left
1928 advertisement

Below
Martin 2-17H

Weissenborn

Herman Weissenborn was a steel guitar visionary. The body shape and hollow necks of his Los Angeles-made Hawaiian guitars offer a significant improvement in volume over that of standard flat top guitars. Often described as "cello-like" or "piano-like", the original Weissenborns have a tonal magic that is unduplicated by other instruments despite their sometimes sloppy interior construction. Weissenborns were made of Hawaiian koa wood and came in four styles offering higher grade woods and increasing levels of decoration, such as fancy inlays and a distinctive "rope" binding made from contrasting colors of wood. Solid-neck models were available under the name "Kona" and offer a tighter sound than the hollow-necked models. Players such as David Lindley and Ben Harper have made Weissenborn guitars collectible and prices for rare, original examples have risen sharply over the last decade.

Facing Page & Above
Weissenborn Style-1 belonging to Ed Gerhard

Center
Weissenborn Style-1

Left
1940's Hawaiian postcard

Electric Steel Guitars

Oahu

The Oahu Publishing Company of Cleveland, Ohio was a retail empire for all things related to lap steel guitars from approximately the early 1930's through the mid 1960's. The company offered Hawaiian and Spanish acoustic and electric guitars, sheet music, and a wide range of accessories. The instruments that carried the Oahu name were manufactured by Gretsch, Harmony, Washburn, Gibson, Kay, and Epiphone. Working through Oahu sheet music was something of a rite of passage for many budding steelers during the heyday of Hawaiian music.

Oahu acoustic instruments range from fairly unimpressive student models to fancy, inlaid instructor models that feature outstanding tone. Tonemaster, Diana, and Iolona electric steel guitars have found favor with players for both their tonal qualities and their design aesthetics. Oahu pickups aren't usually considered as good as those on Fender, Gibson or Rickenbacher guitars.

Left
Oahu guitar & amplifier, 1930's

Above & Right
Oahu Diana, 1940s
Tonemaster advertisement, 1940s
Oahu guitar/amp advertisement 1940s
Lesson tablature, 1940s

Rickenbacher

From its earliest inception, Rickenbacher never followed the crowd. Their aluminum "frypan" steel guitar was probably the earliest production electric guitar and proved immediately popular with professional musicans. The thick, rich sound of the Rickenbacher horseshoe pickup (the strings go directly through the magnetic field) emphasizes harmonics and is considered by many steel players to be the finest pickup ever manufactured for steel guitars. Frypans were offered in A22 [22.5"] "short-scale" and A25 [25"] "long-scale" models.

Collector/player Rick Aiello currently manufactures new magnets in collaboration with luthier Jason Lollar who winds pickups that are exact replacements for the original Rickenbacher horseshoe pickups.

According to Rick: "There were three different Rickenbacher horseshoe magnet widths: $1 \frac{1}{2}$", $1 \frac{1}{4}$", and $1\frac{1}{8}$". The earliest Rickys had "shoes" that were $\frac{3}{8}$" thick.

The magnetization of steel is different from that of other permanent magnets. In steel, it is a surface phenomenon only, meaning the domains that align in response to a magnetic field occur only at the surface of the steel, the internal domains remain random. In Alnico and other permanent magnets, all domains throughout get aligned. In Ricky magnets it is the *surface* area that is important. Thats why $1\frac{1}{2}$" shoes are preferred over $1\frac{1}{4}$".

Above
International Steel Guitar Convention founder, Dewitt Scott, Sr., with his long-scale frypan
1934 Frypan (22.5" scale)

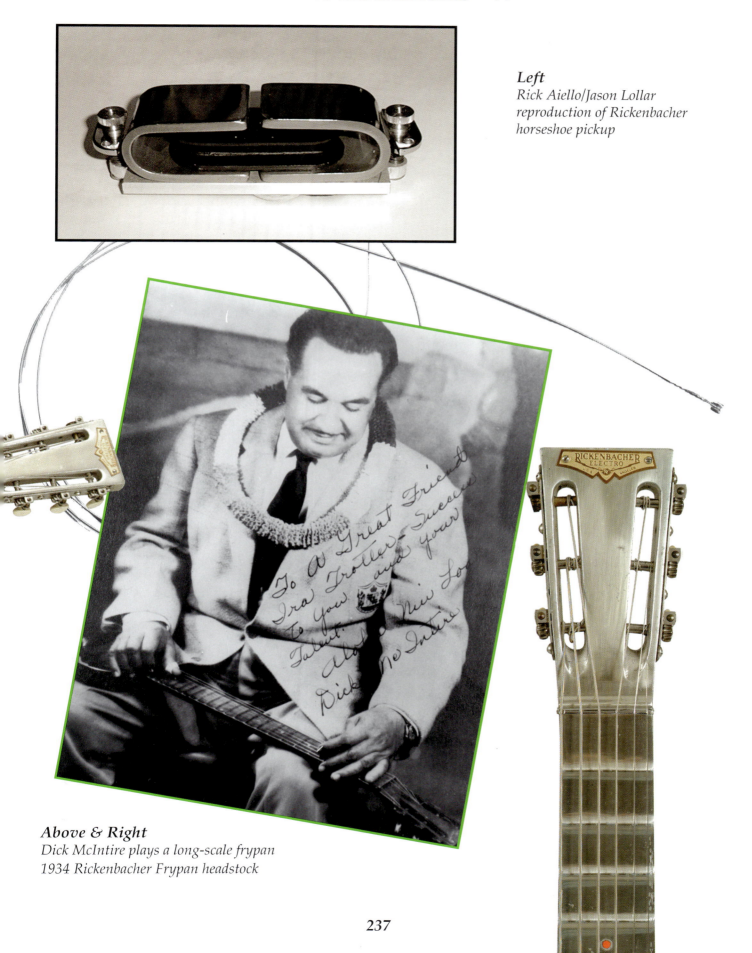

Left
*Rick Aiello/Jason Lollar
reproduction of Rickenbacher
horseshoe pickup*

Above & Right
*Dick McIntire plays a long-scale frypan
1934 Rickenbacher Frypan headstock*

Because the aluminum frypans were subject to detuning due to temperature changes, Rickenbacher developed a new line of instruments in the mid-1930s made from molded Bakelite - the first commercial plastic. The Bakelite guitars are nonetheless subject to some of the same temperature sensitivity as the frypans and their fragility can mean a broken neck if dropped. These drawbacks are well compensated by the rich tone and striking design aesthetics of the Bakelite guitars.

Jerry Byrd used 6 and 7-string Bakelites on radio and recordings in the 1940s & 1950s, inspiring many players around the world and thus increasing both the profile and desirability of these steels. David Lindley on Jackson Browne's records, and G.E. Smith in his tenure with the *Saturday Night Live Band*, proved the power of the Bakelite steels in a rock context during the 1970s & 1980s.

The early Model-B guitars feature chrome plates, thru-the-body stringing and removable necks. Later models added a metal truss rod and tailpiece, as well as white, painted or molded Bakelite plates. While the postwar models with 1 ¼" pickups are excellent instruments, the pre-war Bakelite guitars with 1½" pickups remain among the most sought after of all vintage lap steels.

Left
Circa 1939 Rickenbacher Bakelite with molded Bakelite plates

Above
1950's Rickenbacker metal body double-8. [While not as sought after as the frypans and bakelite models, the metal body guitars are nonetheless well regarded by players]. Vernon Hester, seen here in 1951, played his Rick on early 50's television broadcasts.

Left
Late 1930's Rickenbacher Bakelite with Chrome plates. [The earliest models had one volume knob and no tone knob. Circa 1939, white lines were painted on the molded frets to make them easier to see].

Center
Detail of circa 1939 Bakelite shown on page 238

Gibson

Gibson's reputation as one of the foremost guitar makers of the 20th century was earned by the exceptional high quality and consistency of its instruments and a history of innovation in instrument design. From the F-style mandolin, and the Super 400 archtop to the Les Paul solid body and hundreds of other models, Gibson has created many instruments that have become classics for both musicians and collectors. Jazz guitar legend Charlie Christian's use of a Gibson ES-150 electric Spanish guitar on his records with Benny Goodman started an electric guitar revolution that continues to this day. The single-coil pickup he used came to be called the *Charlie Christian* pickup. First crafted in aluminum, Gibson's EH-150 lap steel reflected the company's use of sunburst finishes on Michigan curly maple & high quality bindings. EH-150s were available in 6, 7, 8 and 10-string models. They were immediately popular with musicians for both their visual appeal, playability, and rich tone. The EH-150 remains a historically important guitar for vintage collectors, as well as the steel of choice for many players.

GUITARS - BANJOS - MANDOLINS - UKULELES

Gibson

ELECTRICAL INSTRUMENTS - STRINGS

THE EH-150 AMPLIFIER

A masterpiece in electrical tone reproduction—strongly made of the finest materials money can buy to give faultless performance hour after hour—an all-purpose amplifier that will take two instruments, a microphone and an extra speaker.

7 tubes with tremendous reserve power which guarantees maximum volume with ease and no distortion. 4 stage amplification with fifteen watt output, undistorted. Amplifier has high gain so that it can be used successfully with any type of microphone.

A new 12" Ultrasonic High Fidelity speaker especially de-

signed for this unit—the voice coil is sealed to prevent any dirt from getting in and causing distortion.

New design case, covered with wear-proof Aeroplane cloth, strong luggage catches and leather bumpers, easy grip handle. Removable back. Waterproof slip cover to protect amplifier from weather.

15 foot instrument cord—exceptionally strong and shielded, heavy nickel plated shielded plugs and spring protectors. 10 foot shielded amplifier cord.

Size—16½" wide, 15½" high and 8¾" deep.

CONTROL PANEL EQUIPMENT
from left to right

1. On-off switch; 2. Replaceable fuse; 3. Extra speaker socket; 4. Control dial for microphone; 5. New ruby light on-off indicator; 6. Control dial for instruments; 7. Socket for microphone; 8. Sockets for two instruments; 9. (Below instrument sockets) Bass or Normal tone control.

FOR AC-DC CURRENT
EH-160 MODEL — Same as EH-150 model but with special unit to be used with either AC or DC current. See prices to right of regular AC sets.

PRICES

	AC	AC-DC
Complete 6 string outfit—Instrument, Case, Amplifier and Cords	$160.00	$170.00
Complete 7 string outfit—Instrument, Case, Amplifier and Cords	165.00	175.00
6 string instrument only, with cord	75.00	75.00
7 string instrument only, with cord	80.00	80.00
Amplifier only	75.00	85.00
Instrument case	10.00	10.00

[35]

Below
*Gibson EH-275, early 1940s
(Only a limited number of these
guitars were made)*

Left & Above
*1937 Gibson catalog cover &
spread showing the EH-150 & amp*

Gibson EH-150, late 1930s

*Aiello/Lollar reproduction Charlie
Christian pickup*

Recording King (made by Gibson)

Gibson's 1947 catalog first featured the Ultratone model lap-steel guitar designed by the Chicago industrial design firm, Barnes & Reinecke. The Ultratone's bright colors, sleek lines and asymmetry reflected the design trends of the time, visible in such non-musical areas as furniture, kitchen appliances, automobiles and architecture. Hinged cover plates concealed the tuning pegs, pickup, bridge, and tailpiece, adding to the unique visual appeal of these guitars.

The pickups on Ultratone guitars are considered by most players to be inadequate. Their chief appeal to collectors stems almost entirely from their design aesthetics that seems to sum up the cultural ethos of the late 1940s and early 1950s.

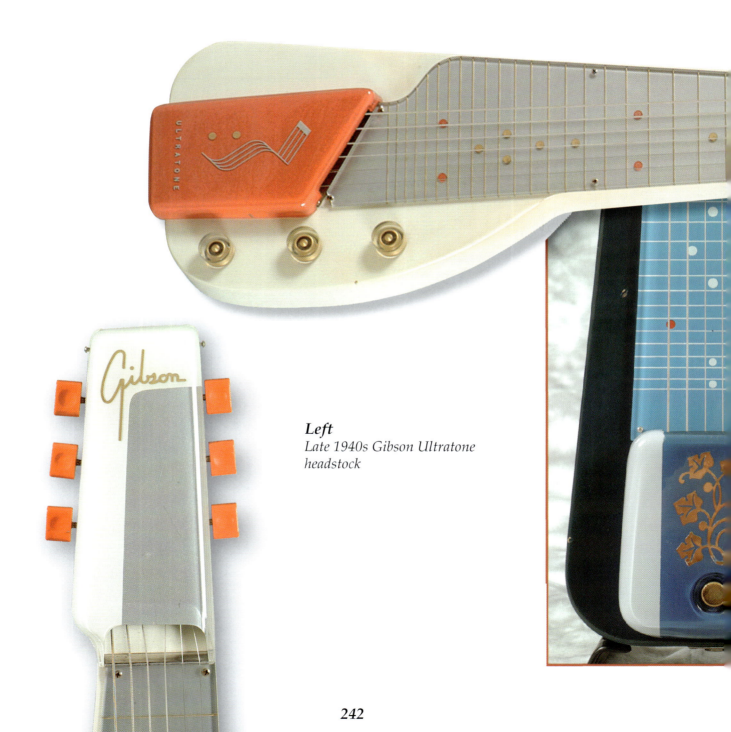

Left
Late 1940s Gibson Ultratone headstock

Below
*Two views of the unique color schemes
of the late 1940's Gibson Ultratone lap steels*

Right
1951 Gibson price list

ELECTRIC HAWAIIAN GUITARS

			PRICE (Tax. Incl.)
BR-9 9	6-string Hawaiian Guitar		$ 60.00
	Hard Shell Oblong Case for above model		10.75
BR-6 6	6-string Hawaiian Guitar		90.00
	Hard Shell Oblong Case for above model		10.75
Royaltone 6	6-string Hawaiian Guitar		90.00
	Hard Shell Oblong Case for above model		10.75
	6-string Hawaiian Guitar		115.00
	Faultless Case for above model		27.50
	10-string Hawaiian Guitar		172.50
	Faultless Case for above models		30.00
	6-string Hawaiian Guitar		174.50
	Faultless Case for above models		27.50

DOUBLE NECK GUITARS

CG CGN 13 ZCG	Console Grande (with detachable stand)—Regular Finish	$290.00
	Console Grande (with detachable stand)—Natural Finish	305.00
	Faultless Case (Flannel) for above	45.00
	Zipper Cover for above model	15.00

EXTRA EQUIPMENT

Now made with four legs in special length (40") for playing in standing position

ELECTRAHARP

Electraharp—Four pedals	$450.00
Case for above model	45.00

AMPLIFIERS
Prices Effective September 20, 1951

BR-9 9-C	Amplifier	$ 82.00
	Cover for above amplifier	3.75
BR-6 6-C	Amplifier	95.00
	Cover for above amplifier	4.00
GA-20 20-C	Amplifier	116.50
	Cover for above amplifier	4.50
GA-30 30-C	Amplifier—twin speakers	147.50
	Cover for above amplifier	5.25
GA-50 GA-50T	Amplifier—twin speakers (inc. cover)	203.50
	Amplifier—twin speakers with built-in tremolo (inc. cover)	225.00
GA-75 GA-CB	Amplifier—15" speaker (inc. cover)	225.00
	Custom Built Amplifier—15" Co-axial speaker with built-in tremolo (inc. cover)	450.00

SPECIAL ELECTRIC HAWAIIAN OUTFIT
(Amp. and instrument available separately at slight increase in price)

BR-9 9 9-C	Complete with 6-string guitar and amplifier	$126.00
	Case for above guitar	10.75
	Cover for above amplifier	3.75

Bigsby

Paul Bigsby of Downy, California, deserves credit for a long list of innovative guitar and accessory designs. His work reflects a California tradition of self-reliant, idiosyncratic builders pushing the design envelope and, in turn, having wide influence on their peers. Bigsby's contributions include an in-line headstock design that pre-dated Leo Fender's, an industry-standard tailpiece/vibrato, aluminum hardware, volume pedals and pickups. He also created a number of unique standard and steel guitars that featured master craftsmanship, hand-made parts, exceptional tonal qualities and beautifully figured curly maple bodies.

Legendary artists such as Merle Travis, Grady Martin, Speedy West, Joaquin Murphey, Marian Hall, and many others all played Bigsby guitars. Paul Bigsby's early training as a machinist and pattern maker for the Crocker Motor Cycle Company, combined with his innate design skills, helped him create instruments that were considered state-of-the-art for their time and command high prices today.

Left
Bigsby double-8 originally built for Joaquin Murphey now owned & restored by collector-musician Chas Smith

- ¤   The Instruments   ¤ -

Most of the top steel players on the California scene of the late 1940s & early '50s either played a Bigsby or wished they did. Bigsby was also a pioneer in adding pedals to his instruments. Pedals were used initially as a way to offer players access to multiple tunings. It wasn't until Bud Isaac's landmark playing on Web Pierce's 1953 hit, *Slowly*, that using pedals as a primary way to achieve moving tones in musical phrases became a trademark of the instrument.

Today, original Bigsbys remain highly sought-after though they rarely appear on the market. Ry Cooder's 2003 CD release *Mambo Sinuendo* features a Bigsby tripleneck steel built by Paul Warnick from original Bigsby parts.

Top
Bigsby triple-10 belonging to Chas Smith who added the lettering in keeping with Bigsby's practice of customizing his instruments with the names of their owners

Left
Joaquin Murphy playing his double-neck Bigsby lap steel with the Spade Cooley Band, late 1940s

Right
Murphey in the studio with Bigsby steel guitar and volume pedal and Standel amplifiers

Fender

Leo Fender was the Thomas Edison of guitar makers because, like Edison, Fender's inventions and refinements to existing technology were so innovative that they extended beyond their initial market to influence the popular culture virtually worldwide.

Initially, only a handful of country and western swing musicians were interested in Fender's solid body instruments. Fender was aggressive in seeking input from working musicians and his blend of futuristic form, function, treble-dominated tone, and unprecedented durability eventually made his instruments the choice of many professional standard and steel guitarists. Herb Remington, Speedy West, and especially Noel Boggs had important consulting roles in the design and on-going refinement of Fender's steel line.

The earliest Fender lap steels were crudely made and are of interest today primarily to collectors because of their historical value. The Fender *Dual Professional* and triple-neck *Custom* 8-string steels introduced in the late 1940s, however, caught the imagination of steel guitarists everywhere and remain in demand today. It's a tribute to Fender's quality that many are still in perfect working order after more than fifty years.

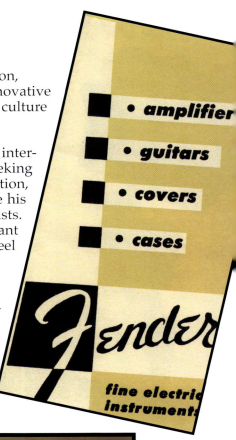

- **amplifier**
- **guitars**
- **covers**
- **cases**

Fender

fine electric instruments

- ¤ The Instruments   ¤ -

In 1949 Fender replaced his early "boxcar" pickups with new asymmetrical "direct string" pickups. Like Rickenbacher's horseshoe, the strings went directly through the magnetic field yielding a rich tone that emphasized the bass and treble. The modern-looking pickups complemented the instrument's clean, lines - not unlike the Danish furniture of the time. While these steels remain very desirable with players, some feel that the pickup design inhibits their right hand positioning.

Left
Early 1950's Dual-8 Professional in walnut with Tremolux amp

Above
1953 Fender Catalog & 1952 Custom tripleneck in blonde

- ¤ The Instruments ¤ -

Leo Fender intended the Stringmaster guitars to make obsolete all previous non-pedal electric steel guitars. In many respects, he succeed in that aim. Stringmasters were made from 1953 through about 1980 in single, double, triple and four-neck models. The single-neck guitar with Stringmaster features was called the Deluxe-6 or Deluxe-8. The standard Fender established with the Stringmaster guitars for tone, design and durability remains a benchmark even today.

Stringmasters came in 22.5", 24.5" and 26" scale lengths. The latter offers tremendous tone but makes slant bar work impractical on the lower frets. One of the most innovative features is a pair of counterbalanced pickups wound for a humbucking effect with two magnetic fields that oppose and cancel each other. Each neck also has a blend control used to balance the tone of the pickups to suit the preference of the individual player. Players like Noel Boggs, Johnny Siebert, and Santo Farina found Fender Stringmasters essential to their music. For many modern players enamored of vintage steel guitars, the Stringmaster remains unsurpassed.

Below
Early 1970's double & triple-neck Stringmasters in gloss ivory &
gloss black (The chrome diamonds hide the bolts that connect the
multiple necks together)

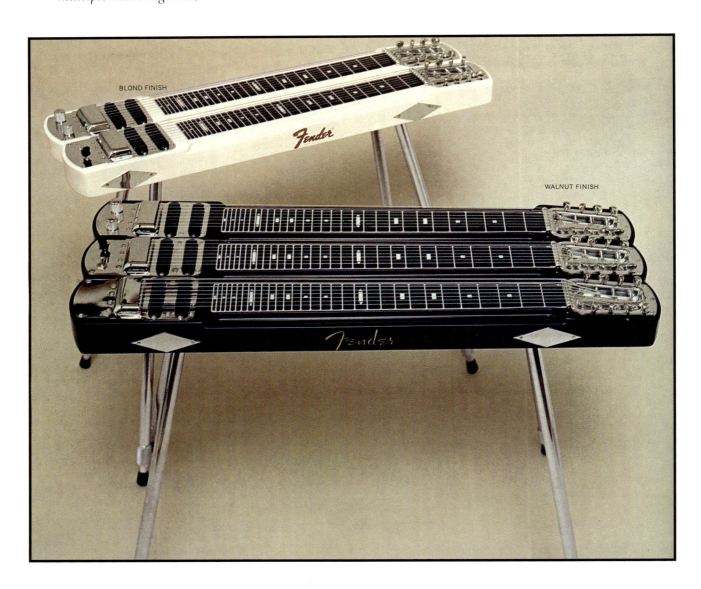

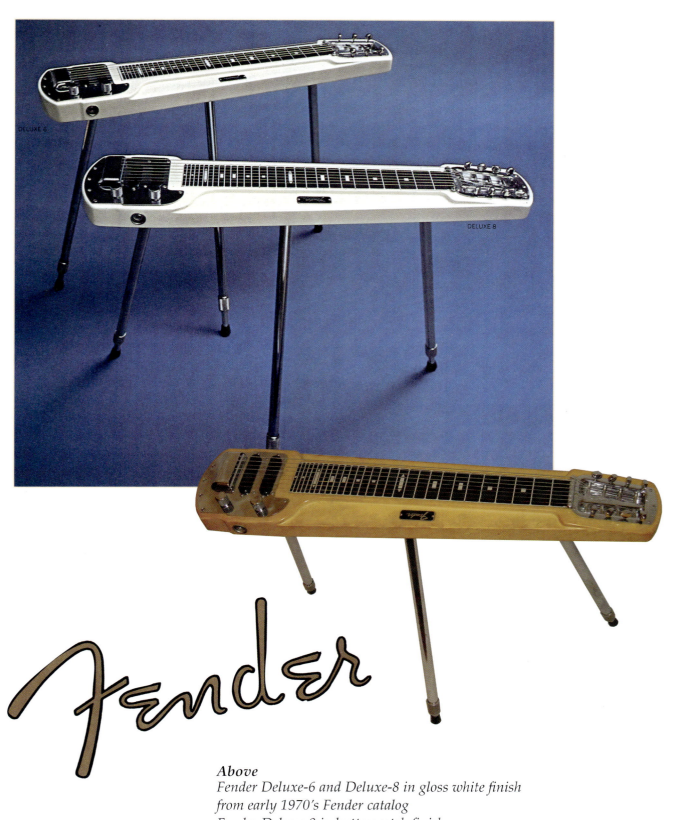

Above
Fender Deluxe-6 and Deluxe-8 in gloss white finish
from early 1970's Fender catalog
Fender Deluxe-8 in butterscotch finish

National-Supro-Valco

The evolution of the original National Guitar Company into the Valco company has a long and convoluted history. National, as it exisited in the 1920s and '30s, is well regarded today among vintage guitar players and collectors for its superb resophonic instruments designed by John Dopyera and George Beauchamp.

After merging with Dobro and relocating to Chicago in the mid-1930s, National produced several electric steel guitars that are appreciated today by musicians for their tone and Art Deco design elements - especialy National's New Yorker lap steel. Supro (and later Valco) was the National Dobro company's budget brand. Supro guitars were

also sold by the Montgomery Ward department stores under the brand name Airline. Supro and Valco instruments are most highly regarded by musicians who play rock and blues styles using high-gain, overdriven sounds. The inexpensive components of the Supro/Valco pickups, which may sound mediocre for clean sounds, lend a rawness to the tone that seems appropriate to certain roots-oriented musical genres.

Left
1940's National New Yorker
lap steel

Above
1950's Supro steel

Right
1950 Valco Owner's Manual
advised: "If you will give
your guitar the care a fine
musical instrument should
receive, normal wear on
strings, controls, and cord
will probably be your only
concern during its lifetime."

THINGS YOU SHOULD KNOW ABOUT YOUR

Electric Guitar

NAMES OF PRINCIPAL PARTS OF YOUR ELECTRIC HAWAIIAN GUITAR

Name Plate
Treble Patent Head
Patent Head Buttons
Nut
Fingerboard
Frets
1st
2nd
3rd
4th Strings
5th
6th

Key Covers

String
Post
Head
Bass Patent Head
Position Markers

Neck

Keeper
Tone Control
Magnet
Unit Plate
Tailpiece
Bridge
Pick-Up Unit
(Under Hand Rest)
Adjustment Screws
Body

Volume Control
Cord Connecting Jack
Hand Rest Knobs
Hand Rest

VALCO MANUFACTURING COMPANY
4700 W. Belton St., Chicago 51, Illinois
The Makers of Fine
NATIONAL and SUPRO ELECTRIC GUITARS
Copyright 1950

CONTEMPORARY STEEL GUITAR MAKERS

Never before in the history of the instrument have there been so many options available to steel guitar players. High-quality vintage instruments are still available at reasonable prices. Fine *modern* guitars by a new generation of factory and small builders offer musicians a dizzying array of choices from the traditional to the cutting edge. Here is a selected gallery of some of today's most interesting new steel guitars.

¤

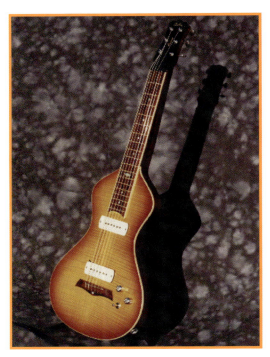

Left
Asher Electro Hawaiian Series II with 25" scale, hand made pickups, koa, mahogany & maple body.

Right
Asher Electro Hawaiian with 25" scale, hand made pickups, curly maple, mahogany & rosewood body.

Asher

Bill Asher's Guitar Traditions
2554 Lincoln Blvd. #1037
Venice, CA 90291
Phone: 310-821-2888
Web: www.guitartraditions.com

Luthier Bill Asher created his first lap steels in collaboration with musician Ben Harper in 1998. Since then he has continued to refine his instruments which combine the body shape of the Weissenborn guitars of the 1920s with modern electronics, quality hardwoods, and exceptional craftsmanship. The eight internal sound chambers (shown at left) are the result of much experimentation in an effort to achieve a lap steel with more sustain, greater tonal variation, and modern pickup configurations. The Asher Electro Hawaiian comes with a Honduras mahogany neck & body, 25" scale, figured koa top, inlaid pearl frets & custom made, double-coil stacked pickups.

Bear Creek

Bear Creek Guitars, Bill & BJ Hardin
29 Palena Place, Kula, HI 96790
Phone: 808-878-8082
E-mail: bcguitar@bcguitar.com
Web: www.bcguitar.com

A master craftsman who honed his guitar making skills in stints with OMI/Dobro and Santa Cruz Guitars, Bill Hardin's Bear Creek guitars are superb modern updates of the designs of Hermann Weissenborn. He endeavors to re-create the classic tone of the early Weissenborns enhanced by additional volume, modern building techniques and top-quality tonewoods.

Bear Creek's best known endorser is Bob Brozman who says, "The Bear Creek is beautifully crafted and captures the mysterious sound of the original Weissenborn, but with greater volume, depth, and clarity." Bear Creek also makes solid-neck Kona models, standard guitars, and ukuleles.

Above
Rope-bound hollow neck of highly figured koa with style-4 inlays

Left (front to back)
Rosewood & spruce Kona model

Figured koa hollow-neck

Mahogany MK model

Blattenberger

Rex Blattenberger - We Need The Money Guitars - Custom Lap Steels
118 Mid Town Court Bldg. F
Hendersonville , TN 37075
E-mail: rxguitar@comcast.net
Web: www.weneedthemoneyguitars.com

Rex Blattenberger's custom electric lap steels feature a chambered body and neck intended to produce a deep, resonant tone. They are available in 6, 7, 8, 10, 12 and 14-string models with either flat or carved tops. String spacing and scale length can be modified to suit the player. Guitars come with George-L , Bill Lawrence, or custom wound pickups.

Above & Detail
RB 10-string in maple & mahogany with natural finish

Left
Sunburst 10-string (photographed prior to stringing)

Natural finished maple 10-string

Bojorquez Guitars

Estaban Bojorquez
23455 Welby Way
West Hills, CA 91307
Phone: 818-340-7023
E-mail: rkripper@aol.com

The guitars of Estaban Bojorquez are some of the most strikingly original designs for lap-style instruments by any modern maker. They represent a fine arts aesthetic in concept and use of materials. Each instrument is custom made and unique. Beyond their appeal as musical instruments, they represent the latest link in a continuous chain of design ingenuity that has flowered in the steel guitar arena for more than one hundred years.

Top Left
Royal Hawaiian
(mahogany, ash & lacewood)

Middle
Yaegermeister
(oak, brass & zebrawood)

Top Right
Lotus (maple & zebrawood)

Bottom Left
Paniolo (balsa w/ koa top & back)

Bottom Right
Manta (brass w/ hollow neck
& body)

Celtic Cross

Neil Russell
1441 Jamaica Road
Victoria, BC Canada V8N 2C9
Phone: 250- 721-0712
Emial: neilcelticcross@shaw.ca
Web: http://hem.passagen.se/
cittern/celtic/

Canadian luthier Neil Russell specializes in mandolin-family instruments and Weissenborn-style acoustic steel guitars that combine fine woods with updated traditional designs. Neil's goal is an even tone - not too over-powerful in bass or treble or weak in the midrange. According to Neil, "I like a sound that goes from one note to the next without a major change in volume sustain or clarity, much like climbing a ladder where each step takes you a bit higher without a change in the rung space. I find this best to obtain with an all-mahogany body."

Below
Mahogany Celtic Cross Weissenborn. All Celtic Cross lap-style guitars feature a 25" scale.

Above & Left
Celtic Cross Weis-senborn-influenced double-6 of mahogany with maple & purple-heart rope binding & headstock veneer. This instrument was made for Canadian musician, Doug Cox.

Chandler

One of the real bargains in today's new lap steels, Chandler guitars offer attractive solid wood bodies, high quality hardware, and unique design touches. Chandler's Weissenbornshaped RH-series lap steels are available in a variety of finishes and come standard with faux pearl or tortoise trim and Art Deco-style fretboard inlays. The versatile pickup looks and sounds like a cross between Gibson's *Charlie Christian* and P-90 guitar pickups. The RH steel was voted an "Editor's Pick" by *Guitar Player Magazine*.

Chandler Guitars
P.O. Box 3637
Chico, CA 95927
Phone: 530-899-1503
E-mail: Paul@chandlerguitars.com
Web: www.chanfdlerguitars.com

Left
Chandler Royal Hawaiian lap steel in maple with faux tortoise shell fretboard

Above
Pickup detail on maple guitar & Inlay detail on mahogany RH with white pearl fretboard

GeorgeBoards

George Piburn's approach to lap steel design combines the traditional with the high-tech. He uses state-of-the-art, computer-controlled CNC machines to carve the guitar bodies made of beautifully figured walnut, Hawaiian koa, African kahya, or bubinga wood. The see-through, laser-etched plexiglass fretboards feature retro-looking "hula girl" position markers. Some models feature a tiny light bulb at the top of the fretboard that illuminates the dancers. GeorgeBoards feature CNC lathed brass rollers, wooden roller trays, Grover tuners, a CAB acrylic lacquer finish and a precision 22.5" scale length. According to George, "The instruments are intended to eliminate the need to roll off the highs via the tone control" offering a "distinctly better sound and overtones without being too twangy."

GeorgeBoards conducts its business via the internet: www.georgeboards.com
Email: george@georgeboards.com

Below:
Single-8 console model of Australian silky oak with plexiglass fretboard.

Below:
Single-8 lap steel of solid African kahya with black mirror-glaze finish on the back and sides, and a solid koa top.

Gold Tone

Founded by former professional folk musicians, Wayne & Robyn Rogers, Gold Tone originally manufactured banjos. Their lap steel is modeled after the Oahu Tonemaster lap steel of the 1950s combined with knobs similar to those found on vintage Gibson guitars. The Gold Tone lap steel offers a marriage of high quality and bargain price. It has received many favorable reviews from players who have posted their comments on internet bulletin boards, such as www.steelguitarforum.com. Gold Tone steels feature a P-90-style single-coil pickup, a 26" scale, and a solid hardwood body with a tobacco sunburst finish.

Gold Tone Instrument Company
3554 Hopkins Ave.
Titusville, FL 32780
Phone: (321) 264-1970
Fax: (321) 269-4910
E-mail: contact@goldtone.com

Above & Left
Gold Tone lap steel with details of bridge, pickup cover, and Gibson-style "speed knobs"

Harmos

Harmos Music, Ltd.
5899 West Branch Road
Mound, MN 55364
info@harmosmusic.com
Phone: 612-695-4107
Fax: 702-995-8908
Web: www.harmosmusic.com

What is that thing? Sage Harmos' mind-blowing, carbon-fiber space frame lap steel guitars radically expand the notion of what a lap steel can be. These visionary instruments utilize a carbon fiber frame with struts that intertwine tetrahedra and octahedra shapes in a pattern developed by R. Buckminster Fuller and others. This "Octet Truss" offers high efficiency in transmitting clear, transparent fundamentals and harmonics with long sustain in a body that's practically impervious to temperature and humidity changes. Harmos steels are available with one or two Jason Lollar pickups and endcaps in maple, koa or swamp ash. Fretboards have pearl inlay and "ivoroid" binding.

Players as stylistically diverse as Sacred Steeler, Robert Randolph, Hawaiian artist Bobby Igano, and bluegrass legend Jerry Douglas have embraced these revolutionary instruments.

Left & Below
Harmos Hawaiian (top view & end view) available with koa or acacia ends, silicon bronze bridge & nut, P-90-style pickups, and keyless tuners

Below
Harmos Americana with maple ends, titanium bridge & nut, Jason Lollar "Chicago Steel" pickup in bridge position, Tele™/Strat™-style pickup by neck, and keyless tuners

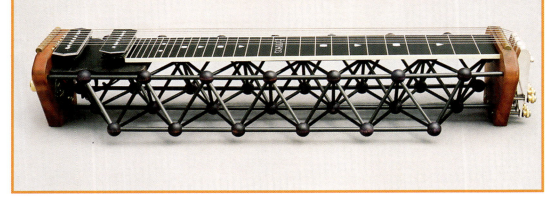

Lapdancer

Lapdancer conducts its
business via the internet:
www.lapdancerguitars.com
E-mail: info@lapdancerguitars.com

Luthier Loni Specter of Lapdancer Guitars isn't content to simply build on existing lap steel design traditions. His instruments offer a pleasing and original take on steel guitar design that combine organic shapes, reminiscent of Gibson's Firebird and Explorer guitars, with beautiful hardwoods and wooden pickup covers.

Below
Lapdancer "Slippery Slides" made of glass. Each is unique.

Lapdancer "Redneck" replacement neck. These ingenious maple bolt-on necks use existing hardware to convert any Tele™ or Strat™-style guitar into a lap steel.

Above
Lapdancer 6-string with custom finish

Left
(top) Lapdancer 7-string of solid swamp ash.

Left
(bottom) Hollow-body Lapdancer 6-string of koa and maho.

Melobar

A family-owned shop in business since the 1960s, Melobar always walked its own somewhat eccentric path. Relatively indifferent to fads and trends, the company did it's own thing and waited for the world to come to its doorstep. In the 1990s, more players began to do just that as Melobar introduced many new models into the line that offered quality, handmade guitars at very reasonable prices. Steelers David Lindley, Paul Franklin, and Cindy Cashdollar have used Melobar guitars on stage. Melobar continues to refine and innovate - their latest models feature Ned Steinberger's patented open guitar head design.

Smith Family Music
9175 Butte Road
Sweet, Idaho 83670
Phone: 800-942-6509
Web: www.melobar.com

Top
Melobar Skreemer - allows the player to stand, wearing the guitar on a strap

Middle
Melobar Teleratt lap steel

Right
Melobar SLS 6-string lap steel

Mermer

Rich Mermer has been designing, building, and repairing fretted string instruments since 1983. He builds a variety of standard guitars as well as Weissenborn and Kona-style lap-style guitars, which often feature distinctive circular soundholes in the upper bout of the instruments. The Maalaea features a modified internal bracing pattern designed to take advantage of the large resonating cavity as well as a "trap door" at the butt of the instrument that allows for access to the interior and serves as a platform for mounting electronics. The Maalaea is available with a single, double offset, or traditional soundhole. The master-quality construction and beautiful tone of his instruments has found favor with a number of professional players including Cyril Pahinui, son of Hawaiian music legend, Gabby Pahinui.

Mermer Guitars .
P.O. Box 782132
Sebastian, FL 32978
Phone: 772-388-0317
E-mail: *rmermer@mermerguitars.com*
www.mermerguitars.com

Top
Mermer Maalaea of koa with ebony bridge & fretboard owned by Bob Taylor of Taylor Guitars

Left
Mermer Maalaea of koa, with rosewood bridge & fretboard

Right
Mermer Baritone

Remington

Herb Remington is a living legend. As a member of Bob Will's *Texas Playboys*, Herb was one of the pioneers of western swing. In 1986, he started his own line of pedal and non-pedal steel guitars. The Steelmaster console model is available with single, double, or triple 8-string necks in many colors and finishes. It comes standard with George-L pickups and a 24$^{1/4}$" scale (22$^{1/2}$" scale available as a special order.) Remington's new budget-priced Playboy lap steel offers a 6 or 8-string neck, a natural finish ash body, and George-L pickups. Telescoping legs are available as an option.

Herb Remington
2102 Jean St.
Houston, Texas 77023
Phone: 713-923-8435
Fax: 713-923-4102
www.remingtonsteelguitar.com

Top
Remington Steelmaster double-8 in gloss black

Right
Remington Playboy 8-string lap steel in natural ash

SS Hawaiian

Ricky Davis
1325 E. Logan St.
Round Rock, Texas 78664
Phone: 512-671-8891
Email: sshawaiian@aol.com

Available only by custom order, the SS Hawaiian is a boutique update of the classic Fender Stringmaster built by Archie Cox & Ricky Davis, former pedal steel guitarist with Dale Watson. The guitar features the tonewood of the customer's choice , a 24" scale, polished stainless steel fretboards, silk screened black, with high-contrast colored palm tree fret markers. The tuning pans are machined from solid brass with gold Kluson-type tuners. Jason Lollar designed the Stringmaster-style pickups which offer volume, tone and a blend knob.

Above
S.S. Hawaiian made of Australian silky oak with gold-plated parts

Right
Koa Scheerhorn Weissenborn-style guitar

Scheerhorn

Tim Scheerhorn, Luthier
120 Sam Hollow Rd
Dickson, TN 37055
Phone: 615-441-5935
E-mail: tscheerhorn@worldnet.att.net

Tim Scheerhorn's resophonic guitars are found in the hands of some of the best acoustic steel players in the world. Jerry Douglas, Rob Ickes & Sally Van Meter are a few proud owners. Sheerhorn's take on the Weissenborn design features a koa top & body with a maple headstock face.

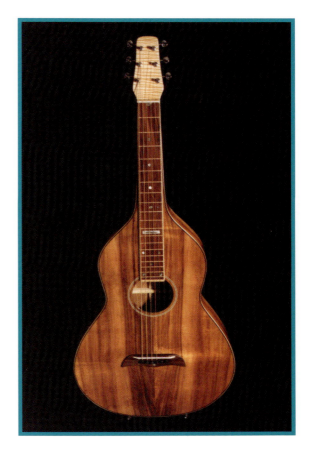

Sea To Sky Travel Instruments

Rory Dafoe
7216 Ridge Drive
Burnaby, BC, Canada V5A 1B5
Phone: 604-299-0019
E-mail: rorydafoe@telus.net
www.travelinstruments.com

Rory Dafoe designs and builds stringed instruments intended specifically for travelling and backpacking. Sea to Sky concentrates on high-quality, affordable travel guitars, mandolin family instruments, fiddles, banjos and lap-style guitars. Dafoe's goal is to achieve the best possible tone out of the smallest possible instrument. Most instruments are designed with full size scale lengths, so they play as closely as possible to their full size counterparts and feature solid, quality tonewoods.

Top, Right & Bottom right
Three detail views of a Sea to Sky koa Weissenborn-inspired baritone travel guitar built for musican Dwight Mark

Below
Optional "belly extender" that clamps onto the guitar for stand up playing

Sierra

Sierra Instrument Company
P.O. Box 19049
Portland, OR 97280-0049
Phone (503) 761-9632
www.sierrasteelguitar.com

Sierra's pedal steel guitars have been among the most respected in the industry for many years. In the late 1990s, they introduced a new line of non-pedal steel guitars that have been garnering rave reviews from players. Sierra's 8- String LapTop was the first in the line to feature an innovative aluminum plate that runs the length of the neck sandwiched between two layers of wood. The strings attach to the aluminum plate at both ends of the guitar. These guitars have been described by one player as "a Rickenbacher Bakelite on steroids" because of their outstanding sustain, tone and playability. Newer models feature combinations of different hardwoods, options for up to 12 strings, and telescoping legs.

Top
Sierra maple & mahogany 8-string with George-L pickup

Above
Sierra 8-string in black lacquer

Superior

Berkley Musical Instrument Exchange
Phone: (866) 548-7538
E-mail: bmie@berkleymusic.com
www.berkleymusic.com

Handmade in Mexico and distributed by Berkley Music, Superior Hawaiian guitars represent a real value for players seeking an all-hardwood, hollowneck, Weissenborn-style instrument with good tone and quality craftsmanship for a price that won't break the bank. A wide variety of options are available including spruce or cedar tops, rope binding, and complex abalone soundhole inlays. Their website sports an endorsement from David Lindley.

Top & Above
Superior Hawaiian guitar with spruce top and abalone soundhole inlay

Right
Rope-bound Superior Hawaiian with cedar top

Tradewinds

Tradewinds Guitars
Elva West
5201 E Crescent Dr.
Anaheim, CA 92807
Phone: 714-637-4084
Email: elvawest@hotmail.com

Like Leo Fender, Elva West was a radio repairman who built his first steel guitars in 1947. Today, he builds a limited number of custom guitars under the name Tradewinds. The instruments are available in a variety of shapes and finishes in ash, poplar and mahogany with handmade pickups. They offer clean, geometric lines and excellent tone according to several musicians of the author's acquaintance who own West's instruments.

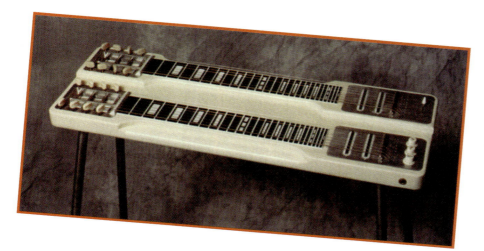

Above
Tradewinds single & double-8 lap steels in natural finish

Left
Tradewinds double-8 console model with gloss white finish

Weissonator™

Mike Dotson
Maricopa Guitar Company.
Phoenix, Az
E-mail: terapln@aol.com
Web: www.maricopaguitarco.com

Luthier Mike Dotson's Weissonator™ guitar combines aspects of the designs of Hermann Weissenborn with those of the early National Tricone resonator instruments. The Weissonator™ model is made from all solid wood and features a 25.5″ scale. It is available on a limited, custom basis in 6 and 7-string models. Dotson also makes round-neck and square-neck, wood and metal, single and tricone guitars in the style of National's guitars.

Left & Below
Three views of a Weissonator made of flamed koa with maple purfling and fret markers, ebony fretboard, handguard and tailpiece. The guitar also features Gotoh mini tuners, bone nut, maple saddle, and a gloss nitrocellulose lacquer finish.

Yanuziello

The guitars of Canadian luthier, Joseph Yanuziello combine master woodworking skills with a keen eye for design and detail. His Hawaiian King models are available in a variety of tonewoods with rope binding. From all accounts these guitars have exceptional tone. Yanuziello describes the tone of the Hawaiian King as "... darker and more bass-responsive than a Weissenborn, like a good sounding flat top with lots of sustain." Don Rook, of the Canadian band, *The Henry's*, plays a Yanuziello.

Yanuziello Guitars
81A Parkway Avenue
Toronto, Ontario M6R-IT6
Canada
E-mail: ysi@ca.inter.net

Left
Rope bound Hawaiian King in koa with ebony bridge & fretboard

Below
Koa & mahogany Hawaiian King guitars

Steel Guitar Tone Bars

It would be difficult to find an accessory in the entire milieu of the guitar that's more personal than a steel guitarist's tone bar. Ask any five steel guitarists for their tone bar recommendations and you're likely to get five completely different answers. This contributes to the charm of the instrument but makes it difficult to know what bar is right for the music you want to play. In general, Hawaiian, country, jazz and western swing players have traditionally used bullet bars because they allow easy movement between strings and facilitate slant bar technique. Resophonic players have traditionally used "Stevens-style" bars that feature a groove for the player's index finger. Listed below are just *some* of the available options. "Buying and trying" is the only way to find your ideal bar (see page 276 for manufacturer contact info).

Left to Right: *Dunlop Jerry Byrd bar, Black Phoenix coated bar, Red Rajah coated bar, Red Rajah pedal steel bar, John Pearse Thermo-Cryonic bar*

Above: *Dunlop 901 & 918 tonebars*

Below: *Gary Swallows tone bars with Hardwood caps*

Above: *Dunlop 925 "Ergo" bar & 926 "LapDawg" bar*

Left: *Lapdancer Slippery Slide*

Below: *wooden tone bars by Michael Werner*

- ☼ -

LAP STEEL GUITAR RESOURCES

- ☼ -

Selected Steel Guitar Dealers

Billy Cooper's Music, Inc.
20504 Constitution Highway
Orange, VA 22960
Phone: 540-854-5940

A steel guitar specialty store.

Elderly Instruments
Showroom:
1100 N. Washington Street
Lansing, MI 48906
Phone: 888- 473-5810
Customer Service: 517-372-7890
Fax: 517-372-5155
Email: web@elderly.com
Web: www.elderly.com

One of the largest dealers and a good source for vintage lap steels at fair market prices.

Gruhn Guitars
400 Broadway
Nashville, TN 37203
Phone: 615- 256-2033
Fax: 615-255-2021

One of the largest and more expensive dealers. While George Gruhn has likely forgotten more about vintage instruments than any of us will ever know, steel guitars are not Gruhn's specialty.

London Resonator Centre
44 Duncan Street
London N1 8BW England
Phone: 020-7833-9881
Email: sales@resocentre.com
Web: www.resocentre.com

One of the best and most knowledgeable dealers in Europe for resonator and lap steel guitars. Their website features extensive information on instruments from many instrument makers from around the world.

Mandolin Brothers
629 Forest Avenue
Staten Island, NY 10310-2576
Phone: 718-981-8585
Fax: 718-816-4416

The largest US dealer of Dobro and National guitars, Mandolin Brothers is one of the premier and most knowledgeable vintage instrument dealers in the world and their prices reflect this.

Resophonic Outfitters
Paul Beard
14122 Marsh Pike
Hagerstown, MD 21742
Phone: 301-733-8271
Email: sales@beardguitars.com
Web: www.beardguitars.com

An excellent source for resophonic parts, info and instruments.

Scotty's Music, Inc.
9535 Midland Boulevard
St. Louis, MO 63114
Phone: 314-427-7794
Fax: 314- 427-0516
Email: scotty@scottysmusic.com
Web: www.scottysmusic.com

Probably the most respected dealer in the world for steel guitars, they specialize in pedal and non-pedal instruments.

Steel Guitar Nashville
Bobbe Seymour
123 Midtown Court
Hendersonville, TN 37075
Phone: 615-822-5555
Email: sales@steelguitar.net

If it's an electric pedal or non-pedal steel guitar, steel guitarist, producer and raconteur Bobbe Seymour has probably owned it, sold it or traded it at one time or another.

A Word About eBay (www.ebay.com)

It is still possible to obtain high quality acoustic and electric instruments on eBay at fair prices but it's becoming more difficult. Sellers may have unrealistic price expectations, be grossly misinformed, uneducated, or even outright deceitful about the instruments they list for auction. Some sellers are less than forthcoming regarding problems that may or not be fixable. Competition is generally fierce for highly desirable vintage guitars except in rare instances, when they are listed in such a way that a keyword search doesn't immediately reveal their presence on the site. The best possible advice is Caveat Emptor — let the buyer beware. Do your research, read the seller's feedback, and educate yourself thoroughly before you bid. Decide your bid limit for a given instrument and then stick to it.

Steel Guitar Pickups

Seymour Duncan
5427 Hollister Avenue
Santa Barbara, CA 93111-2345
Phone: 805-964-9610
Fax: 805-964-9749
Email: tech@seymourduncan.com

Makes a replacement Stringmaster pickup.

Fishman Transducers, Inc.
340-D Fordham Road
Wilmington, MA 01887
Phone: 978-988-9199
Fax: 978-988-0770
Email: fishmail@fishman.com
Web: www.fishman.com

Makes well-regarded pickups for acoustic instruments.

Fralin Pickups
Lindy Fralin
2015 West Laburnum Ave.
Richmond, VA 23227
Phone: 804-358-2699
Fax: 804-358-3431
Web: www.fralinpickups.com/index.htm

Bill Lawrence Designs
613 East Broad Street
Bethlehem, PA 18018
Phone: 610-974-9544
Email: becky@billlawrence.com

Fralin & Lawrence are both well-respected for their pickup designs. Fralin offers custom rewinding.

Jason Lollar
P.O. Box 2450
Vashon, WA 98070
Phone: 206-462-9838
Email: info@lollarguitars.com
Web: www.lollarguitars.com

Custom steel guitar pickups, replacement pickups and rewinding. The first stop for vintage steel replacement pickups including the Rickenbacher Horseshoe & Charlie Christian reissue pickups.

McIntyre Pickups
5618 E. Oak Island Drive
Oak Island, NC 28465
Phone: 910-278-5540
Fax: 910-278-5565
Web: www.mcintyrepickups.com

Highly regarded pickups for acoustic instruments used by many professional resophonic players.

Sunrise Pickup Systems
Jim Kaufman
15740 Stagg Street
Van Nuys, CA 91406-1913
Phone: 818-785-3428
Email: jimsunrise@earthlink.net
Web: www.sunrisepickups.com

Exceptional sounding pickups for acoustic instruments used by players such as David Lindley, Bob Brozman and Martin Simpson.

Tonebars

B.J.S. Tonebars
8886 Highway 22
Route 1, Box 151
Dresden, TN 38225
Phone: 901-364-3519
Fax: 901-364-5750

B.J.S. bars are the choice of many professional pedal steel players.

Breezy Ridge® Instruments, Ltd.
John Pearse
P.O. Box 295
Center Valley, PA 18034
Phone: 610-691-3302
Fax: 610-691-3304
Email: Jpinfo@aol.com
Web: jpstrings.com

John Pearse Thermo Cryonic tone bars have found favor with many lap steelers including Cindy Cashdollar.

Bullet Bars
Jim Burden
4525 Hwy 64 NE
Georgetown, IN 47122
Email: jdadb@aol.com

Custom made bullet bars.

BullsEye Bars
Jerry Hilburn
Phone: 832-746-5220
Buddy Hilburn
Phone: 318-724-6151
Email: jerrywayne@bullseyebars.com
Web: www.bullseyebars.com

Custom made bullet bars.

Carter Steel Guitars
617 West Kearney Street, Suite 101
Mesquite, TX 75149-3200
Phone: 800-969-7332
Email: psgbuilder@steelguitar.com
Web: www.steelguitar.com

Makes the Sacred Steeler GrooveTone Bar in 10 & 12-string sizes.

Jim Dunlop Manufacturing, Inc.
P.O. Box 846
Benicia, CA 94510
Phone: 707-745-2722
Email: customerservice@jimdunlop.com
Web: www.jimdunlop.com

Makes the Jerry Byrd bar, among many others.

GS Steels
Email: gswallows@yahoo.com
Web: www.gssteels.com

Gary Swallows builds unique Stevens-style bars customized to fit the individual player's hand. He offers 10 to 15 different hardwood options on a stainless steel base. The weight can be varied to suit each player's preference. Swallows has also developed special bars for handicapped players using leather straps to assist the player in holding onto the bar.

Latch Lake Music Products
3115 Mike Collins Drive
St. Paul, MN 55121
Phone: 612-688-7502 or 800-528-2437

Makers of the Broz-o-Phonic Authentic Hawaiian Steel Bar Slide"

Brittain Guitar Products
Chuck Brittain
11206 Lake June, Suite C
Balch Springs, TX 75180
Phone: 972-286-9703
chuckguitar@msn.com

*The Black Raja tone bars of the 1950s were highly coveted by lap steel players. Long out of production, Chuck Brittain has created a bar that has many of the same qualities. These unique tone bars are coated with a synthetic resin that imparts warmer tone than an all-metal bar while substantially reducing friction on the strings. The **Black Phoenix** bars have a hard, glossy surface while the **Red Rajah** has a hard, matte surface. Resin-coated fingerpicks are also available.*

Tim Scheerhorn
120 Sam Hollow Road
Dickson, TN 37055
Phone: 615-441-5935

Makes the Sheerhorn bar, an improvement on the classic Stevens bar of old. The bar of choice of many pro resophonic players, such as Rob Ickes.

The Shubb Company
14471 Highway One
Valley Ford, CA 94972
Phone: 707-876-3001
Fax: 707-876-3034
Email: shubb@shubb.com
Web: www.shubb.com

The Shubb-Pierce bar combines the feel of a Stevens bar with some of the characteristics of a bullet bar.

Loni Specter Productions
7104 Deveron Ridge Road
West Hills, CA 91307
Phone: 818 992-0745
Email: lonster@earthlink.com
Web: www.LapdancerGuitars.com

*Loni Specter's **Slipperyslides** are individually crafted tone bars that feature an art glass approach. They're made from hand-formed, solid glass, and no two exactly are exactly alike in color or design. They feature a ground edge on one side for Sitar-like sounds or a traditional steel guitar tone by rotating the bar.*

Michael Werner Wooden Tone Bars
16528 Marine Drive
Stanwood, WA 98292
Phone: 360- 652-7515
Fax: 360-652-0795
Email: wernerme@earthlink.net

Michael Werner makes hand-turned tone bars out of exotic solid hardwoods such as lignum vitae and cocobola. Wooden bars offer a much different tone color than metal, often, with much less sustain.

- ¤ -

Bridges, Volume Pedals, Cables, etc.

Ernie Ball, Inc.
51 Suburban Road
San Luis Obispo, CA 93401
Phone: 805-544-7726
Fax: 805-544-7275
Web: www.ernieball.com

Bigsby Guitars (owned by Fred Gretsch Enterprises, Inc.)
PO Box 2468
Savannah, GA 31402
Email: info@bigsbyguitars.com

Designed by legendary steel guitar designer Paul Bigsby, these high profile pedals are still being manufactured.

Goodrich Sound Company
8733 Silver Creek Road
Whitehall, MI 49461
Phone: 231-893-5702

Maker of well-regarded volume pedals.

George L's
P. O. Box 238
Madison, TN 37116
Phone: 615-868-6976
Web: www.georgels.com

George L guitar cables are the industry standard among steel guitar players. Guitar Player Magazine voted their cables #1 for sound clarity in a side-by-side test with cables from 25 manufacturers. Cables are available in custom lengths using solderless plugs with convenient screw-on connectors.

Hilton Electronics
248 Laurel Road
Ozark, MO 65721
Phone: 417- 581-1265
Email: klhilton@aol.com
Web: www.hiltonelectronics.net

Makes volume pedals that are popular with pedal steel players.

HipShot Products, Inc.
8248 Route 96
Interlaken, NY 14847
Phone: 800-262-5630
Fax: 607-532-9530
Email: hipshot@hipshotproducts.com
Web: www.hipshotproducts.com

Makers of the innovative Trilogy replacement bridge that allows instant and precise re-tuning of each string to three notes pre-set by the player by means of six cam levers.

Amplifiers

Choosing an amplifier is much like choosing a guitar: a matter of personal preference. The electric steel guitar, however, presents an amp with a unique set of demands beyond those of standard guitars. High-gain pickups and the close voicings of certain steel guitar tunings can make it more difficult to accurately reproduce the entire spectrum of sound generated by a given instrument. This is especially true for 8, 10, and 12-string guitars.

Players who seek distorted or crunch tones may have a different set of needs from those who seek accurate clean sounds. While many steel guitarists use a host of new and vintage amps designed for standard guitar, several manufacturers make amplifiers specifically intended for steel guitar.

Evans Custom Amplifiers
2734 Woodbury Drive
Burlington, NC 27217
Phone: 336-437-0703
Web: www.evansamps.com

One of the earliest makers of amps targeted to steel players, Evans amps are noted for their clean, warm tone and ability to enhance string separation with close-voiced steel guitar tunings. In the 1990s, they began to find favor with jazz guitarists in addition to their core base of steel guitar players.

Fender
Web: www.fender.com

Fender tube amplifiers have been used by steel guitarists on many classic country, folk, rock, blues and Hawaiian recordings and live performances for more than 50 years. Twin Reverbs, Deluxe Reverbs, and Bassman amps have remained sought after by steel players in both vintage and reissue models. The Fender Custom Shop has also created new amps that have found favor with steel players.

Peavey Electronics Corporation
711 A Street
Meridian, MS 39301
Phone: 601-483-5365
Fax: 601-486-1278
Email: customerservice@peavey.com
Web: www.peavey.com

Probably the industry standard amplifier for pedal steel players. Peavey offers a full range of amplification.

Requisite Audio Engineering (Standel)
Los Angeles, CA
Phone: 818-247-2047
Fax: 818-247-4498
Web: www.requisiteaudio.com

Standel amplifiers were used by Joaquin Murphey, Merle Travis, Buddy Emmons, Chet Atkins, Wes Montgomery and other influential recording artists. While the original Standel Company ceased production in the 1970s, the new company has received extremely positive reviews for their high-quality "boutique" amps.

Webb Amplifiers
100 West 6th Street
Antioch, CA 94509
Phone: 925-757-1198
Fax: 925-757-5312
Web: www.webamps.com

Designed by Jimmie Webb, these amps are noted for their powerful, clean sound.

Amps for Practice or Jam Sessions

Songworks Systems & Products
32158 Camino Capistrano, #A274
San Juan Capistrano, CA 92675
Phone/Fax: 949-582-7720
Email: tris@songworks.com
Web: www.songworks.com

Songwork's Little Laneli is a powerful, compact, all-tube amp that delivers surprising tone for its size. They are available in 7, 30, and 50-watt versions. The 50-watt version is recommended for players desiring a clean sound without distortion.

Magnasynch Moviola URS Amplifiers

Want to own an all-tube amp with incredible tone that's about the size of a lunch box? These all-metal industrial-looking green boxes were manufactured in the 1960s to amplify the audio tracks in 16mm film editing. They can be found for about $50 on eBay or from used film equipment dealers. For approximately $60 -$75, a qualified technician can outfit them with a 1/4" plug and extra long cord with a grounded plug. These little amps have a warm sound that makes them ideal as practice amps and they offer surprisingly good tone and enough volume for a small jam session. There is minimal headroom however, before they begin to distort. (Thanks to steel guitar tinkerer and all-around steel guitar science guru, Rick Aiello for introducing the author to these wonderful amps).

Instructional Materials

Henry Kaleialoha Allen
Book: *Learning to Play the Hawaiian Way*
Polynesian Promotions
5161-D Kohi Street
Lahaina, HI 96761
Web: www.galaxymall.com/retail/steelguitar

Tom Bradshaw
Pedal Steel Guitar Products
P.O. Box 931
Concord, CA 94522
Email orders preferred:
bradshaw@california.com.
Web: www.songwriter.com/bradshaw

Tom Bradshaw has an extensive catalog of steel guitar-related products and recordings.

Jerry Byrd
The Jerry Byrd Instruction Book For Steel Guitar, 5th edition. 60 lessons in A, E, C#m, F#m, B11th, C6th tunings. All Byrd's students such as Alan Akaka, Greg Sardinha, and Casey Olsen, learned from this course. One hour instruction video available too from:
Steel Guitar International
9535 Midland Boulevard
St. Louis, MO 63114
Phone: 314-427-7794

Jerry Byrd's *Complete List of Professional Steel Guitar Solos* is available directly from him. 180 different professional arrangements are listed and include Hawaiian, country and popular standards which Byrd has recorded over the years. Prices per arrangement run from $2.00 to $5.00. There is a minimum order of ten arrangements. Order from:
Jerry Byrd, P.O. Box 15026
Honolulu, Hawaii 96830

Leavitt Tuning Arrangements
William Leavitt, late Chairman of the Guitar Department at Berklee College of Music in Boston, developed a unique tuning (C# E G Bb C D) that allows complex jazz harmony without bar slants. Mike Ihde, Associate Professor of Guitar at Berklee, has arranged many standard tunes for the Leavitt tuning. Mike sells recordings of these tunes, tablature and notation, and a play-along cassette. More information can be obtained by writing:

Mike Ihde
P.O. Box 143, Berklee College
1140 Boylston St.
Boston, MA 02215
Fax: 617-247-6878
Email: mihde@berklee.edu email

- ¤ Lap Steel Guitar Resources ¤ -

Georgeboards
Email: george@georgeboards.com
Web: www.georgeboards.com

George Piburn has produced a series of CD-Rom and DVD training discs for C6ᵗʰ lap steel that covers blues, jazz and country styles. Quicktime movies and on-screen graphics and animations enable students to learn both visually and aurally at their own pace.

Homespun Tapes, Ltd.
P.O. Box 340
Woodstock, NY 12498
Phone: 845-246-2550
Fax: 845- 246-5282
Web: www.homespuntapes.com

Happy Traum's Homespun Tapes was one of the earliest companies to use video-based media to teach music. Their products are uniformly well done. They include lessons by world-class players like Bob Brozman, Cindy Cashdollar, and Jerry Douglas.

HotlLicks Productions
Web: www.hotlicks.com

Well-produced instructional videotapes.

Mel Bay Publications, Inc.
Web: www.melbay.com

Publishers of a number of fine instructional books for non-pedal steel.

Jeff Newman/Jeffran Music
Web: www.jeffran.com

Well-respected teacher & provider of instructional materials, oriented toward pedal steel guitar.

Denny Turner
Web: www.homestead.com/dennysguitars

Mind-boggling site that details a comprehensive method for modal improvisation on C6ᵗʰ lap steel.

Joe Wright
Web: www.pedalsteel.com

Extensive instructional material oriented toward pedal steel, much of it applicable to non-pedal.

Websites

It's a reality of the Internet that websites come and go, which raises important questions about the archival survival of information from web-published content in this new century. Nevertheless, as of the publication date of this book, the following selected websites (active as of publication of this book) offer some of the most interesting and helpful information for people interested in acoustic and electric lap steel guitar.

Parts

Finding replacement parts for older guitars can be a daunting process. Here are a few reliable sources to try:

- **www.wdmusicproducts.com**
- **www.guitar-parts.com**
- **www.stewmac.com**
- **www.angela.com**
- **www.lmii.com**
- **www.lollarguitars.com**

General Info

www.steelguitarforum.com
This is your first stop on the information highway.

www.well.com/user/wellvis/steel.html
Brad's Page of Steel was the first, and still the best, personal web page devoted to all aspects of lap steel guitar.

www.hsga.org
The Hawaiian Steel Guitar Association's site.

www.hawaiiansteel.com
John Ely's helpful site has tuning & string gauge info.

www.users.voicenet.com/~vanallen/hcoahome.html
Dave Van Allen's tribute to the Hot Club of America, a fascinating history of Jody Carver & Johnny Cucci's musical odyssey.

www.notecannons.com
Excellent British site features extensive info on National string instruments.

www.horseshoemagnets.com
Rick Aiello's horseshoe pickups.

www.billchaviers.com
Bill Chaviers' non-pedal steel tablature site

www.wideopenwest.com/~steelgtr
John Tipka's site offers excellent info on Fender Stringmaster guitars as well as tab and educational materials for building your own guitar.

Artist Web Pages

Mike Auldridge: *www.mikeauldridge.com*

Bob Brozman: *www.bobbrozman.com*

Campbell Brothers:
www.campbellbrothers.com/sacredsteel

David Lindley: *www.davidlindley.com*

Stacy Phillips: *www.stacyphillips.com*

Mike Scott: *www.hawaiianaires.com*

Bud Tutmarc: *www.marcrecords.com*

Ken Emerson: *www.kenemerson.com*

Selected Discography

It's a frustrating reality of record collecting that albums that don't fit into mainstream categories or aren't released on large, well-funded labels tend to go in and out of print with alarming frequency, especially those featuring exclusively steel guitar instrumentals. The "good stuff" sometimes reappears on Japanese or European labels or as part of exhaustive (and expensive) box sets or even, posted on someone's website. Therefore, the cardinal rule is: if you want it, buy it when you see it 'cause it may not be available later.

The following list contains some of the best lap steel guitar-related recordings currently available on compact disc. This list is by no means all-encompassing or definitive but rather, represents a sampling of the music of some of the artists featured in this book.

Hawaiian Music

Jerry Byrd
• *By Request (Mountain Apple)*
• *Steel Guitar Hawaiian Style (Lehua Records)*
• *Master of Touch and Tone (Midland)*
• *Jazz From the Hills (Bear Family)*

These CDs and many other of Byrd's early albums (on cassette) are available from Scotty's Music.

John Ely
• *How The West Was Swung, Vol. 7, No Peddlers Allowed (W.R. Records, Tom Morrell/Producer)*

Billy Hew Len
• *Steel Guitar Magic Hawaiian Style (w/ Barney Isaacs (Jack de Mello)*
• *Hawaiian Songbird: Lena Machado (Billy is on eight of the cuts from 1962) (Cord International)*

Sol Hoopii
• *Master of the Hawaiian Guitar Volume 1 (Rounder Select)*
• *Master of the Hawaiian Guitar Volume 2 (Rounder Select)*

Andy Iona
- *At Night, By The Ocean - Andy Iona and His Islanders #1 (Cumquat)*
- *South Sea Lullabies - Andy Iona and His Islanders #2 (Cumquat)*
- *Hula Girl - Andy Iona and His Islanders #3 (Cumquat)*
- *Songs Of Old Hawaii - Andy Iona and His Islanders #4 (Cumquat)*

Ralph Kolsiana
- *Several cuts with the Waikiki Swingsters appear on the MP3 CD compilation: Waikiki Is Good Enough For Me (Beer Records)*

Dick McIntire
- *Honey, Let's Go For Broke - Dick McIntire & His Harmony Hawaiians #1 (Cumquat)*
- *Trade Winds - Dick McIntire & His Harmony Hawaiians #2 (Cumquat)*
- *South Sea Moon - Dick McIntire & His Harmony Hawaiians #3 (Cumquat)*
- *Royal Hawaiian Hotel - Dick McIntire & His Harmony Hawaiians #4 (Cumquat)*

David Feet Rogers
- *Sons of Hawaii: The Folk Music of Hawaii (Panini)*
- *The Best of the Sons of Hawaii - Volume 1 (Panini)*

Hawaiian Compilations
- *Vintage Hawaiian Steel Guitar Masters (Import on P-Vine Label)*
- *Hawaiian Steel Guitar Classics: 1927-1938 (Arhoolie)*
- *Waikiki Is Good Enough For Me: 188 tracks of Hawaiian style steel guitar spanning the years from 1921 to 1940. Record collector Dave Stewart has put together an amazing collection of tracks from his private collection on one MP3 disc. An incredible value.*
- *Hawaiian Steel Volume 1 (Cord International)*
- *Hawaiian Steel Volume 2 (Cord International)*
- *The History of Hawaiian Steel Guitar (Cord International)*

Western Swing

Cindy Cashdollar
- *Tribute to the Music of Bob Wills - Asleep At The Wheel (Liberty)*
- *Wheel Keeps on Rollin' - Asleep At The Wheel (Capitol)*
- *Ride with Bob - Asleep At The Wheel (Dreamworks)*
- *Dance Hall Dreams - Rosie Flores (Rounder)*
- *Bob Dylan: Time Out of Mind (Columbia)*
- *Lyle Lovett : Pearls in the Snow (Kinajou)*
- *Leon Redbone: Up a Lazy River (Private Music)*
- *Artie Traum: Cayenne (Rounder)*
- *Artie Traum: Letters from Joubee' (Shanachie)*

John Ely
- *Western Standard Time - Asleep At The Wheel (Sony)*
- *Keepin' Me Up Nights - Asleep At The Wheel (Arista)*

Leon McAuliffe
- *Take it Away the Leon Way! Leon McAuliffe and His Cimarron Boys (Jasmine)*
- *Hillbilly Boogie (Compilation) (Sony)*
- *Bob Wills and His Texas Playboys - the King of Western Swing: 25 Hits 1935-1945 (ASV Living Era)*

Tom Morrell and the Time Warp Tophands:
(Vol. 1 - 11 on WR Records)
- *Volume 1 - How The West Was Swung*
- *Volumes 2 and 3 - Let's Ride With Bob & Tommy (with Bobby Koefer)*
- *Volume 4 - Pterodactyl Ptales*
- *Volume 5 - Go Uptown*
- *Volume 6 - Smoke A Little Of This*
- *Volume 7 - No Peddlers Allowed*
- *Volume 8 - On The Money*
- *Volume 9 - Son Of No Peddlers Allowed*
- *Volume 10 - Win Place & Show*
- *Volume 11 - Jugglin' Cats*
- *Wolf Tracks (Shanachie)*

Joaquin Murphey
- *Murph (Class Act Records) Recorded just before Joaquin's death - available from Scotty's Music.*
- *Tex Williams On The Air (1947-1949) (Country Routes)*

- ¤ Lap Steel Guitar Resources ¤ -

Joaquin Murphey (continued)
- *Tex Williams Vintage Collections Series (EMD/Capitol)*
- *Spade Cooley: Spadella! (Sony)*
- *Spade Cooley: Shame on You (Bloodshot Records)*

Herb Remington
- *Bob Wills and His Texas Playboys: The Tiffany Transcriptions: Vol. 3 & 5*
  On pedal steel:
- *Steeling Memories (Glad Music)*
- *Steeling Dreams (Glad Music)*
- *Herb Ellis: Texas Swings (Justice)*

Vance Terry
- *Billy Jack Wills and his Western Swing Band (Joaquin)*
- *Billy Jack Wills and his Western Swing Band Crazy Man Crazy (Joaquin)*
  On pedal steel:
- *Brisbane Bop (with Jimmy Rivers) (Joaquin)*

Country

Marian Hall
- *Town Hall Party: 1958-61 (Country Routes)*

Don Helms
- *Hank Williams Instrumentals: Original Drifting Cowboys Band (Landmark)*
- *Hank Williams Sr. - 40 Greatest Hits (Polygram)*
- *Hank Williams Sr. - The Ultimate Collection (Universal)*

Kayton Roberts
- *The Cox Family: Everybody's Reaching Out for Someone (Rounder)*
- *The Derailers: Here Come the Derailers (Sony)*
- *Riders in the Sky: Cowboy Songs (Easydisc)*

Billy Robinson
- *Lap Steel Guitar (CRF) (available from Scotty's Music or Steel Guitar Nashville)*
- *Lap Steel Instrumentals Volume 1 & 2 (Cassette) (available from Scotty's Music or Steel Guitar Nashville)*

American Roots Music

Masters of the Incredible Lap Steel Guitar
- *Compilation of recordings by a diverse group of contemporary players. (Horserock Records)*

Jody Carver
- *Jody Carver and Johnny Cucci: the Hot Club of America (out of print; a reissue is planned)*

Ed Gerhard
- *House of Guitars (Virtue)*
- *Live Album (Virtue)*
- *Counting the Ways (Virtue)*

Pete Grant
- *Might As Well: The Persuasions Sing The Grateful Dead (Artista)*
- *Hoyt Axton: Free Sailing (Edsel Records UK)*
- *Chuck McCabe: Bad Gravity Day (Blah Blah Woof Woof)*
- *Jay Howlett: Jay Howlett (Blah Blah Woof Woof)*
- *Paul Edward Sanchez: Yesterday's Clothes (Wynema Music)*

Lee Jeffriess
- *Big Sandy & His Fly-Rite Boys: Jumping from 6 to 6 (HighTone)*
- *Big Sandy & His Fly-Rite Boys: Swingin' West (HighTone)*
- *Big Sandy & His Fly Rite Boys: Feelin' Kinda Lucky (HighTone)*
- *Big Sandy Presents The Fly Rite Boys (HighTone)*

Greg Leisz
- *Bill Frisell: Good Dog Happy Man (Nonesuch)*
- *Bill Frisell: The Intercontinentals (Nonesuch)*
- *Bill Frisell: Blues Dream (Nonesuch)*
- *k.d. lang: Ingenue (Warner Brothers)*
- *k.d. lang: Absolute Torch and Twang (Warner Brothers)*
- *Joni Mitchell: Taming the Tiger (Reprise)*
- *Joni Mitchell: Turbulent Indigo (Reprise)*
- *Mary Black: Shine (Curb)*
- *Dave Alvin: Public Domain: Songs From the Wild Land (Hightone)*
- *Dave Alvin: Blackjack David (Hightone)*

- ¤ Lap Steel Guitar Resources ¤ -

Kelly Joe Phelps
- *Lead Me On (Burnside)*
- *Roll Away the Stone (Ryodisc)*

Freddie Roulette
- *Back in Chicago (Hi Horse Records)*
- *Spirit of Steel (German release available only from www.indigo.de)*

Jeremy Wakefield
- *The Hot Guitars of Biller and Wakefield (HighTone)*

Sacred Music

Darick Campbell
- *None But The Righteous: The Masters of Sacred Steel (Ropeadope)*
- *The Campbell Brothers: Sacred Steel for the Holidays (Arhoolie)*
- *The Campbell Brothers: Pass Me Not: Sacred Steel Guitars Volume 2 (Arhoolie)*

Aubrey Ghent
- *None But The Righteous: The Masters of Sacred Steel (Ropeadope)*
- *Can't Nobody Do Me Like Jesus (Arhoolie)*
- *Traditional Sacred African-American Steel Guitar Music in Florida (Arhoolie)*

Cajun Music

Clarence "Junior" Martin
- *Jo-El Sonnier: Cajun Pride (Rounder)*
- *Vin Bruce: Cajuns of the Bayou (Cajun Sounds)*
- *Cajun Heat Zydeco Beat (Sampler) (Easydisc)*

Rock & Roll

Gary Brandin
- *The Vanduras (Pascal Records)*
- *The Blue Hawaiians: Sway (Pascal Records)*
- *The Blue Hawaiians: Savage Night (Interscope Records)*

SpongeBob SquarePants episodes on DVD:
- *Sea Stories*
- *Sponge Buddies/Nautical Nonsense*
- *Halloween*
- *Tales From the Deep*

Ben Harper
- *Live from Mars (Virgin Records)*
- *Fight for Your Mind (Virgin Records)*
- *Burn to Shine (Virgin Records)*
- *Welcome to the Cruel World (Virgin Records)*
- *The Will to Live (Virgin Records)*

Steve Howe
- *Skyline (Inside Out Music)*
- *Natural Timbre (Spitfire)*
- *Homebrew 2 (Cleopatra)*
- *Yes: Relayer (Atlantic)*
- *Masterpiece Guitars: Steve Howe & Martin Taylor (Limited edition available only from 20th Century Guitar: (phone): 631-273-1674*

David Lindley
- *Win This Record (Elektra Asylum)*
- *El Rayo-X (Elektra Asylum)*
- *Very Greasy (Elektra Asylum)*
- *A World Out of Time: Henry Kaiser & David Lindley in Madagascar (Shanachie)*
- *The Sweet Sunny North: Henry Kaiser & David Lindley in Norway (Shanachie)*
- *El Rayo-X Live (Pleemhead)*
- *Twango Bango III: David Lindley & Wally Ingram*
- *Twango Bango Deluxe: David Lindley & Wally Ingram*
- *David Lindley & Hani Nasar Live in Tokyo Playing Real Good*
- *David Lindley & Hani Nasar #2 - Playing Even Better*

The last 5 CDs (above) are available from:
David Lindley, Inc.
PO Box 370
Upland, CA, 91785-0370
www.davidlindley.com

Santo & Johnny
- *The Best of Santo & Johnny (Stardust)*
- *I Grandi Successi Originali (Italian import)*

World Music

Harry Manx
- *Wise and Otherwise (Northern Blues)*
- *Dog My Cat (Northern Blues)*

Bob Brozman

- *DigDig (with Rene' Lacaille; La Reunion Island) (World Music Network)*
- *Live Now in the USA and Australia (available from www.bobbrozman.com)*
- *Nankuru Naisa with Takashi Hirayasu (Okinawa) (Riverboat)*
- *Jin Jin Firefly with Takashi Hirayasu (Okinawa) (Riverboat)*
- *Ocean Blues with Djeli Moussa Diawara (Guinea) (Celluloid/Melodie)*
- *Tone Poems III with Mike Auldridge & David Grisman (Acoustic Disc)*
- *In the Saddle with Ledward Kaapana (Dancing Cat)*
- *Four Hands Sweet and Hot with Cyril Pahinui (Dancing Cat)*
- *Kika Kila Meets Ki Ho'Alu with Ledward Kaapana (Dancing Cat)*

Debashish Bhattacharya

- *Hindustani Slide Guitar (India Archives)*
- *Raga Saraswati (India Archives)*
- *Debashish Bhattacharya with Bob Brozman: Sunrise (Sagarika)*

Sources for Steel Guitar Music on Compact Disc:

Beer Records
Dave Stewart
1321 Lincoln Street
Fairfield, CA 94533
Web: www.beerrecords.com

Pedal Steel Guitar Products
Tom Bradshaw
P.O. Box 931
Concord, CA 94522
Email: bradshaw@california.com
Web:www.songwriter.com/bradshaw

Cord International
P.O. Box 152
Ventura, CA 93002
Toll Free: 1-877-648-7881
Web: www.cordinternational.com

Cumquat Records
Box 963, Central Park Post Office, Burke Road
Malvern East, Victoria 3145.
Australia
Email: sales@cumquatrecords.com.au
Web: www.cumquatrecords.com.au

Down Home Music Store
10341 San Pablo Avenue
El Cerrito, CA 94530
Phone: 510-525-2129
Fax: 510-525-4827
Email: mail@downhomemusic.com
Web: www.downhomemusic.com

Hawaiian Music Island
P. O. Box 223399
Princeville, HI 96722
Phone/Fax: 808-826-1446
Web: www.mele.com
Email: auntie@mele.com

Scotty's Music, Inc.
9535 Midland Boulevard
St. Louis, MO 63114-3314
Phone: 314-427-7794
Web: www.scottysmusic.com
Email: scotty@scottysmusic.com

Steel Guitar Nashville
123 Midtown Court
Hendersonville, TN. 37075
Phone: 615-822-5555
Web: www.steelguitar.net
Email: sales@steelguitar.net

- ¤ -

Bibliography

Every effort has been made to credit all sources and obtain clearance for copyrighted materials. In some cases, copyright holders are no longer living, companies no longer in business, or no contact information was available.

Books:

Charles Alexander & Nick Freeth, *The Acoustic Guitar,* Quadrillion Publishing, 1999

Keoki Awai, *The Superior Collection of Steel Guitar Solos,* Sherman Clay & Co. SF, 1917

Tony Bacon & Paul Day, *The Ultimate Guitar Book,* Alfred Knopf, 1991

Jim Beloff, *The Ukulele, A Visual History,* Miller Freeman, 1997

Julius Bellson, *The Gibson Story,* Self-published, 1973

Bob Brozman, *The History & Artistry of National Resonator Instruments,* Centerstream, 1994

Jerry Byrd, *It Was a Trip on Wings of Music* (autobiography), Centerstream, 2003

Jerry Byrd, *The Jerry Byrd Instruction Course for Steel Guitar – A Complete Study for the Serious Student,* Isa Wado, Oudensha Company Ltd., Kawasaki, Japan, 1983

Walter Carter & George Gruhn, *Gruhn's Guide to Vintage Guitars,* Miller Freeman, 1991

Richard Chapman, *Guitar: Music, History, Players,* Dorling Kindersley, 2000

Kevin Coffey, *Steel Colossus, the Bob Dunn Story,* published in *The Country Reader: Twenty Five Years of the Journal of Country Music,* Vanderbilt Univ. Press, 2000

Jim Ferguson Ed., *The Guitar Player Book,* GPI Publications, 1978

Tim Gracyk, *Popular American Recording Pioneers: 1895-1925,* Haworth Press, 2000

Hugh Gregory, *1000 Great Guitarists,* GPI Miller Freeman, 1994

George Gruhn & Walter Carter, *Acoustic Guitars & Other Fretted Instruments: A Photographic History,* Miller Freeman, 1993

Kamiki Hawaiian Guitar Method, William J. Smith, 1928

George Kanahele, *Hawaiian Music and Musicians, An Illustrated History,* U. of Hawaii Press, 1979

Darcy Kuronen, *Dangerous Curves – The Art of the Guitar,* MFA Publications, Boston Museum of Fine Art, 2000

Robert Oberman, *A Century of Country – An Illustrated History of Country Music,* TV Books, 1999

Stacy Phillips, *The Dobro Book,* Oak Publications, 1996, *The Complete Dobro Player,* Mel Bay Publications, 2002, *The Art of Hawaiian Steel Guitar,* Mel Bay Publications, 1991

Lorene Ruymar, *The Hawaiian Steel Guitar and its Great Hawaiian Musicians,* Centerstream, 1996

Ann Allen Savoy, *Cajun Music, a Reflection of a People,* Bluebird Press, 1984

Dewitt Scott, *Basic C6th Non-pedal Lap Steel Method,* Mel Bay Publications, Inc., 1996

Richard Smith, *The History of Rickenbacker Guitars,* Centerstream, 1987, *Fender – The Sound Heard 'Round The World,* Garfish Publishing, 1995

Jim Washburn & Richard Johnston, *Martin Guitars: An Illustrated Celebration of America's Premier Guitarmaker,* Rodale Press, 1997

Forrest White, *Fender: The Inside Story,* Miller Freeman, 1994

Eldon Whitford, David Vinopal & Dan Erlewine, *Gibson's Fabulous Flat-Top Guitars,* Miller Freeman, 1994

David Winters, *Artificial & Natural Harmonics for the Guitar,* Self-published, 1985

Catalogs

Carvin 1956
Fender 1953 & 1972
Gibson 1937, 1940, 1951 (price list)

- ¤ Lap Steel Guitar Resources ¤ -

Magazines
Much information and inspiration was found in the following periodicals:

Guitar Player Magazine, 1982-2003
Acoustic Guitar Magazine, 1992-2003
Frets (out of print), 1980s
20ᵗʰ Century Guitar, 1990s
Vintage Guitar, 1990s
The Hawaiian Steel Guitar Association Newsletter, 1984-1990
Hawaiian Guitar Music Review, Fred Gagner, Self-published, 1988-89

Websites:
www.allmusicguide.com, Essays by:
  Sandra Brennan (Leon McAuliffe),
  Eugene Chadbourne (Papa Cairo),
  Charlotte Dillon (Tom Morrell),
  Craig Harris (David Lindley),
  Don Helms (discography),
  Ritchie Unterberger (Shirley Bergeron)
www.mikeauldridge.com
www.bluebookinc.com
www.b0b.com
www.bobbrozman.com
www.campbellbrothers.com/sacredsteel.html
www.well.com/user/wellvis/steel.html
www.cajunculture.com (key source for author's intro
  to Cajun music section)
www.dancingcatrecords.com
www.davidlindley.com
www.elderly.com
www.horseshoemagnets.com
www.kenemerson.com
www.gruhn.com
www.hawaiiansteel.com
www.hsga.org
www.home.earthlink.net/~chrisknutsen
www.marcrecords.tripod.com
www.notecannons.com
www.rhull.freeserve.com.uk (Bill Haley)
www.rockville-international.com (copyrighted interview with Scotty Moore)
www.scottysmusic.com
www.steelguitarforum.com
www.uhpresshawaii.org
www.wideopenwest.com/~steelgtr/stringmaster.html
www.users.voicenet.com/~vanallen/hcoahome.html

Liner Notes

Sol Hoopii, Master of the Hawaiian Guitar Vols. I & 2 (Notes: Bob Brozman) Rounder Select
Sacred Steel, None But the Righteous: The Masters of Sacred Steel (Notes: Robert Stone) Ropeadope
Chuck Guillory & The Rhythm Boys (Notes: Chris Strachwitz) Arhoolie
Source for David Feet Rogers photo & info: The Sons of Hawaii, Island Heritage Limited, Norfolk
Island, Australia and Panini Productions, photos: Robert B. Goodman, notes: Carl Lundquist,
Copyright 1971.

Other Sources

Music has been handed down by word of mouth from musician to musician for thousands of years
of human history. The author is grateful to the many players and guitarmakers who have shared
information, personal histories, photographs, memories, and opinions in personal conversations
and correspondence. This kind of communication is priceless and often, as valid as that found in
published sources.

Ralph Kolsiana with Fender Dual Professional, Hollywood, 1940's

- ¤ Photo & Illustration Credits ¤ -

Front Cover,
Gibson Ultratone, Rickenbacher Frypan, Weissenborn Style-1 headstocks, courtesy Stan Werbin, Elderly Instruments, Lansing, MI

By Page Number,

3 Gary Brandin's hands, courtesy Gary Brandin, photo, Steven Dipinto

5 Illustration from Oahu sheet music, circa 1947, courtesy Tim Ausburn

7 Illustration from Oahu sheet music, circa 1947, courtesy Tim Ausburn

10 Leonard Stadler, mid-1950s, courtesy Ken Latchum

11 Matson Steamship Company menu art, 1930s, reproduced courtesy Matson Navigation Company

12 Sol Hoopii w/Bakelite Rickenbacher, courtesy Dirk Vogel

13 Sol Hoopii Trio, 1920s; writing music, courtesy Dirk Vogel

14 Ralph Kolsiana in a nightclub, 1940s, author's collection

16 Waikiki Swingsters RCA Bluebird 78 RPM record label, courtesy Dave Stewart

17 Ralph Kolsiana & the Waikiki Swingsters, mid-1930s, author's collection

18 Keoki Awai group, circa 1915, author's collection

19 Dick McIntire w/Rickenbacher frypan, courtesy Dirk Vogel

20 Dick McIntire and his Harmony Hawaiians, courtesy Dirk Vogel

21 Andy Iona (Andy Iona's Folio of Hawaiian Songs, 1937), courtesy Tim Ausburn

22 David Feet Rogers, photo, Robert B. Goodman; Copyright 1971 Panini Records/Island Heritage Ltd., Norfolk Island, Australia

23 Barney Isaacs with resonator guitar; Isaacs with slack key guitarist, George Kuo, courtesy Dancing Cat Records; Matson Steamship Company menu art, 1930s, reproduced courtesy Matson Navigation Company

24 Billy Hew Len, 1980s, courtesy John Marsden, photo, Dewitt Scott, Sr.

26 Billy Hew Len w/ Rickenbacher frypan, courtesy John Marsden

27 Jerry Byrd at NAMM, mid-1950s, courtesy Ken Latchum, photo, Leonard Stadler

32 Jerry Byrd 1997, digital photomontage courtesy Mike Idhe

35 Rickenbacher B-6, circa 1940; photo, author; Jerry Byrd from Rickenbacker catalog, circa 1960

36 Greg Sardinha w/ Gordon Freitas (b) & Rick Rickard (g), courtesy Greg Sardinha

41 Kamiki Hawaiian Guitar Method, 1928, author's collection

42 John Ely w/ Fender console steel, courtesy John Ely

48 Illustration from Oahu sheet music, 1940s, courtesy Tim Ausburn

49 Bruce Clarke & the Hawaiian Hotshots, 1947, courtesy Bruce Clarke

52 Bruce Clarke w/ Herb Ellis, mid-1980s, courtesy Bruce Clarke

55 Cumquat Records Sol Hoopii CD cover, courtesy Bruce Clarke

56 Billy Robinson at the Grand Ole Opry, late 1940s, courtesy WJM/Billy Robinson

57 Don Helms w/ the Drifting Cowboys, 1940s, courtesy Don Helms

62 Don Helms, 1990s, courtesy Don Helms

63 Carvin guitar catalog page, 1956, courtesy Ron Preston

64 Billy Robinson, courtesy Billy Robinson

68 Billy Robinson on WSM/Grand Ole Opry radio, late 1940s, courtesy WJM/Billy Robinson

71 Marian Hall w/ Tex Williams, circa 1960, courtesy Marian Hall

74 Town Hall Party Cast, mid-1950s; Spade Cooley's All-Girl Orchestra, circa 1957/1958, courtesy Marian Hall

76 Marian Hall w/Merle Travis & Joe Maphis, courtesy Marian Hall

77 Marian Hall w/ Randy Price & Jubilaires, 1970; with Spade Cooley, 1958, courtesy Marian Hall

78 Kayton Roberts at ISGC, 1990s, courtesy Dewitt Scott, Sr.

80 Kayton & Iva Lee Roberts w/ Roger Carroll (b), 1990s, courtesy Keith DeLong

81 Fender logo, courtesy Bobbe Seymour

82 Jeremy Wakefield, courtesy Jeremy Wakefield

86 Bigsby string package, courtesy Ron Middlebrook

87 Junior Brown, courtesy Tanya Rae Brown

88 Joaquin Murphey w/ Spade Cooley, courtesy Michael Johnstone

89 Bob Dunn with on KXYZ Radio, Texas, 1938, courtesy Kevin Coffey/Cliff Bruner

92 Bob Dunn's Vagabonds, El Toro Club, Texas, 1938, courtesy Kevin Coffey/Cliff Bruner

93 Volutone amplifier, early 1930s, courtesy, Gary Schireson & Neville Hanson, Volutone Distributing Company

94 Leon McAuliffe, courtesy Western Swing Journal, Jesse Morris, Editor

97 Panhandle Rag 78, author's collection

99 Panhandle Rag, Oahu sheet music, courtesy Tim Ausburn

101 Leon McAuliffe, courtesy Western Swing Journal, Jesse Morris, Editor

- ¤ Photo & Illustration Credits ¤ -

102 Joaquin Murphey, 1954, courtesy Jody Carver, photo, Jody Carver

103 Joaquin Murphey w/ Spade Cooley, courtesy Michael Johnstone

106 Joaquin Murphey, 1997, courtesy Michael Johnstone

107 Joaquin Murphey with The Plainsmen, 1940s, courtesy Michael Johnstone

108 Cindy Cashdollar, courtesy Cindy Cashdollar, photo, Emily Joyce

110 Cindy Cashdollar, courtesy Cindy Cashdollar, photo, Herb Remington

115 Herb Remington with the Tony Landry Big Band, courtesy Herb Remington

123 Tom Morrell at ISGC, courtesy Dewitt Scott, Sr.

126 Tom Morell at ISCG, courtesy Tom Morrell

128 Bigsby steel guitar tuning booklet & logo, courtesy Ron Middlebrook

129 Guitar still life, courtesy Loni Specter, photo, Loni Specter

130 Ed Gerhard at Star Pines Café, Tokyo, courtesy Virtue Records, Photo, Isato Nakagawa

134 Recording King headstock, courtesy Stan Werbin, Elderly Instruments, Lansing, MI

135 Pete Grant, courtesy Pete Grant

141 Greg Leisz w/ Bill Frisell; photo, Jerry Gleason

147 Magic Steel Guitarist book cover, 1935, courtesy Loni Specter, photo, Loni Specter

148 Freddie Roulette, courtesy Fritz Svacina, photo, copyright Fritz Svacina

152 Freddie Roulette at ISGC, courtesy Dewitt Scott Sr.

153 Illustration of a tone bar from Oahu sheet music, 1940s, courtesy Tim Ausburn

154 Lee Jeffriess, courtesy Old Timey Artists, photo, Jesse Wuorenma

158 Vance Terry, 1950s, courtesy Brad Bechtel; Bigsby steel guitar tuning booklet & logo, courtesy Ron Middlebrook

159 Bigsby string packaging, courtesy Ron Middlebrook

160 Jody Carver, courtesy Jody Carver

160 Hot Club of America LP cover, 1959, courtesy Dave Van Allen

161 Walter Johnson Poster, 1940, courtesy Robert L. Stone

162 African American churchgoers, circa 1900, Library of Congress

163 Darick Campbell, copyright Robert L. Stone

163 Darick Campbell's hands, copyright Robert L. Stone

169 Aubrey Ghent, copyright Robert L. Stone

172 Vermont Ave. Baptist Church, circa 1900, Library of Congress

173 Cajun Steel Guitar player, Louisiana, 1938, Library of Congress, photo, Russell Lee

174 Papa Cairo, courtesy Arhoolie.com, photo, Chris Strachwitz

175 Shirley Bergeron, courtesy Roger Armstrong, Ace Records, London

176 Clarence "Junior" Martin on stage, 1950s, courtesy Clarence "Junior" Martin

181 Gary Brandin, courtesy Gary Brandin

182 Santo & Johnny, late 1950s, courtesy Robert L. Stone

183 David Lindley in Concert, courtesy Martin Abend/UlfTone Music, Photo, Ina Kuschel, copyright UlfTone Music

191 David Lindley in Concert, courtesy Martin Abend/UlfTone Music Photo, Ina Kuschel, copyright UlfTone Music

193 Elton steel guitar bar, photo, Loni Specter; Bear Creek guitar headstock, Photo, author

194 Gary Brandin in Capitol Records Studio B 1998, courtesy Gary Brandin

197 The Vanduras, courtesy Pascal Records, David Pascal

199 Steve Howe, courtesy of Doug Gottleib, copyright Gottlieb Brothers 2002

204 Gibson catalog, 1937, courtesy Tim Ausburn

205 Mexican Musicians, Library of Congress

211 Illustrations from the Nick Manoloff Method for Hawaiian Guitar, 1936, author's collection

212 Bob Brozman in convertible, courtesy Bob Brozman, Photo, Ali Madjdi

219 Bob Brozman's hands, Photo, Ali Madjdi

220 Debashish Bhattacharya, courtesy Debashish Battacharya, photo, Parsupati Rudra Pal, Kolkata, India

223 Debashish Bhattacharya with Brij Bushan Kabra, courtesy Debashish Bhattacharya, photo, copyright Prashant Arora, Kolkata, India

226 Debashish Bhattacharya, courtesy Debashish Battacharya, (photo), Parsupati Rudra Pal, Kolkata, India

227 Gibson Ultratone, courtesy Stan Werbin, Elderly Instruments, Lansing, MI

228 Martin Price List, 1929, courtesy Dick Boak, C. F. Martin Guitar Co., Nazareth, PA

229 Martin 00-40H, 0040-H (detail), courtesy Dick Boak, C. F. Martin Guitar Co.

230 Martin 00-28H & 1921 flyer, courtesy Dick Boak, C.F. Martin Guitar Co., Nazareth, PA

231 Martin 2-17H & 1928 flyer, courtesy Dick Boak, C.F. Martin Guitar Co., Nazareth, PA

232/233 Weissenborn Style-1, courtesy Ed Gerhard

232/233 Weissenborn Style-1, courtesy Stan Werbin, Elderly Instruments, Lansing, MI

233 Hawaiian postcard, 1940s, author's collection

234 Oahu lap steel & amplifier, courtesy Stan Werbin, Elderly Instruments, Lansing, MI

- ¤ Photo & Illustration Credits ¤ -

234/235 Oahu Diana lap steel, courtesy Stan Werbin, Elderly Instruments, Lansing, MI; Oahu Tonemaster & guitar spread, 1940s, courtesy Tim Ausburn

235 Oahu Advanced Harmony Course, 1940s, author's collection

236 Dewitt "Scotty" Scott w/ long-scale frypan, courtesy Dewitt Scott, Sr.

236/237 Rickenbacher frypan lap steel, 1934, courtesy Stan Werbin, Elderly Instruments, Lansing, MI

237 Lollar/Aiello re-issue horseshoe pickup, courtesy Jason Lollar; Dick McIntire, courtesy Dirk Vogel

238/239 Rickenbacher Bakelite lap steel, circa 1940, Photo, author

239 Rickenbacher double-8 metal body lap steel, courtesy Stan Werbin, Elderly Instruments, Lansing, MI; Rickenbacher Bakelite lap steel (chrome plates), courtesy Rick Aiello; Vernon Hester, 1951, courtesy Vernon Hester

240 1937 Gibson logo & catalog page, courtesy Tim Ausburn

240/241 Recording King lap steel, courtesy Stan Werbin, Elderly Instruments, Lansing, MI; Gibson EH-150 & case, courtesy Harry Deitrich

241 Gibson EH-275, courtesy Howard Reinleib; Lollar/Aiello Charlie Christian re-issue pickup, courtesy Jason Lollar

242/243 Gibson Ultratone lap steels, circa 1949, courtesy Stan Werbin, Elderly Instruments, Lansing, MI

243 Gibson price list, 1951, courtesy John Bechtel

244 Joaquin Murphey's Bigsby lap steel, courtesy Chas Smith

244/245 Joaquin Murphey w/ Spade Cooley; Joaquin in studio, courtesy Michael Johnstone

245 Bigsby triple neck, courtesy Chas Smith

246 Fender Dual-Professional & amplifier, courtesy Ron Randall; 1953 Fender catalog cover, author's collection

247 1953 Fender catalog interior & 1952 Fender Custom steel, author's collection

248 Fender Stringmasters & 1972 Fender catalog, courtesy Ron Preston

249 Fender Deluxe-6 & Deluxe-8, 1972 Fender catalog, courtesy Ron Preston

250 National New Yorker lap steel, courtesy Stan Werbin, Elderly Instruments, Lansing, MI

251 Supro console steel, 1950s, courtesy Mike Idhe; Valco owner's manual, 1950, courtesy John Bechtel

252 Asher lap steels, courtesy Bill Asher

253 Bear Creek guitars, courtesy BJ Hardin, Bear Creek Guitars

254 Blattenberger guitars, courtesy Marci Blattenberger

255 Estaban Bojorquez guitars, courtesy Amy Dakos

256 Celtic Cross guitars, courtesy Neil Russell, Celtic Cross Guitars

257 Chandler RH lap steel, courtesy David Siegler; Chandler fretboard, photo, author

258 GeorgeBoards guitars, courtesy George Piburn, GeorgeBoards

259 Gold Tone lap steel, courtesy David Siegler

260 Harmos guitars, courtesy T. Sage Harmos, Harmos Guitars

261 Lapdancer guitars, courtesy Loni Specter, Lapdancer Guitars

262 Melobar guitars, courtesy Ted Smith, Smith Family Music

263 Mermer guitars, courtesy Richard Mermer

264 Remington Steel guitars, courtesy Herb Remington

265 SS Hawaiian, courtesy Ricky Davis

265 Sheerhorn Weissenborn, courtesy Tim Sheerhorn

266 Sea To Sky guitars, courtesy Rory Dafoe/Dwight Mark

267 Sierra guitars, courtesy Sierra Instrument Company

268 Superior guitars, courtesy Berkley Musical Instrument Exchange

269 Tradewinds guitars, courtesy Elva West, Tradewinds Guitars

270 Weissonator guitar, courtesy Mike Dotson, Maraicopa Guitar Company

271 Hawaiian King guitars, courtesy Joseph Yanuziello, Yanuziello Guitars

272 Tone bars still life, photo, author; Dunlop, Slippery Slide & Werner bars, courtesy Jim Dunlop Company, Lapdancer Guitars, and Michael Werner

273 Volutone amplifier, 1930s, courtesy Gary Schireson & Neville Hanson, Volutone Distributing Company

288 Ralph Kolsiana in a Hollywood nightclub, 1940s, author's collection

273 Volutone lap steel, 1930s, Courtesy Gary Schireson & Neville Hanson, Volutone Distributing Company

296 Harry Dietrich w/ the Dick Saintclair Troubadors, 1951, courtesy Harry Dietrich, Alan Akaka at ISGC, courtesy Dewitt Scott, Sr.

297 David Keli'i, photo, Bob Waters

Back Cover, (photographs attributed above),
L, Santo & Johnny, Darick Campbell, Cindy Cashdollar, Harry Manx, Debashish Bhattacharya
R, Sol Hoopii, Bob Brozman, Gary Brandin, Jerry Byrd, Freddie Roulette

- ¤ Index ¤ -

- ¤ Index ¤ -

- ¤ Index ¤ -

- ¤ Index ¤ -

Harry Dietrich on Supro steel with the Dick Saintclair Troubadors, 1951

Alan Akaka at the International Steel Guitar Convention, mid-1990's

Andy Volk is a freelance television producer, writer, and graphic designer based in Massachusetts. His has written and produced award-winning television programs about finance, medicine, technology, and music including the documentary video, *Ralph Kolsiana: A Life in Hawaiian Music*. Andy's writing has appeared in *Steel Guitar World*, *Acoustic Guitar Magazine*, and various online venues. His graphic art career includes book, compact disc, and video animation design. After thirty years of playing standard and lap-style guitar, he's still searching for the ultimate steel guitar tuning.